THE HUMAN DRAMA

THE HUMAN DRAMA

World History: From the Beginning to 500 C.E.

Jean Elliott Johnson
and Donald James Johnson

Markus Wiener Publishers
Princeton

For information write to:
Markus Wiener Publishers
231 Nassau Street, Princeton, NJ 08542

Book Design by Cheryl Mirkin

Printed in the United States of America on acid-free paper

CONTENTS

ACKNOWLEDGEMENTS

The authors are indebted to many people for their support, expertise, prodding and constructive criticisms. We especially want to acknowledge the inspiration of William McNeill, Ross Dunn, and Jerry Bentley who have motivated countless students and colleagues to attempt to conceptualize the world's history. Insights too numerous to mention have also come from members of the World History Association and the faculty and participants at the Woodrow Wilson World History Summer Institute. We gratefully acknowledge special scholarly advice from Morris Rossabi, Queens College and Columbia University, and Larisa Bonfonte, Moss Roberts, and Rita Wright, New York University.

The faculty and administration of Friends Seminary, New York City—particularly Barclay Palmer, Joyce McCray, Phil Allen, Joseph Gosler, Charles Blank, and Richard Eldridge—deserve special credit for supporting the use of early versions of this text in ninth grade world history classes. Exemplary history teachers who offered critical evaluations of the text include Michele Forman, Middlebury Union High School, Vermont; William Skowronski, Msg. Bonner High School, Philadelphia; Lorne Swarthout, Berkeley Carroll School, New York City; and Timothy Connell, The Laurel School, Shaker Heights, Ohio. Susan Meeker and Joan Kenyon used early versions of the text in their Hunter College High School world history classes and offered encouragement and support. Many other teachers have made helpful suggestions; Gwen Johnson, Scarsdale High School, New York, and Mary Rossabi, Fieldston School, New York deserve special recognition.

We thank Markus Wiener for his faith in this project, his constant advice on content, and his assistance in locating resources. Editorial and layout expertise has been provided by Cheryl Mirkin, Susie Van Doren, and Patricia Emerson. Finally, we want to thank our son Keith Johnson; without his patience and support this text would not have been completed.

*Dedicated to the ninth grade students
at Friends Seminary
whose insights are incorporated in this text
and whose lives are shaping
the ongoing human drama.*

SETTING THE STAGE

History tells a story about what happened in the past, what choices people made, and how things changed over time. Material remains, what people create, and the stories they tell or have written down are all important sources historians use as they try to figure out what was going on "long ago and far away." Many sources have been lost; others reflect only one viewpoint or are ambiguous, capable of being interpreted in various ways. For that reason historians try to gather multiple sources about past events and periods—especially those that reflect more than one perspective—rather than relying on any single source.

Examining more than one source is important for local history, but even more so for world history. World history allows us to examine how similar events might have looked to people in very different

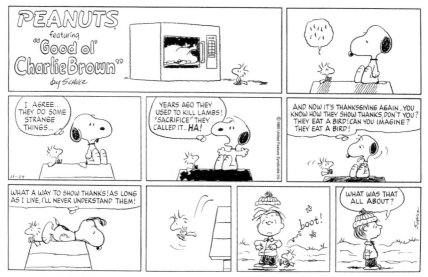

PEANUTS *reprinted by permission of United Feature Syndicate, Inc.*

places around the globe. It also forces us to be aware of our own biases as we try to figure out what "really happened."

Imagine telling your life story or your family's history. Besides looking for sources and then evaluating them, you would have to select the events and people you think are important. Obviously what you include and what you leave out make an enormous difference. If you had to write a history of the whole United States with its millions of families, you certainly could not include everyone or even all the groups that have lived in the States: you would have to leave out a great deal. Yet our country's history is only a small part of world history stretching back to when human life first appeared on the earth. Imagine trying to select and interpret events from the experiences of billions of people over thousands of years. World history involves doing just that.

Questions Historians Ask

Perhaps gathering and evaluating information are relatively easy aspects of the historians' job. Next they must ask those sources questions. Questions may stress economic factors, or political, social, or cultural information.

The questions historians ask determine which aspects of human experience they will emphasize. Many historians ask political questions. They search documents for names of kings and dynasties and examine records to find out what gave leaders the right to rule. Some historians ask economic questions. They want to know about the production and distribution of wealth, who controlled the land, how people made a living, and how they were paid. They look for class divisions and specialization. Others focus on the military and examine how various groups extended and defended their territories. Some ask social questions, identifying people's roles and how they got along with one another. Some ask cultural and religious questions, attempting to determine people's beliefs, what values shaped their lives, and their expressions of ultimate meaning. Some ask questions about technology and examine how people controlled their environment and what they invented.

The same source, such as a letter or newspaper article, can provide information in different areas. Sometimes the absence of information also can provide insight. Why, we might ask, are there relatively few records about what women did or thought, about the lives of average farmers, or about those who were very poor?

As you study the past, you will probably discover that you are more interested in some aspects of human life than in others. Like any historian, you must decide which questions you want to ask and which you will leave for others. Analyze the kinds of questions you ask about any given time or place. You may find that getting answers is relatively easy; deciding on what questions to ask may be the real challenge.

Change Over Time

History is the story of change over time. But what is time? Does it move? If so, how? Cycles in nature—phases of the moon, the seasons, the growth, death, and rebirth of plants—suggest time moves in circles. Time that appears to move in circles is called cyclical time. Nature follows cyclical time, and agricultural communities usually follow the rhythms of the seasons. Myths from India tell of great cycles during which the world comes into being and dissolves, over and over again. The present universe has existed before and will come into being again. In these stories, there is no "In the beginning . . ." Where does a circle begin?

Some communities in Africa have two kinds of time: one covers what a person has experienced or is about to experience, and the other encompasses a community's past, most of which no one remembers very clearly any longer. Events move backwards, away from memory, into the "graveyard of time."

Most people in the United States assume time moves forward in a straight line from a fixed beginning into the future. This is called linear time. The study of history assumes linear time because historians are interested in cause and effect and how things change. Some people who believe in linear time also assume that as things change they get better. They may study the past in order to see how things have improved and progressed, how our present way of life is superior to earlier times.

To record events in linear time requires starting at some point.

Logically, we should start with creation, but when did that take place? Events are often dated from the birth of some extremely important person or the start of a ruler's reign. The Greeks used the Olympics as the basis of their calendar. For Muslims, year one was when the first Muslim community fled from Mecca to Medina, and they use a lunar calendar with twelve 28-day months. The birth of Jesus is at the center of the designations B.C. (before Christ) and A.D. (*anno Domini*, "in the year of the Lord"). We will follow this dating but use the more general terms B.C.E. (before the common era) and C.E. (of the common era).

Calendar	Year	New Year's Day
Gregorian	2000 C.E.	January 1
Islamic	1420–1421	April 6
Hebrew	5761	September 29
Chinese	4697 (year of the rabbit) –4698 (year of the dragon)	February 5

All the World's Our Stage

Soon after the first moon landing, many people realized that from outer space, the earth looks small and vulnerable. We began to speak of Spaceship Earth. Nearly three fourths of the earth's surface is water. Two massive oceans separate the habitable land into two hemispheres. There are impressive mountain ranges, and a vast desert highway extends from the Sahara Desert all the way to the Gobi Desert. A belt of rich grasslands lies south of the desert in Africa and north of the deserts in Asia.

Viewed from space it is easier to realize that all life on earth exists in one interconnected system with global weather patterns, ocean currents, and seasonal winds. What happens in one part of the globe affects what is going on in other areas. While we usually focus on communities, cities, nations, and regions, it is important to remember that weather patterns, rivers systems, mountain ranges, deserts, grasslands, and plains know no political boundaries. Humans overlay the earth with boundaries.

As we try to trace our history, we should remember that the bound-aries that now divide groups into political units, such as the nations of the world, the states of the United States, and even our own towns and cities, have changed over time. Boundaries are fluid and shift or even dissolve as people move, power centers change, and new areas are settled. Rivers or mountains that once divided groups may no longer be significant. But the borders between different groups and ecological zones are important zones of interchange. As one civiliza-tion expands, it meets other cultures, and the exchanges and adap-tions that result often create new boundaries as well as new ways of life.

World Maps Lie Because They Lie

Most of the time we are not aware that we live on Spaceship Earth. Instead of thinking about life on a globe, we think of land stretching north, south, east, and west from where we are. How we conceptual-ize space—what is near and what is far away—and how we view the world depends on who we are and where we are standing.

Cartographers—scholars who make maps—who want to draw the globe on a flat piece of paper must figure out how to represent a three-dimensional sphere on a two-dimensional surface. Because no two-dimensional map can record the earth accurately, all two-dimen-sional world maps distort the earth.

What point should be the center of a world map? Most people put their country at the center. Ancient Greeks considered Delphi to be the center of the world, while Israelites thought Jerusalem was. Chinese call their land the Middle Kingdom. Residents of Teotihua-can, near present-day Mexico City, thought their city was the birth-place of the gods. Maps in many U.S. schools have the Western Hemisphere in the middle of the world, even though that means half of South Asia appears to the west and half to the east. Chinese maps, which put the Middle Kingdom in the center of the world, turn the eastern seaboard of the United States into the "Far East."

The Power to Name

Deciding what information to include or omit, thinking about time

A North American view of the world   *A Chinese view of the world*

and progress, and identifying what to put at the center of the world are only a few of the myriad decisions world historians must make. Naming things is another category of decisions. The names we give people, places, and events reflect our perspectives and values. For example, we will try to avoid terms such as "Middle East" or "Far East," because they assume a specific vantage point, and use instead West Asia and East Asia. We will call the area that includes Europe and Asia "Eurasia" and the whole Eastern Hemisphere "Afro-Eurasia."

Many of the names we use today are not what people in the past called themselves. For example, the Chinese thought of themselves as the People of Han and called their country the Middle Kingdom, not China, which reflects the Qin [Ch'in], the first dynasty to unite their land. When Romans called people Greeks, they meant dishonest traders. Greeks called themselves Hellenes. Moreover, people who lived in various places in the past did not think of themselves as British, Polish, or Russians nor that they were living in Europe or Asia until very recently.

The right to give something a name usually reflects power. Often smaller or weaker countries, peoples, and individuals have to accept the names more powerful neighbors give them. Less powerful groups have to accept belittling or even insulting names. When studying about people in the past, we need to think about what names signify, who used them, and why.

Many people have fought for the right to name themselves. The first Spanish explorers in the Western Hemisphere called the people they met Indians because they thought they had reached Asia, instead of calling them Inca, Aztec, Maya, Pequot, or the other names these people called themselves. Europeans and Americans in the eighteenth and nineteenth centuries used "blacks" as a term of derision for enslaved Africans. However, in the 1960s African Americans proudly adopted the term and, in doing so, reversed its original meaning.

Scholars exercise power not only when they choose what to include but also when they decide how to identify events, groups, or time periods. Think, for example, of words such as "civilized" and "civilization." Who is civilized? What do you mean when you say a person is uncivilized? When and why should a society be called a civilization? Who should make these designations? Who decides whether a battle was a mutiny, an insurrection, or a war? What do terms such as "primitive," "third world," "underdeveloped," or "modern" imply? Who has the right to identify areas of the world by those terms?

Terms such as "primitive," "civilized," "uncivilized" and "modern" are social constructs. Many social constructs reflect value judgments and are not just descriptions. Maps are also social constructs as is the idea of time and how it moves along with designations such as B.C. and B.C.E. Why should non-Christians mark events by the birth of Jesus? Geographic terms, such as continent or longitude, are social constructs as well. Why, for example, do we call Europe a continent but call South Asia a subcontinent? Why does the prime meridian run through Greenwich, England?

As we examine the world's history, it is important to understand the many ways people have viewed and labeled the land, its inhabitants, and events. We will try to note how people describe themselves, their homes, and their communities as well as the way they refer to others who are different, and we will consider how and why names change over time. We must be especially sensitive to how historians have named people, places, and periods, and analyze the perspectives and values these terms reflect.

From the history of many individuals and groups comes an integrated story about our shared past. The drama of human history encompasses us all and is informed and enriched by many different languages, beliefs, and cultures. Keep in mind that what you read here is only one way of organizing past events. Perhaps as you become involved in world history, you will want to join the intriguing debate on the best way to organize information about the past. At the very least we hope that you think about these questions as you study the greatest of all dramas, that of our common history.

The Origins of the Human Community: Learning to Cooperate (from earliest times to 3500 B.C.E.)

How did it all begin? How did the universe materialize? Can something come out of nothing? What happens at the end and after? Throughout history people from all over the world have asked similar questions and have expressed their ideas about origins through stories and myths.

Creation: How Did the World Come into Being?

Creation stories reflect the values of the people who tell them, and they shape the values of individuals who learn them. They are a model of what people believe and a model for new generations.

For example, some people tell stories about the world coming into being through the process of birth from a cosmic egg or lotus. In some India and Chinese accounts an undifferentiated oneness "falls apart" into finite forms (suggesting, perhaps, what modern scientists identify as the Big Bang). For some, creation resulted from the actions of a divine force fabricating the cosmos. The Greek goddess Athena emerged from Zeus's head, suggesting inspiration can be a source of creation as well.

Humans, animals, the earth, and stars all come from the same Self (to use the Indian term) and therefore are all originally from the same

Three views of creation:

Procreation
Fabrication
Inspiration

*Path fashions the egg of the world
upon a potter's wheel*

Lajja Gauri, a Hindu lotus goddess

Birth of Athena

substance. Many creation stories establish the relationship between humans and the rest of the natural world. In a Chinese story of creation, humans come from insects in the hair of the original cosmic being called Pan Ku. In several Indian versions, humans and all other aspects of the universe are all part of the same ultimate reality. In the biblical story in Genesis, the Lord is totally other than the world he creates. Humankind was made in the image of God and given dominion over the earth and each thing that creeps upon it.

Evolution: How Did We Get to Be Human?

Scientists who believe that human beings evolved over many millions of years are called evolutionists. Evolutionists generally do not focus on what came before the Big Bang. They contend that very gradually, over eons, the universe and life as we know it evolved and became more and more complex as time moved on (note the conception of time). They rely on science to demonstrate that humans evolved from earlier forms of life and believe progress actually takes place. Evolved and progressed are important concepts in evolutionists' worldview. However, they disagree among themselves about the exact process of human development, offering varying pictures of what makes us truly human.

Most evolutionists build their theories on the work of Charles Darwin, a nineteenth-century English biologist. In 1859 Darwin published *The Origin of the Species,* in which he explained how all kinds of life had evolved from earlier, simpler forms. Those that could adapt as conditions changed were "more fit" and survived in larger numbers; most of those that did not died out. Darwin called this process "natural selection."

Subsequent scientists observed that certain species changed dramatically, all of a sudden, and they called these changes mutations. The next generation would inherit the mutations, and if they made a species more fit, offspring were more likely to survive. If a mutation was very drastic, a new species had come into being.

Life began with one-celled organisms a billion years ago, evolutionists say. Millions of years passed, and gradually life became more complex. Fishlike marine vertebrates, then great reptiles, and then the first mammals developed. By fifty million years ago, apelike, four-legged primates (the most highly developed mammals) with tails were living in trees, moving through the forest by swinging from branch to branch.

Africa: Birthplace of Human Life

At least four million years ago, some primates began to stand up, supporting their weight solely on their two hind legs. Human beings evolved from these bipedal primates, identified as hominids. Between four million and one million years ago, a hominid species called

Lucy and her mate

Australopithecus evolved in Africa. One of the most exciting discoveries of this species occurred in 1974, when anthropologists excavated part of the skeleton of a 3,5 million-year-old woman that they named Lucy. These beings, including Lucy, were short, quite hairy, and had limited intelligence, but they were able to use their free hands to carry things and make simple scraping and chopping tools that helped them survive.

Then about a million years ago, a new species, under the general category of *Homo*, replaced earlier ones. *Homo erectus* (beings walking upright), the most important, had a brain much larger that *Australopithecus*, and they created better tools, including hand axes. *Homo erectus* also knew how to use fire. They probably also could use language and coordinate group activities. *Homo erectus* ventured north, far from their original home in East Africa.

About 250,000 years ago *Homo sapiens* (thinking beings) first appeared. They had still larger brains than *Homo erectus* and communicated with one another and manipulated their environment in new and creative ways. They could conceptualize far better than other species and could communicate these thoughts to others. *Homo sapiens* established larger cooperative communities and could adapt and survive in much more challenging climates.

Gradually our human ancestors migrated out of Africa and into central and western Eurasia. Many areas of land now separated by water were once connected. Gibraltar was a landbridge 100,000 years ago, and humans could walk from Africa into southern Europe. Humans, perhaps following herds of large animals, probably walked from Siberia to Alaska, and their descendants gradually moved southward as far as Chile. Still other humans may have traveled by sea to the Indian subcontinent, the islands of Indonesia, Australia, and perhaps even North America.

After about 100,000 years, humans began to endure a series of harsh ice ages caused by glaciers that covered much of the northern latitudes. Relying on their superior intelligence to adapt to very new conditions, they settled most of the globe, including the Western Hemisphere. By 40,000 years ago, *Homo sapiens* had developed fully into human beings who biologically are much the same as the people who now live throughout the world.

What Does It Mean to Be Human?

Calling the earliest humans *Homo sapiens* implies that the ability to think is the most important human characteristic. Closely related to thinking is the ability to create symbols, especially words and a language, and to group things into categories. Language makes it possible for thinking beings to communicate and create culture: the shared meaning and ideas common to a specific group of people. In order to survive, humans must learn the culture from older members of their groups, including their language, religious symbols, and values as well as what it means to be fully human in that particular culture. They learn to control their biological needs, defer instant gratification, and make choices about how they will fulfill their desires. Because humans migrated all around the world and settled in many different environments, the human family quickly became very diverse and created a wide variety of cultures.

One of the cultural differences among people is how they define what it means to be human. What are the most important characteristics of human beings? Are people human because they can make tools and shape the environment? If we stress early humans as toolmakers we might call them *Homo faber*, beings who make things. Some would argue that weapons were the most important early tools and only Man the killer was able to survive.

"Looks O.K. But how are you going to hit people with it?"

But we might also ask, "Is the most important quality of being human the ability to communicate and remember the past, or must a person have compassion or want to cooperate with others in order to be called human? Are those who believe in one god or live in a democracy more human than those who believe that no one can own part of the earth? Are people in industrial societies more fully human than farmers and hunter-gatherers? What are the qualities that make up our humanness?"

What Color Is the Human Race?

Everyone now living on the globe developed from those earliest African ancestors who were probably dark skinned. In tropical climates, dark skin helps a person survive because it filters out cancer-producing rays from the sun. But in cooler, darker climates, such as western Eurasia, where exposure to the sun is limited, darker skin is a liability because, for one thing, it inhibits the production of vitamin D. Over the millennia, the skin color of some of these early migrants may have lightened as they adapted to cooler environments, while others who found homes in warmer climates that were similar to Africa remained dark skinned.

As a result of adaptation to different environments, humans now have a variety of skin colors, but that is only one kind of adaptation. Another is additional protection for the eye in dry climates, or differences in bone structure as a result of diet. In spite of all the physical differences among people around the world, there is only one race: the human race.

In whatever ways the large group of scientists— including physicists, bone and dental specialists, chemists, geologists, biologists, anthropologists, as well as historians—resolve the questions they are asking about earliest times, we can agree that more than 50,000 years ago, thinking beings were living in many parts of the world. They understood time and place and shared food, tools, and ideas with one another. The story of how they survived and the meanings they attached to their efforts to cooperate is the focus of the first act of the human drama.

"Joe, these people say they want flesh-colored band-Aids."

GATHERING AND HUNTING: HUMANS SHARE RESOURCES

Setting the Stage

Of the 50,000 years that thinking human beings have lived on the earth, recorded history covers only about 5,000, less than one tenth of the total human experience. The earliest surviving writing comes from about 3500 B.C.E., which must be considered current events in the whole span of human experience. Historians used to call the time before people kept written records prehistory, because they had nothing written down to tell them what was happening. That term reflects the historian's traditional bias in favor of written records. Calling that period prehistory could imply that nothing significant happens unless people write it down. In fact, the period known as prehistory may be the most important in the whole human drama because our ancestors who lived at that time developed the basic social features that people continue to use today.

Unfortunately, we know least about this earliest period of history, since we must rely on artifacts, fossils, and half-forgotten memories embedded in myths as our sources. Even though we may make many mistakes in deriving so much from so little evidence, we must try to reconstruct what happened during our earliest history, because it was extremely important.

The timeline some historians suggest for the history of these early times reflects their interest in humans a toolmakers.

> Stone Age: 2,000,000 B.C.E. to 3500 B.C.E.
> Paleolithic (Old Stone Age): 2,000,000 B.C.E. to 9000 B.C.E.
> Mesolithic (Middle Stone Age): 9000 B.C.E. to 6000 B.C.E.
> Neolithic (New Stone Age): 6000 B.C.E. to 3500 B.C.E.
> Bronze Age: 3500 to 1400 B.C.E.
> Iron Age: 1400 B.C.E. to 800 B.C.E.

Who Were the Earliest Humans?

The earliest humans probably evolved in east Africa and migrated over the globe. We assume that they survived and developed because they formed social groups, devised home bases, collected and shared food, and protected and nursed those who were young, old, or sick. Early men and women formed their first social groups while they were gathering and scavenging for food, not hunting it. Putting others' needs before their own, they fed helpless infants and brought both plants and meat back to share with other members of the group. Both men and women probably picked up seeds, nuts, and roots to eat. Both probably scavenged for dead animals, and men hunted only in times of severe droughts, when they were able to kill feeble animals weakened by lack of water or food.

The first "families" may have been groups of women and children in which all the women protected all the children. Girls and boys the same age were like sisters and brothers. The important relationships were most likely mother-child and sister-brother. Adult males may have lived separately in their own groups.

Hunting-gathering groups usually included between twelve and forty people. When they could find lots of food, more infants survived and the numbers increased. But more people put a strain on the food supply, and if they couldn't find enough food, some starved. Sometimes mothers must have practiced infanticide—killing newborn infants—in an effort to keep a balance between their food and the number of people they had to feed. This life cycle continued for tens of thousands of years.

How Did Humans Survive?

Culture, particularly language, helped human beings survive. As women nursed their infants, they experimented with ways to communicate with their babies, and perhaps language developed from these early efforts. The earliest tools were probably used in caring for the children and gathering food. A sling of bark to hold a baby was perhaps the first human invention, and containers for food were also among the earliest tools. Both men and women probably used sticks or pieces of stone to dig up roots. In addition, women had to pound or scrape many plants before humans could digest them, and they may have invented tools for these purposes as well.

At first, the meat people ate came from animals that had died or other animals had killed. Men probably concentrated on finding dead animals. As they learned to communicate and cooperate and/or as game became scarcer, men most likely traveled farther to hunt and spent a lot of time hunting, even though the meat they brought back probably accounted for very little of the diet.

Gradually men and women performed different roles, especially when men traveled long distances to hunt. They developed ways to transport animals they had scavenged and later created weapons for catching and killing live animals. Women concentrated on gathering nearby roots, plants, nuts, and grains, caring for children and the elderly, and maintaining the home base.

Cave painting of a deer hunt

Our early ancestors began to use fire, an extremely important technological advance, about 50,000 years ago. Lightning or spontaneous combustion provided this important source of protection and warmth long before early humans could produce it themselves, and early people may have considered fire a sacred gift from the gods. Since they could not produce fire, they must have carefully preserved and guarded fires they found. As men wandered off to scavenge and later hunt for meat, women must have guarded the hearth and kept the valuable fire burning. (Millennia later, women were still guarding the sacred flame in temples. Perhaps the eternal flame burning at President John Kennedy's grave is a continuation of the early reverence for fire.)

Fire gave warmth, and it could keep large animals away as well as drive them out of caves. Fire allowed women to cook food, softening it for toothless elders or small children. Women figured out how to use fire to preserve foods and make some otherwise poisonous plants safe and edible.

The ill and old found a safe haven at the home base. When human bands were constantly on the move, a sprained ankle or fever could prove fatal. Once bands established home bases, they could better care for one another, and, judging from the number of very ancient healing goddesses, perhaps women created the first medicines from herbs and plants. Women probably also devised ways to ease childbirth and determined which plants were effective laxatives (rhubarb) or heart stimulants (digitalis).

Art Suggests a Sacred Dimension to Life

Figurines and wall paintings in cave sanctuaries and burial sites that have survived reveal that after about 30,000 B.C.E. some groups were beginning to draw, paint, and sculpt. The first artists must have invested a great deal of time and energy creating images in caves, and the cooperation required to support their efforts suggest early gathering-hunting communities not only shared food and cared for the young but also cooperated in the performance of ceremonies that strengthened the community.

Pictures of animals and a few human figures cover the walls of many ceremonial caves. Many of the caves went deep into the interior of the earth and could be reached only through narrow passageways. Perhaps the passages represented the channel through which a child enters the world. If so, the caves may have represented the womb of the earth goddess, and the humans and animals pictured in them were the creatures to which the goddess was going to give birth. This would suggest that people were practicing sympathetic magic. They would draw or act out an event in hopes that what they represented would actually take place. By drawing animals emerging from these caves, perhaps they were attempting to help the earth produce game.

A Goddess?

Archaeologists have unearthed countless small female figures at many ancient sites throughout the world. The so-called Venus of Willendorf, a four-inch-tall limestone carving made about 20,000 B.C.E., came from western Eurasia. She is quite fat and has no feet or facial features. Although archaeologists call her Venus, that is obviously not what early people called her. We can wonder whether she represented the goddess and whether her shape symbolized fertility. Her lack of feet may symbolize that she rose from the earth or perhaps it simply made it easier to prop her up. Might her hairstyle suggest that the people who made her came from Africa? These and other questions intrigue scholars.

Ancient ceremonies may have celebrated the cycle of life and death. Worship of the goddess and symbols of transformation associated with her could have helped people face death by suggesting a transformation back to life. Many very old drawings found in northwest Eurasia show snakes and butterflies, both symbols of the goddess and transformation. (Think of a caterpillar becoming a butterfly or a snake shedding its skin.) The earth might also have symbolized the womb and tomb of the world, inexhaustibly pouring forth new life, as new plants arose from "dead" seeds. Giant trees that shed their leaves in the fall and produced new ones in the spring also may have seemed to hold the secret of life and death.

Early humans must have been fascinated with women's ability to give birth and the fact that their menstrual cycles reflect those of the moon. Before people realized how and why women became pregnant, men may have looked at women with awe and dread as well as reverence. Many must have marveled that women could bleed but not die and wondered how they created life within their bodies.

The Middle Stone Age

Around 10,000 B.C.E. the gathering-hunting way of life started to change, and for several thousand years, at least in western Eurasia, people produced fewer artifacts of any kind and almost no art and or figurines that suggest worship activities. Archaeologists call this period of transition from about 9000 to 6000 B.C.E. the Mesolithic, or Middle Stone, Age. Pottery is an important artifact from this era. It first appears around 6500 B.C.E. It may have developed from woven containers in which people not only stored food but also tried to cook it. They may have coated branches with mud in order to keep them from burning. When they realized the mud hardened, they had invented pottery.

Learning to communicate, to use fire, to cooperate and care for one another enabled early humans to survive. The evidence of pottery suggests people were producing a surplus and needed places to store it. But how did they start to produce a surplus? What new ways to get food did people discover? What did they do with the surplus? These questions and the new possibilities they suggest are central to the next scene in the human drama.

REVOLUTIONARY CHANGES BROUGHT BY AGRICULTURE

SCENE TWO

Setting the Stage

For tens of thousands of years, generation after generation, humans had been gathering roots and plants to eat and scavenging and hunting for game. Imagine what happened once they realized what made plants grow and how to control the birth of babies and young animals. People in several areas across Afro-Eurasia began to settle down and raise food or follow a pastoral way of life centered on herding.

This dramatic breakthrough in human understanding probably began around 8000 B.C.E. in the hills of western Asia near the Zagros Mountains. Historians call these discoveries the start of the Agricultural Revolution because knowledge of agriculture and breeding animals resulted in numerous dramatic changes in how humans live. This knowledge also changed how men and women thought of themselves and their environment, and, as a result, they created new symbols and adopted new attitudes toward the land, animals, and one another.

Women were probably the first to realize that plants grew from seeds. While men were hunting, women foraged for food near their home bases, paying close attention to details of the landscape. Some must have noticed that plants they had gathered appeared at the same place the next year. Perhaps they wondered if there were any relationship between seeds they had dropped and new plants. Eventually someone must have experimented with putting seeds into the ground. Soon they realized they could control which plants grew. Gradually people discovered how to select hardier strains of grain and save the best seeds for planting. They also may have determined that ashes from fires helped make crops grow.

The other great breakthrough, learning how to breed animals, was closely related to domesticating animals, a process that spanned ten thousand years. Men probably domesticated reindeer and dogs first, then cows, sheep, pigs, and goats. These animals provided meat and milk, and their skins could be used as clothing. Early humans used dogs to control other animals and for protection and experimented with using larger animals to carry loads.

Perhaps men first figured out how animals bred. Communities must have tried to keep live animals around for food and sacrifices. Men, watching over the animals, eventu-

Species	Domesticated (year BP)	Area
Reindeer	14 000	Northern Europe/Germany
Dog	11 500	Northern Iran
Goat	9 000	Middle East/Jordan
Sheep	8 000	Northern Iran/Jordan
Cattle	7 000	Europe
Donkey	5 500	Nile Valley
Buffalo	5 000	? India
Pig	5 000	Mesopotamia
Horse	5 000	Turkestan
Cat	5 000	Nile Valley
Silkworm	5 000	China
Bee	5 000	Nile Valley
Fowl	4 500	Indus Valley/East Asia
Elephant	4 500	Indus Valley
Onager	4 000	Mesopotamia
Camel	4 000	South Arabia

Earliest radio-carbon dates in BP (before the present) for domesticated animals.

ally must have realized what happened when animals mated. From that discovery they learned how to control the breeding of animals. (It is intriguing to speculate what happened to the status of women when men and women realized the role men play in procreation.)

People Settle Down and Farm

People who farm have to stay in one place, so the agricultural way of life transformed some nomadic and seminomadic gatherers and hunters into settled farmers. Men and women began to clear forests and plant crops. People stayed put at least until the soil became exhausted, so they started to build sturdier, more permanent homes out of wood, where it was available, or bricks made of dried mud, and eventually bricks fired in ovens. Women had the primary responsibility for constructing shelters for nomadic groups, and they probably also helped build permanent homes. Catal Huyuk, a 32-acre village settlement in Anatolia (present-day Turkey), is one of the best preserved early agricultural settlements.

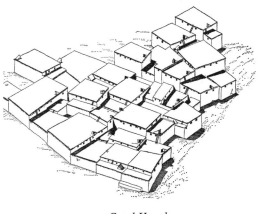

Catul Huyuk

Early farming communities were probable largely a woman's world. Men were responsible for looking after the animals and tending the herds and often hunted far away from their settlements. Women added farming to their other tasks, working in the fields with each other.

These early communities may have been both matrilineal (determining descent through the mother) and matrilocal (in which a married couple lives with the wife's family). In a matrilocal community the oldest women and their families owned the property. Children probably lost their carefree life as agriculture developed. Instead of just being responsible for finding food for themselves, they had to work on the land and learn to help grow food to feed others.

Surplus and Specialization

For many centuries these farming communities probably practiced subsistence farming, producing just enough for their own immediate needs. Almost everyone must have been involved in either raising food or tending animals. Gradually people developed better tools, including hoes to loosen the soil and make holes or furrows into which they could drop seeds. As people became experienced farmers, some communities began to produce a surplus and the population increased.

Surplus food led to specialization, another radical change from gathering and hunting times. Specialization means people perform particular jobs or roles in the community and requires cooperation. Individuals who do nonagricultural work need food, while farmers need the services of others, such as the blacksmith or priestess. Men probably specialized more than women, becoming millers, brewers, and traders, while women performed the numerous jobs associated with the family and land.

Women's activities revolved around three areas: the hearth, where they cooked and cared for small infants; the courtyard, the area in the middle of a home that was open to the sky where women carried out activities such as sewing, weaving, making baskets, pottery, jewelry, and cosmetics, teaching young boys and girls, and organizing social activities; and the field, where they gathered food, cleared, planted, cultivated, and harvested crops, found fuel for hearth fires, and collected building materials. Added to these functions were the full-time jobs of childbearing and raising the young. Women also had a special place in developing the musical tradition, singing together as they worked. Singing not only built a sense of solidarity but was also a way to pass on knowledge and wisdom to the young. Women also sang songs during public rituals and entertainment events, organized singing groups, and served as wailers at funerals.

Who Has the Most Prestige?

As greater specialization developed, so did social stratification, which involves ranking or classifying people according to status or prestige. There are several criteria by which people may be ranked. Perhaps, at first, people associated with the gods and goddesses had the most prestige. Priests or priestesses who knew how to please the divinities usually had a great deal of ritual or divine power. In hunting-gathering societies, as we have seen, a woman's ability to give birth resulted in a great deal of status. Women probably served the goddess, and some scholars suggest that the role of priestess was the only specialized work that women in these communities performed. If women were responsible for many of the religious ceremonies, men would have respected them even more.

Communities have to decide who will control the surplus and how they will divide it. Those who own the surplus are wealthier, so they often have greater status. Wealth in products such as food, animals, or jewelry serves as an important status marker. Possessing rare items not available locally would also add to an individual's status.

Land ownership is an important source of wealth, and people who control large areas of fertile land often have a great deal of status. Families and groups began owning sections of land, so boundaries became important. Individuals or families wanted to pass their land down to their sons. To do this, men had to know who their sons were, and this may help explain why men began to keep tighter control over their wives. This notion of individual ownership of plots of land likely led to both patriarchal families (controlled by men) and lower status for women when men owned the land.

Political power is another source of status. Someone or some group has to ensure individuals do not hurt each other and that the community is safe from outside attack. As communities became bigger and people were no longer members of the same family or clan, they had to follow rules to prevent fighting among themselves, settling disagreements peacefully. Those who made the rules had a great deal of power. They could decide what to do with the surplus, how much people had to give to support the community, and who had to fight and when. Men who enforced those rules and supervised the collection, storage, and distribution of food also had a great deal of power.

Gradually and relatively peacefully powerful men who could enforce the rules and protect the goods assumed the responsibility for the community's well-being. No pictures from Neolithic times depict battle scenes, soldiers fighting, or heroic conquerors. Men are pictured spearing animals, but no pictures depict military weapons or fortifications. Art historians also have had difficulty finding any images of rulers.

After the first agricultural breakthrough in western Asia, farming began to be carried on in many different parts of the world. As people supported themselves by farming, their populations increased. Some villages supported the development of the first cities, and some grew into cities themselves. But before we turn to examine how cities developed, we must consider herding, the other way of life that started during this revolutionary period in the human drama.

SCENE THREE

PASTORIALISM: AN ALTERNATIVE LIFESTYLE

Setting the Stage

Oh give me a home where the buffalo roam,
Where the deer and the antelope play,
Where seldom is heard, a discouraging word,
And the skies are not cloudy all day.

That's the cowboy song about "Home on the Range." His way of life began as part of the Agricultural Revolution. While many people were settling down and forming farming communities and villages, knowledge of how to breed animals enabled some to live by raising animals. Their way of life is called pastoralism. Pastoralists depend on their animals for survival, and they must find grassland so their animals can graze.

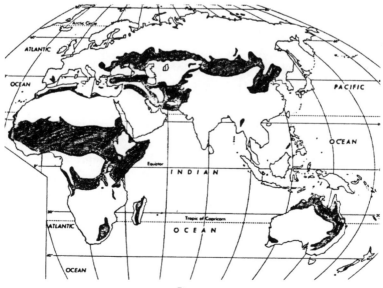

Steppes

Pastoralists lead a seminomadic life, maintaining home bases and periodically taking their herds to new grazing land. Their herding lifestyle is not a stage on the way to becoming farmers. It is a highly complicated way of life that has existed alongside agricultural communities from the time of the Agricultural Revolution to the present. Most pastoralists also hunt to supplement their diet, and, where geography permits, some do a little farming as well.

Geography largely defines where pastoralists can live. In areas such as Arabia and the steppes of Eurasia, rainfall is too sparse and the soil generally too poor to support agriculture. A tall feathery grass grows in the spring and summer months on the steppes, on which herds of sheep, goats, and cattle can graze. Inner Asia, the most extensive steppe, includes areas of the former Soviet Union plus Mongolia and parts of western China.

Indo-European and Semitic Pastoralists Depend on Their Herds and Flocks

Pastoralists in central and western Eurasia were called Indo-Europeans, and those in Arabia were known as Semites. Both Indo-Europeans and Semites had to figure out ways to survive on the scarce food these harsh environments provided. Early pastoralists struggled against wild animals, the threat of disease, hostile groups competing for the same pasturelands, and natural disasters, as well as challenging climates and little food.

Whether Semites or Indo-Europeans, herders' lives revolved around their animals, which were their source of food, clothing, shelter, transportation, wealth, and status. Pastoralists were almost like parasites living off their animals. Sheep and cattle, then horses, and eventually camels, provided meat and milk, which they fermented. ("Cattle" refers to cows, bulls, and oxen but is often used to indicate all domesticated herded or farm animals.) Women sewed animal skins into clothes. Sheep were used for their wool and their hides served as covers for shelters, and dogs provided protection and controlled other animals, but early pastoralists did not know how to harness cattle and horses to pull heavy loads or for transportation without choking them. Pastoralists also exchanged animals for other goods they needed.

Pastoralists living in inner Asia herded horses, cattle, sheep and goats. Semites in Arabia mainly herded sheep. The number of animals a man had, particularly horses, not the land where they grazed, determined his status in the community. Nomads developed a deep affection for and intimate knowledge of their animals. Herders and their animals were inseparable. Hebrew herders claimed they could recognize their sheep and their sheep could recognize them.

Challenges of the Pastoralist Way of Life

Life for these early herders was difficult and dangerous, and they became skilled fighters. They fought other pastoralists for new grazing land and to keep the land on which their herds already grazed. They also raided each other's herds. The land, by and large, provided no natural defenses such as trees, hills, or mountains. Pastoralists became adept at both defensive and offensive fighting techniques and developed innovative military strategies and technologies.

Both men and women must have shared some of the qualities we still associate with masculinity, such as aggression and physical strength. They had to be ready to fight at a minute's notice, and they endured many hardships.

Hunting was important, particularly for Indo-European pastoralists. Animals they hunted provided extra food, so herders did not have

Nomad life

to kill off as many from their own stock. Hunting was good training for fighting as it involved tracking, marksmanship, and skilled shooting. In addition, pastoralists often treated the hunt as sport.

Young boys received strict training. A boy had to learn how to train dogs and falcons as well as the habits of animals and birds. He had to understand the unwritten science of animal breeding, be able to orient himself in the endless spaces of the great steppe by day or night using the stars, the sun, and landmarks, and know by sight not only his own cattle, but those of his neighbor. He would have to cut up the carcasses of domestic and wild animals, determine the area required to feed one animal in a 24-hour period, and calculate how long he could live at a chosen encampment. He had to know what to do in times of drought, heavy rainfall, or unforeseen epidemics; know what vegetation the cattle, sheep, and goats liked at different times of the year; and be able to plan migrations so that the animals would get the necessary food and mineral supplements. He had to identify signs of disease and possible herbs and other remedies; be able to treat wounds, including an animal's broken bones; forecast changes in the weather, floods and drought by the behavior of the animals; and recognize and read both animal and human tracks.

While men were responsible for herding, hunting, and fighting, women maintained the home bases. They hauled water and collected and dried dung (manure) for fuel, made cheese and other milk products, and sewed clothes, rugs, cushions, and coverings for their homes. Women took care of children and old people as well as small animals at the home base when men drove the animals to pasture. Except for times of war or extremes of weather, pastoral men probably had an easier life and more leisure time than women.

Between 8000 B.C.E. and 6000 B.C.E., settled agriculturist and pastoralist ways of life developed in many areas of Eurasia. Their interaction, to which we now turn, is one of the main themes of the human drama.

ACT ONE – ORIGINS OF THE HUMAN COMMUNITY: LEARNING TO COOPERATE (FROM EARLY TIMES TO 3500 B.C.E.)

Setting the Stage

1. Compare how the world came to be in any two creation stories.
2. What is the relationship between people and the rest of the natural world in creation stories?
3. What does "survival of the fittest" mean? How did mutations make early primates "more fit"?
4. How many races are there? What evidence do you have for your answer?
5. If there is only one race, why is there so much variation around the world in people's skin color and appearance?
6. Do you believe in progress? If so, what do you mean by progress and what evidence can you offer to show that it exists?
7. How do you explain the origin of the world and how people came to be?

SCENE ONE
Gathering and Hunting: Humans Share the Resources

1. What is meant by Prehistory? What other name could you suggest for this period in the past?
2. Explain the differences between scavenging, gathering, and hunting for food. Why did early humans change from one way of getting food to another?
3. Why was learning to speak so important to early humans? Try to be around others and go without speaking for fifteen minutes. Explain your experience.
4. In what ways did early humans get and use fire?
5. What are the possible meanings of the cave paintings that early humans made? What do goddess figurines and drawings suggest about what early humans believed?
6. What did the tree represent to early humans? Why?
7. Why might early human males have looked on women with both awe and dread?

SCENE TWO
Revolutionary Changes Brought by Agriculture

1. What was the Agricultural Revolution? Why is it called a revolution? Do

you agree? Why or why not?

2. Explain the roles of men and women in the early agricultural communities.

3. What kinds of geography would have been good for farming? What aspects of the land and climate would make farming difficult?

4. What does specialization mean? Why must there be surplus food before there can be specialization? Why did men have more specialized roles than women had?

5. What does social stratification mean? Who probably had the most prestige in the early agricultural communities? Who has the most prestige in your community? What groups have the most prestige in the United States? What groups do you think should have the most respect? Why?

6. Why do you think early farming communities may have been relatively peaceful?

SCENE THREE
Pastoralism: An Alternate Lifestyle

1. What is the relationship between geography and the pastoral way of life? How do pastoralists take advantage of steppe lands? Why don't pastoralists farm? Why are pastoralists semi-nomadic?

2. What are the differences between Indo-European and Semitic pastoralists?

3. Explain at least five ways pastoralists make use of their animals.

4. What are the major differences between the way you live and the way pastoralists live? Which do you think is more exciting? Why do many of us romanticize the life of people on the move, such as cowboys, businessmen who travel, those who freely wander, etc.?

Summing up

1. Make a chart that compares the lifestyle and beliefs of pastoralists and agriculturists. Include things such as daily life, jobs, homes, food, who is respected, and beliefs.

2. How did gatherers, farmers, and pastoralists adapt to different geographic environments?

3. Construct a conversation between a woman living in a scavenging-gathering community with a woman living in a farming community. What might they discover was the same about their lives? What was different?

4. If you were a woman living at the time of the Agricultural Revolution, would you rather be a farmer or a pastoralist? If you were a man living at the time of the Agricultural Revolution, would you rather be a farmer or a pastoralist? Explain your answers.

5. Evaluate this statement using at least three examples from this act: "Early humans survived because they cooperated."

ACT TWO

Surplus, Specialization and Cities (third millennium B.C.E.)

For several thousand years after the Agricultural Revolution, farming and pastoral communities developed throughout Eurasia. Each group created tools, skills, customs, arts, and values—a way of life identified as their culture. Over the millennia, populations grew, and groups built complex societies, many of which revolved around cities. The urban cultures that developed between 3500 B.C.E. and 2000 B.C.E. in the Tigris-

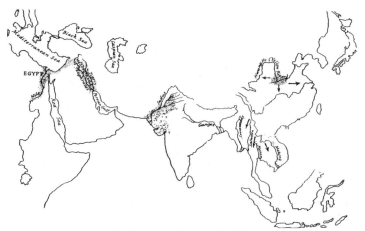

Early river valley civilizations

Euphrates, Nile, and Indus river valleys, and around the Aegean Sea, as well as agricultural settlements along the Yellow River, are the focus of this act of the human drama.

What Is So Special About River Valleys?

Even before cities appeared, many agricultural communities had grown up along the banks of large rivers, where surplus food could be found. Rivers have a constant supply of fish and waterfowl. If there is not enough rainfall to support agriculture, rivers provide the needed water. They are also a good means of transportation, allowing people to communicate over a relatively large area and making it possible for farmers to ship food to urban centers down river.

Rivers that flood their banks carry fertile silt onto the land, allowing people to farm the same area year after year without the soil losing its fertility. Farmers who settled near these rivers did not have to move to find new fertile land, so they could build larger homes and produce a surplus. But when living near rivers that flood became too dangerous and water for farming was too sparse without irrigation, people had to figure out how to dam the rivers or build irrigation canals. Flood control and irrigation projects demanded a high level of cooperation and centralized planning, both the causes and hallmarks

River valleys provided many resources

of urban life. No wonder the first cities appear to have developed in river valleys.

Characteristics of Cities

Cities are relatively large permanent settlements where a great many diverse people with different skills live close together, sharing resources and specializing in specific occupations and roles. Specialization—people performing different jobs—is an essential characteristic of all cities. Cities attract people with a wide variety of skills because they can find jobs there. Some create goods to sell, others are merchants, while some conduct religious ceremonies, record and collect taxes, keep the peace, or rule.

Specialization results in social stratification, where some people have more status than others. Religious leaders are usually held in high esteem when they seem able to communicate with divine powers. Leaders, who specialize in power, expect to be obeyed. Merchants often are wealthier than other people.

Trade is another significant feature of urban life. Although cities are usually clearly separated from the surrounding countryside, sometimes by walls and gates, urban dwellers depend on the countryside for food and other resources. Without these resources, cities could not survive. In addition, merchants often carry on long distant trade for such things as food, building materials, or luxury items not available in the surrounding area.

Why Should We Cooperate with Strangers?

Specialization, interdependence, and trade require cooperation. City dwellers must depend on others to whom they are not related and they do not know. Unless they are willing to cooperate, there would be no surplus, no specialization, in short, no urban life.

In the United States we tend to idealize individualism and think urban life affords us the most freedom. We cite as evidence that we do not even know who lives down the hall in the high-rise apartment buildings many of us call home. But how long could an urban dweller survive completely on his or her own? Think of the countless ways those of us who live in towns or cities depend on others. In the woods or in a rural community, you might be able to grow your own food, collect your own water, and keep yourself warm or safe, but how can you do that in a city?

Large-scale cooperation is difficult to maintain, so urban political, cultural, and religious leaders must help promote a set of shared cultural symbols, including a common language and beliefs, so that the diverse population will know how to act and be willing to support the city's activities. There must also be a way to keep accurate records, especially records of taxes and the sale of goods.

Should We Call These Societies Civilizations?

The first river valley societies all produced a surplus, built cities, had specialization, trade, and social stratification, created some kind of centralized government, shared values, and kept written records. Historians identify a society with these characteristics as a civilization. That does not mean societies without these characteristics are "uncivilized," a term that has a negative connotation. Nomadic societies also have highly sophisticated ways of supporting themselves, even though they did not construct large buildings or keep written records.

Terms such as "civilization" or "uncivilized" are social constructs, that is, scholars establish definitions for them and then apply the criteria to various groups. Because civilized and uncivilized frequently reflect value judgments, we must be sensitive when we use the terms; we may want to use the term "complex society" instead. While we need categories to make sense of the past and to distinguish among different ways of life, these categories should help us describe what happened rather than judge whether one group was better than another.

Why Did Cities Develop?

Two prominent world historians, Arnold Toynbee and William McNeill, among others, have offered theories on what motivates human beings to create complex societies and why cities developed in certain regions and not others. Although there are many explanations for the birth of cities, their theories may stimulate your thinking not only about this important development but about what causes other significant change over time.

Arnold Toynbee, a famous early twentieth-century English, believed the key to human development lay in "challenge and response." Toynbee argued that difficult conditions challenge a group, causing it to respond with extra effort in order to survive. This response enables people to overcome hardships and build a more complex system or invent new technology. When life is too easy, there is no challenge and therefore no reason to change. One just reaches out and plucks fruit from the tree or fish from the stream: no innovation is necessary. Likewise, Toynbee cautioned, people will be overwhelmed and unable to respond if the challenge is too great. We might add the "Goldilocks Corollary" to his theory of challenge and response: like Goldilocks's porridge, the challenge must be just right—neither too difficult (too hot) nor too easy (too cold)—if humans are to seize the opportunity to make significant break-throughs.

William McNeill, a well-known American world historian, suggests that a major reason for human development is interaction among
groups. When various groups with different lifestyles meet, they stimulate each other, borrowing and adapting new ideas or else developing
ways to protect themselves from those ideas. McNeill believes interaction leads to innovations, particularly new technology, which is the
key to social change. Interaction and the exchange of ideas stimulate
new technological development. Notice that both Toynbee and
McNeill assumed that human beings evolve better ways of doing
things, and both scholars looked for reasons for progress.

Challenge and Response
Along the Tigris and Euphrates Rivers

Let's apply Toynbee's theory of challenge and response and McNeill's
idea that cultural interaction produces new technology to the development of cities in Mesopotamia, the area between the Tigris and
Euphrates rivers. The rivers originate in the Armenian highlands and
run south to the Persian Gulf. Six thousand years ago the land
between the rivers was swampy but very fertile, while the land
beyond the rivers was barren and arid. Cities developed first in
Sumer, the area near the Persian Gulf in southern Mesopotamia.

Unfortunately the Tigris and Euphrates rivers flooded irregularly,
often catastrophically, making life very precarious for those who lived
near their banks. Swampy land had to be drained, and people had to
cooperate to create irrigation and flood control. Sparse rainfall meant
water from the rivers had to be diverted onto the land if agriculture
was to thrive. Furthermore, there were no natural barriers to protect
settled communities from outside threats, so the Sumerians also had
to cooperate to defend themselves.

On the other hand, Mesopotamia had many attractions. Flooding
river water deposited a layer of rich silt onto the land, constantly
renewing its fertility. When the land was properly irrigated, the crop
yield was very high. The rivers made it easy for farmers to trade their
surplus crops, and traders could travel through the Persian Gulf to the
Arabian Sea to find markets for their goods.

Conditions must have been "just right" in Mesopotamia because
people gradually began to work together to build flood control and

irrigation projects. They cooperated to clear swamps and construct dikes and canals to control the floodwaters. During times of drought, which was most of the year, water flowed through these irrigation canals, making possible planting and harvesting crops.

McNeill's theory also applies. Because no natural barriers protected Mesopotamia from nearby areas, and Sumerians produced large surpluses, outsiders were constantly coming into the region in search of food and other goods, bringing new ideas and challenging the Sumerians to figure out how to defend themselves.

Similar reasons could explain the development of cities along the Nile River in north Africa, the Indus River in the Indian subcontinent, and the Yellow River valley in present-day China, and, later, along many rivers, such as the Mekong River in mainland Southeast Asia, the Niger River in west Africa, and the Mississippi River. Each of the complex societies that developed along these rivers created a unique style of life that continues to influence people today. In this act of the human drama we will examine five of these early complex societies.

CITY-STATES IN MESOPOTAMIA

Setting the Stage

"History begins at Sumer," states Samuel Kramer, one of the foremost scholars of ancient history. In the mud flats where the unpredictable Tigris and Euphrates rivers empty into the Persian Gulf, many people worked together to drain the swampy land between the two rivers and control the flooding water. They harvested abundant produce from the fertile soil near the riverbanks, and with this surplus they supported larger dense populations and built cities. People had enough food to reward the goddesses and gods as well as feed the growing population. They also traded with Anatolia, Egypt, and even the Indus valley, for minerals, wood, and stone, which Sumer lacked.

The cities of Sumer all had their own separate governments and rules. Although everyone spoke and wrote the same language and prayed to the same gods and goddesses, each city was under the spe-

Ancient Mesopotamia

cial protection of its own divinity, and they often competed, particularly for water and trading rights. Each city was independent and had sovereignty—final authority over what happened within its boundaries. Because these are the characteristics of a state, we identify Sumer as a collection of city-states.

What Do Written Records Reveal About Sumer?

If history depends on written records, Sumerian history begins around 3600 B.C.E. when people in the urban settlements at the southern end of the Tigris-Euphrates rivers developed writing. Sumerians wrote on clay tablets, using the end of a reed to impress a mark or wedge in the soft clay, which they baked. They first made pictograms, images that looked like the things they were writing about. Later they added ideograms—a single image for a single idea—and phonograms—an image that stood for the sound of a syllable; all three might appear on one tablet. By 3200 B.C.E. the Sumerians had created five to six hundred symbols in the writing system called cuneiform (from the Latin word for wedge: *cuneus*). Many of their clay tablets have survived, and they tell a great deal about life in Sumer.

The oldest written records archaeologists have found report numbers of sheep and goats and amounts of barley and dates, so obviously people recorded their produce. They also put seals on sacks of goods, probably to indicate ownership. Besides commercial records, Sumerians created a rich religious literature including individual prayers, litanies (that both the priest or priestess and people prayed), and hymns of praise. The Sumerians' extensive library contained over 30,000 clay tablets, stacked one on top of another. By 2000 B.C.E. historians were compiling a record of their past, and poets were writing down *Gilgamesh*, the thousand-year-old epic about their god-king.

Lamentations (public expressions of grief) reflect the precarious nature of life in the Tigris-Euphrates valley, where flash floods and devastating winds might erupt at any time. In the view of the Sumerians, a city's patron deity was responsible for both blessings and disasters. Laments reveal men and women mourning because the gods caused storms and blinding hurricanes, which annihilated the land, and brought tempests that beat down and devoured the city's ships. In addition, rival cities or plundering nomadic bands might attack without warning.

Some cuneiform tablets reveal everyday life. For example, a father scolds his son:

> . . . . why do you idle about? Go to school, stand
> before your "school-father," recite your assignment,
> pen your schoolbag, write your tablet, let your "big
> brother" write your new tablet for you. After you
> have finished your assignment and reported to your
> mentor, come to me. . . . Don't stand about in the
> public square or wander about the boulevard. . . . Go
> to school, it will be of benefit to you. . . . I, night and
> day am I tortured because of you. Night and day you
> waste in pleasures. . . .

Inferring Values from How Cities Look

Sumerians believed their gods and goddesses lived in temples called ziggurats. A ziggurat was a massive stepped tower with a huge square or rectangular base and as many as seven similar shaped smaller stories on top of the base. Its foundation was made of stone, but the upper stories were built of baked brick because stone was scarce in Sumer. Homes were clustered around the ziggurat.

City-planning can reveal a great deal about a society's values. The size and position of buildings indicates who had the most status and power. If the ziggurat was in the center of the city and was bigger and

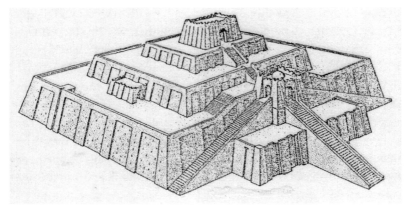

A Ziggurat

more impressive than any other building, then religion must have been central to people's lives. Obviously people worked hard to construct and support such a large building and the rituals performed in it. Cities with a palace as well as a ziggurat suggest political leaders were also important, perhaps even more important than the priests. Whether cities have walls or not is also revealing. They may indicate that people felt threatened and wanted to kept outsiders away. Walls around certain sections of a city can indicate segregated communities, or be a way to control the population or monitor trade.

Serving the Divinities

In the early years of Sumer the ziggurat was the center of city life. The economy has been called a temple economy because much of its activity was directed by and for the ziggurats. Sumerians must have hoped to impress and please their deities by building such grand structures. The god or goddess who lived in the ziggurat was like a great landowner presiding over his or her estate, and much of the land belonged to the deities. Tenants who farmed temple land paid their local deity, the landowner, for its use.

The special group who took care of the deities in the ziggurat-temples had many more duties than those we normally associate with priests or priestesses. Their responsibilities included religious, economic, social, and political activities. They served the gods and goddesses as servants would serve a landlord or as courtiers and courtesans serve a ruler. They tried to anticipate what the gods and goddesses desired by reading heavenly signs and other omens, such as the direction flocks of birds flew or from the intestines of sacrificed animals. Once temple servants had figured out what the divinities wanted, they announced what sacrifices, prayers, or goods people should offer in thanksgiving or supplication (asking for things they wanted).

Temple servants controlled what farmers grew and how that produce was distributed, and they directed peasants and slaves to do the god's or goddess's bidding. They supervised farming, determining when to sow, irrigate, and harvest, and oversaw work draining swamps and constructing irrigation works. They had a monopoly on education and learning, and because they mediated between gods and goddesses and human beings, they had extraordinary economic and political, as well as religious, power.

What Gives Leaders Legitimacy?

Obviously men and women believed the temple servants had the right to rule, and they were willing to obey their commands. When most people obey a ruler's commands, we say he or she has legitimacy. Using weapons and saying "might makes right" are not enough. If people obey only because the ruler has the strongest army and can force them to do what he says, he can be overthrown as soon as someone else amasses more military might. Successful leaders appeal to fundamental values to justify their actions, and most people will obey a ruler they think is legitimate without being threatened.

As long as Sumerians believed the temple servants were in contact with the gods and goddesses and were pleasing them, and could pass on divine wishes and rules, they had legitimacy. But Mesopotamia did not have protective natural barriers, and prayers and sacrifices did not always stop raiders intent on carrying off goods. Sumerians often had to rely on an army for safety, and military leaders began to compete with religious leaders for legitimacy.

Why Marry a Goddess?

The constant threat of attack—either from nomads or other city-states —increased the city-states' need for military leaders. A leader sometimes became a king and established a hereditary monarchy (meaning his son or daughter ruled when he died). The palace was gradually becoming as important as the ziggurat, and the king, his family, and court officials gained control over a lot of land and the people who worked it. But in order to get legitimacy, these rulers had to prove that they had a special relationship with the gods and goddesses, often accomplished by performing a sacred marriage with the goddess. The main priestess would represent the goddess in a marriage ceremony that legitimated the ruler.

The ritual marriage between the would-be ruler and the priestess who represented the goddess became the most important ritual performed in the ziggurat. The Sumerians also believed it insured the fertility of the people, land, and cattle. As a result of this holy marriage:

Plants grew high by their side.
Grains grew high by their side.
Gardens flourished luxuriantly.

Trade, a very important aspect of life in the Sumerian city-states, also helped leaders establish their legitimacy. If only the leader could own or wear lapis lazuli and other rare items that traders brought, these goods helped establish and reflect his importance and status.

Belief in the powers of the gods and goddesses, the effectiveness of the temple servants, and the strength of their armies encouraged people to obey orders from the ziggurat and the palace. When the harvests were good, the floods were controlled, and the city walls and armies kept raiders and invaders out, the Sumerians must have believed the divinities were pleased and that all would be well. But life in Mesopotamia was precarious at best. One never knew when the rivers might flood, when violent storms might come, or when enemies might attack. In the next act we look at how these threats intensify as nomads in increasing numbers try to get some of Mesopotamia's wealth. But first we turn to see how urban life was developing in other areas.

PERMANENCE AND PEACE
ALONG THE NILE

Setting the Stage

The second major river valley civilization developed along the Nile
River in present-day Egypt. Egypt's long history as an independent
civilization is impressive, extending from around 3400 B.C.E. until the
first century of the common era, nearly two-thirds of all recorded
human history. Ancient Greek historians called Egypt the Gift of the
Nile because nearly every aspect of Egyptian life was related to the
river. The bountiful existence that characterized ancient Egypt owed
much to the fertile soil and abundant wildlife of the Nile valley.
Moreover, natural barriers allowed Egyptians to develop a relatively
peaceful way of life.

The Gift of the Nile

The Nile River originates in the Sudan in Ethiopia and flows north (so
on our maps it looks as though it is flowing uphill). Boats can float
north on the river current and sail south, blown by the wind, enabling
the movement of communication and trade to go in either direction
along the 700-mile stretch from the first cataract (a major obstruction
of rocks and currents) to where the river empties into the Mediterranean Sea. Farther south there are additional cataracts.

The Nile floods regularly, mildly, and predictably. The annual
flooding, called an inundation, usually spreads about six feet of water
over a six-to-ten-mile-wide area on both sides of the river, depositing
rich silt that keeps the soil very fertile. Beyond this thin band of irrigated land, arid deserts stretch east toward Saudi Arabia and west for
hundreds of miles into the great Sahara Desert. Both deserts and
cataracts protected Egyptians from outside invaders, in contrast to
Mesopotamia, which had no natural barriers protecting it.

Because the climate in the Nile Valley does not change, Egyptians
had to devise a way to figure out when inundations would occur.

Their calendar was divided into three seasons: inundation, when the river floods (June to September); emergence, when the fields reappear (October to February); and drought, when all is dry (February to June). Sacred days were added periodically to keep the seasons consistent. Egyptians counted the years of a ruler's reign and, when a new ruler came to power, they started over again.

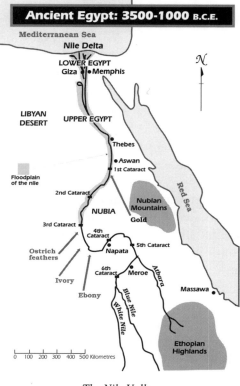

The Nile Valley

Because the Egyptians could plant as the land re-emerged in October and were able to rely on the natural drainage of the Nile valley, supplemented by simple canals, for their summer crops, they did not have to construct monumental irrigation project. They cooperated to control the precious water and distribute it fairly during the long periods of emergence and drought. They kept track of who owned the land and what it produced. Land nearest the river was assessed at a higher tax rate than barren land beyond. Law courts heard disputes over who should have access to the Nile water, and Egyptians believed that at their final judgment, they would have to swear that they had not killed, robbed, or "held up the water in its season or built a dam against running water." Record keeping was also essential in order to dig canals, chart the changing river, construct levees, and locate boundaries obliterated by flooding water.

Egyptians Create Hieroglyphics

Whereas Sumerians developed cuneiform writing, Egyptians created hieroglyphics (from the Greek words for "sacred carvings"). At first a hieroglyph stood for a whole word or even an entire idea. Gradually most of the symbols began to stand for sounds and had little or nothing to do with what was pictured. (It would be as if you drew a picture of a body of water—a sea—and added a picture of a saw to make the word "see-saw".) Egyptians also developed 24 hieroglyphs that stood for the 24 consonants. Recent excavations indicate they created an alphabet as early as 3200 B.C.E., which would make it the first alphabet.

Egyptians wrote on strips of papyrus (water plants from which we get the word paper), slitting the stalks and pressing them into flat sheets. Historians have lots of information about ancient Egypt because records on papyrus and many other artifacts, including buildings and wall paintings, have survived in the dry climate. From these sources historians can infer a great deal about Egyptian society.

Uniting the Communities

In about 3500 B.C.E. many small independent communities along the southern part of the Nile united and became the Kingdom of Upper Egypt. In the north, communities in the Nile delta (the 100-mile triangular-shaped mouth of the river named after the Greek letter delta: Δ) joined to become the Kingdom of Lower Egypt. Unlike Sumer, where priests ruled, powerful chieftains governed both kingdoms.

About 3200 B.C.E. King Menes united Upper and Lower Egypt, making his capital at Memphis where the Nile delta starts. To symbolize this unity, rulers often wore a crown that combined those of both Upper and

Crowns: Lower Egypt, Double Crown, Upper Egypt

Lower Egypt. King Menes established a hereditary monarchy. When Menes died, his son ruled and then his son's son. Egyptians used the thirty dynasties (rule by a single family) to establish dates.

Egypt's ruler was called a pharaoh, and he was considered semidivine. When the pharaoh died, Egyptians believed he joined the other gods and goddesses in the afterworld. Those who had served the pharaoh or who were close to him might hope to continue to serve him in the afterworld as well.

Egypt's Pyramid-Shaped Society

Egyptian society was rather like the pyramids the pharaohs had built. At the top was the pharaoh, who directed the economy, handled relations with both local communities and outsiders, and established the laws. Egyptians believed he was responsible for the inundation of the Nile and the abundance of the soil. The land also belonged to the pharaoh.

Under the pharaoh and directly responsible to him were his advisors and ministers. The vizier, the most important government official next to the pharaoh, presided over the high courts, oversaw the collection of taxes, maintained peace, and headed the police. He was responsible for moving and distributing food and organizing workers on public works projects, such as building pyramids. The vizier had to balance the needs and requests of the forty governors, each of whom controlled a local community. These local governors often did what they pleased, and some of them attained great power, especially when the central government was weak.

Next came the priests who interpreted the will of the gods. Priests had a great deal of power and sometimes competed with the pharaoh and ministers for authority. To keep priests loyal, pharaohs exempted them from paying taxes or sending their servants to work on public building projects.

Scribes, below the vizier and priests, made up the Egyptian bureaucracy. (A bureaucracy does the day-to-day administrative work of the government, and bureaucrats are expected to serve whoever is ruling and not get involved in power struggles. Bureaucrats often survive because they can please any supervisor. We call government bureaucrats civil servants, meaning citizens who serve the government.) Egypt developed one of the world's first bureaucracies and maintained it for two thousand years. A pharaoh, advising his son on whom to appoint as bureaucrats, stated: "Advance thy great men, so they may carry out thy laws. . . . Do not distinguish the son of a noble man from a poor man, but take to thyself a man because of the work of his hands."

Bureaucrats, known as scribes, kept records, collected taxes on land, herds, and the goods that artisans made, and ensured that everyone obeyed the rules. Scribes recorded what each parcel of land produced and who lived there. They surveyed fields, supervised collections, and recorded payments. Payment was made in kind (crops people grew), because there was no money. Any male could become a scribe, but the training was exacting. Boys studied five to twelve years from dawn to dark each day, tediously copying by hand classical manuscripts, sample letters, and government lists.

Below scribes came artisans (craftsmen), who built ships, cut stones, helped construct palaces and pyramids, crafted jewelry, and wove cloth. Each craft had its own pay scale and standards, which were passed on to family members. Artisans were paid in bread, beer, and beans and other vegetables.

Peasants, farming the land, were the largest group and supported the rest of the society. Much of what they grew went to the pharaoh and priests. During periods when they were not plowing, planting, tending crops, and harvesting, peasants were required to work on public works projects, such as irrigation canals and pyramid construction. This kind of work, a form of taxation, is called corvée. Egyptians were required to provide several months of corvée when they were not farming.

Everyday Life Along the Nile

No written records tell about peasant life, but judging from pictures, songs, and stories that have survived, their lives were not especially hard. The soil was rich and the Nile had lots of game and water fowl, so men and women usually had enough to eat. In addition, the government stored food to distribute during periods of scarcity caused by flooding, plagues of locust, or other natural disasters. If the inundation was too high, floods might destroy homes; if the inundation was sparse, there might be a period of famine; but generally the inundation was regular and life-giving. In the most fertile mud-lands, Egyptian farmers grew wheat and barley, which they made into bread and beer. They also spun flax into linen cloth. Papyrus—from which they made paper, canoes, baskets and boxes, and cord—grew in the delta.

Women in Egyptian society were respected and enjoyed many of the same rights as men. Originally, the mother inherited the family's wealth. Women were allowed to own property and even operate a business. They testified in court, served on juries, and could serve as trustees for property rights for their brothers and sisters. Several women became pharaohs, and the pharaoh's sisters and wives had a lot of influence. To ensure passing on "royal blood," sons and daughters of the pharaoh often intermarried, and sisters often influenced their brothers' decisions.

Making Egyptian women more beautiful

Egyptian paintings and sculptures show husbands and wives working, sitting, talking, and eating together, enjoying the company of their children, even hunting together. Wives often managed the household, and couples wanted children. The following advice comes from a father to his son:

> If thou art successful, and hast furnished thy house, and lovest the wife of thy bosom, then fill her stomach and clothe her back .... Make glad her heart during the time thou hast with her, for she is a field profitable to its owner. . . . If thou oppose her it will mean thy ruin. (Instructions of Ptahhotep)

Unmarried young men and women were quite free to have sexual relations with one another, but once they married, husbands and wives were expected to remain completely faithful. Men were cautioned not to have anything to do with another man's wife.

> If you want to make friendship last
> In a house you enter,
> Whether as a lord, or brother, or friend,
> Beware of approaching the women!
> (Instructions of Ptahhotep)

Religion was very important in Egyptian life. Art, agriculture, government, and medicine all depended on the gods. Early Egyptian religion was filled with nature worship and images of animal-like deities. It was also common for each community to have its own special god or goddess that protected the people who lived there.

IMAGINE BUILDING A PYRAMID

The key element linking human life on earth with the life of the gods was the pharaoh, who straddled these two worlds. If the pharaoh continued to exist after his death, he could ensure the well-being of all Egyptians, so building great pyramid tombs to house the dead pharaohs' *ka* (soul) and *ba* (physical vitality) was important.

Sphinx and Great Pyramid at Giza

Immense pyramids symbolized the grandeur of the Egyptian government as well as the seeming permanence of the civilization. The most impressive pyramids were built during the Fourth Dynasty. The greatest pyramids are at Giza; the tallest one is 481 feet high and was probably even higher when it was built. The base is more than 700 feet wide.

These achievements are all the more awesome because the Egyptians had few tools and no pulleys. Talented engineers supervised large crews of workers who carved massive building blocks ranging from 2.5 to 15 tons at Aswan, 450 miles up the Nile. They floated the blocks on barges to Giza, pushed them onto sleds, dragged them to the building site and up mud-brick ramps that went around the sides of the pyramid, and finally hauled each block, which had to be perfectly level and have the right slope, into its proper place.

Imagine what it took to house and feed all those workers. (Herodotus, a Greek historian, was so impressed he estimated it must have taken 100,000 workers 20 years to build one pyramid.) Where would they sleep? How would they get enough food? What would they do in their free time? Recent excavations suggest that near the pyramids the Egyptians may have constructed large dormitory settlements where the huge numbers of administrators, laborers, and support groups required to build the great pyramids lived.

Pyramid and temple construction was extremely expensive and put a strain on the government's resources. In addition, both temple lands and priests were not taxed; local governors collected their own taxes, further reducing the central government's income and power. In response, the government raised taxes, causing unrest. When harvests were poor and famine threatened, and the government could no longer provide sufficient emergency food, peasants revolted. By 2200 B.C.E. the central government could no longer keep the peace, and local leaders had to deal with the unrest.

Linking this World and the World of the Dead

After more than 200 years, leaders in Thebes, a city in southern Egypt, finally regained control of the country, and in about 2040 B.C.E. Egypt began a new era of centralized rule. During this time Egyptians made impressive achievements in the arts and literature.

Farmer and wife in the Egyptian afterlife

They built new irrigation systems, including a canal that connected the Nile valley with the Red Sea. They carried on a lively trade with Nubia, the land along the Upper Nile, south of the first cataract. Egyptian businessmen and merchants were also a common sight in the trading cities of Syria and Palestine.

By the end of the second millennium B.C.E., Egyptians believed even average people could hope to enjoy the afterlife, not just the pharaoh and those who served him. At death, Osiris, the god of the underworld, would weigh a person's virtues and faults. Good people could expect a blissful eternity, while people who had not been as good would die once and for all. A very important and enduring legacy of ancient Egyptian religion was the belief that the way people acted during their lifetime determined their status after death.

The grave was one's eternal home, and people worked long and hard building tombs. They began to imagine the afterlife as a continuation of this world, where leaders were always good and the gods gave each person a source of water and a piece of land. Tomb inscriptions and paintings show healthy, attractive, well-fed people in the world of the dead. The afterlife lasted as long as a person's corpse did not disintegrate, which explains why Egyptians were so concerned with preserving dead bodies and even invented a way of embalming a corpse so that mummies (dead bodies preserved by embalming) would last for thousands of years.

Egyptians devoted most of their talents and energies to building huge irrigation works, monumental pyramids, temples, palaces, and the world's first really effective bureaucracy. Unlike the Sumerians,

they did not have to worry very much about creating and maintaining an efficient army, because the desert and cataracts discouraged invaders. Instead Egyptians could spend a great deal on social programs and public works.

But will the Egyptians be able to maintain their relatively peaceful lifestyle and continue to spend their resources constructing monumental public buildings? Will their weak army make them vulnerable if outsiders decide to attack? When we return to their story in the next act, we shall see what happened to Egyptian society when another struggle for power between the central government and the local communities erupted in about 1800 B.C.E.

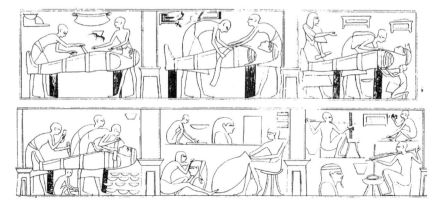

Preparing a body for mummification

SCENE
THREE

CITY PLANNING
IN THE INDUS VALLEY

Setting the Stage

The third and largest river valley civilization developed along the the the
Indus River in what is now Pakistan and the western part of India.
Historians know little about the life and thoughts of the people who
walked the streets of the ancient Indus cities of Harappa and
Mohenjo-Daro more than 5000 years ago. Archaeologists have
unearthed many artifacts, but scholars have not yet deciphered the
Indus script, so historians must try to figure out what life was like
from artifacts such as seals, art work, tools, and toys.

Before the 1920s historians in India and the rest of the world had
no idea there had ever been an Indus civilization and Indians had long
since forgotten that this great civilization was part of their past. A
conquering god who helped his people invade India was identified as
"destroyer of cities," but historians thought that meant he was very
powerful, nothing more. No one looked for the cities he might have
destroyed. Amazement rippled through the scholarly community
when several young Indian archaeologists excavated the remains of
Mohenjo-Daro in 1922 and realized it had flourished in 2500 B.C.E.
and been part of one of the three oldest civilizations.

When the British started building railroads in northern India in the
nineteenth century, they were pleased to find large numbers of baked
bricks near what later proved to be the site of Harappa, one of the
largest Indus cities. Bricks—all the exact same size and spread over a
considerable area—made excellent beds for the British railroad tracks.
Few stopped to question where these bricks had come from, even
though people in the area were not making baked bricks. Indians had
also been using these ancient bricks to build their own homes for generations, thankful they were of better quality than the sun-dried ones
they were producing.

The other clue to Indus cities were numerous small seals that farmers found as they plowed their fields. These baked mud or stone seals, usually about one or two inches square, contained pictures of animals or fish, and some had what looked like writing. Archaeologists have now discovered a great many seals, not only at Indus sites but as far away as Iraq and Egypt, but despite much scholarly effort, no one has figured out the Indus writing system. Even so, the seals offer clues about life in the Indus valley.

What Did Indus Cities Look Like?

The first major Indus cities archaeologists excavated were Mohenjo-Daro, which is located on the Indus River, and Harappa, which lies about 370 miles to the northeast, on the Ravi River. Archaeologists have recently discovered that another river once ran parallel to the Indus, and there were lots of cities along that river as well. More than 1,500 Indus-period towns and cities have now been identified, suggesting that the Indus civilization covered half a million square miles, equal to a triangular area with 1,000-mile sides. The Indus civilization appears to have extended from the border of present-day Iran to Meerut, near the modern city of New Delhi, north to the Himalaya

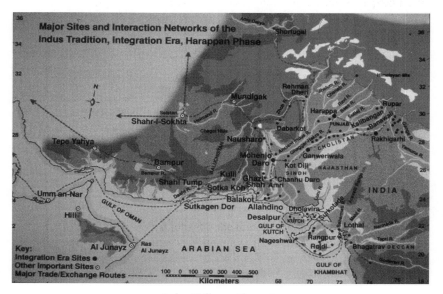

Indus Valley settlements

Mountains and south almost to Bombay. No ancient civilization covered this much territory until the Roman Empire, 2,500 years later.

The Indus people planned their cities carefully, so there must have been some kind of centralized control. Many streets are laid out at right angles on a north-south and east-west grid. The baked bricks, the major building material, are the same size throughout, and builders used the same unique method of laying bricks. Homes were usually two stories, with central courtyards open to the sky. Brick walls around some of the cities might have protected residents from attack, but more likely they were used to control floods and help authorities keep track of who came into the city.

One of the most impressive features of the city planning in Harappa and Mohenjo-Daro is the sophisticated plumbing and drainage system. Many houses in Harappa had latrines and bathing platforms made of water-tight floors with drains. Most homes were connected to the elaborate city-wide drainage system, which carried waste to drains under the main avenues and out of the city. The drains were covered with bricks that people could remove when they wanted to clear away waste. The whole system was interconnected, and the entire city was laid out in a gentle slope to allow gravity to carry excess water and waste beyond the city walls. In areas with very little rainfall, people may also have used some drains to carry water to storage areas.

Drains and a well in Lothal

Harapa was at least 3.5 miles in circumference and probably had from thirty-five to fifty thousand inhabitants. Artisans—such as dye-makers and weavers—probably lived together in separate neighborhoods. Recent excavations suggest various neighborhoods were walled, perhaps to facilitate recording and controlling trade. Streets, running through gateways, connected the neighborhoods, and trade may have taken place near these gateways.

Each housing block in Mohanjo-daro had one or more private wells. Houses faced small alleys connected to large avenues, which were laid out so that wind blowing down the streets served as a natural air conditioning system. Having few windows opening onto the main streets protected inhabitants from dust that otherwise would have blown into their homes and offered privacy from the prying eyes of neighbors.

The Importance of Trade

Trade seems to have been a central feature of the Indus civilization, and trade may have existed in that area as early as 3500 B.C.E. Many Indus seals unearthed at Ur and other Sumerian sites demonstrate significant commerce between the Indus cities and Sumer. One recently discovered Indus seal shows two traders, one a Sumerian and the other a Harappan, standing by what appears to be an interpreter.

Indus seals

Indus farmers grew wheat and barley and were the first to figure out how to make clothe out of cotton plants and grow cotton commercially. They also dyed the cloth and decorated it using wood blocks. Cotton cloth was a major innovation.

Highly skilled artisans processed ivory and shells as well as cotton goods. Craftsmen made tiny bead jewelry of semi-precious stones,

The dock and locks at Lothal

which they traded in Sumer for refined copper and tin. Artisans also produced bronze tools such as saws. An interesting four-inch-tall, stone male figure, with an extended stomach and doweled arms that allowed the arms to rotate, is an example of the skilled workmanship of Indus artists.

Lothal, now about 30 miles inland from the Arabian Sea, was a port city in western India and perhaps the capital of the southern province. Lothal had a carefully designed dockyard, the earliest of its kind in the world. Ships entered the dock at high tide, and a water-locking device in the spillway of its southern wall kept the water level even at low tide. As many as thirty 60-ton ships could dock at Lothal at any one time.

Grain stored in numerous granaries both within the cities and along the river, suggests that Indus merchants traded surplus food. Differences in wealth must have existed, because artisans made both cheap and expensive jewelry, plates, and bowls (not unlike our designer and K-Mart jeans). People did not bury gold or other valuable materials in graves. Instead, they buried cheap bangles and other jewelry made of bone or clay, in order to keep wealth circulating rather than burying it.

The "Great Bath" on the citadel at Mohenjo-Daro

Purity, Pollution, and Power

One of the most interesting buildings at Mohenjo-Daro is the so-called Great Bath on the citadel, the raised area that dominates the northern part of the city. This 39-by-23-foot watertight structure was surrounded by small rooms. Lined drains, connected to the bottom of the central tank, prove it contained water, but what the tank or bath was used for remains a mystery. Perhaps it was similar to modern Japanese public baths, where Indus people relaxed after a hard day on the docks, at the kiln, or in the bead factory. The bath may have had religious significance, with water serving as a purifying element in Indus life. So much attention to drainage may mean people were concerned about cleanliness and perhaps ritual purity as well.

Ritual purity is usually associated with religious beliefs, and priests often have elaborate texts explaining how to maintain it. People who want their food to be ritually pure may insist that animals are butchered in the proper way or require food to be cooked in a particular way. Things that are not ritually pure are not necessarily dirty, but they have not been blessed or prepared according to religious rules. Evidence suggests ritual purity could have been important in Indus cities.

Although we really do not know what the "Great Bath" was for, one eminent Indian historian argues that it served as a pool where lotuses grew and relates it directly to goddess worship because the lotus is a common symbol of the goddess. The small rooms around the pool might have been where priestesses conducted rituals.

Archaeologists have discovered thousands of small figurines throughout the Indus valley that are unmistakable Mother Goddess figures and demonstrate her importance in Indus religion. Trees, also associated with the goddess, were also significant. Some seals picture sacred trees with horned figures, which might represent deities, sitting in or near them. Since no permanent altars have been identified, perhaps worship took place at the foot of sacred trees or in sacred groves.

Who Was In Charge?

Indus homes were modest and, unlike in Egypt and Sumer, people did not spend their resources on impressive temples, palaces, or burial tombs. So far, no one has unearthed any large buildings where persons with a great deal of status or power might have lived. Archaeologists have found only a few representations of human beings in the Indus excavations. One shows the bust of an aristocratic-looking man with eyes half shut, possibly a priest-king or a prosperous merchant.

Was this man a priest, merchant or official?

Horned figure in yoga position

Perhaps priests and priestesses ruled from the Great Bath, or, since trade was so important, maybe merchants ruled.

One intriguing seal shows a man wrapped in a tiger skin and wearing an animal headdress. He is seated with legs crossed and hands relaxed over his thighs, a posture commonly associated with yoga. Yoga, a mystic practice of intense concentration, originated in the Indian subcontinent, and the seal suggests that this important religious practice is 4,500 years old! If the seal is indeed an early yogi, then the figure on the seal may be the earliest known representation of the great Indian god Shiva, who is often shown as a meditating yogi, seated on a tiger skin. Bulls, also pictured on several Indus seals, are associated with the worship of Shiva as well.

Objects that look like modern lingams have also been unearthed. Although some identify the lingam as a phallic symbol, it is an aniconic (non-representational) symbol of Shiva's creative potency. (The lingam is the major form in which Shiva is worshipped in India today and may be the oldest continuing religious sacred symbol in the world.)

Some historians and archaeologists think the Indus civilization may have been composed of semi-autonomous city-states (not unlike Sumer), ruled by local elite groups of merchants, landowners, or religious leaders. There is no evidence that any one individual had power for any period of time, and no images that look like kings have been discovered. Historians have little

A young girl with bangles

knowledge of everyday life. There is a small bronze figurine of a girl. Her smile and posture might say, "Don't mess with me" or "Come hither." Many carefully designed toys, including tiny two-wheel toy carts pulled by miniature clay cattle with moving heads, have been found. They also had dice and a board game that might have been an ancient form of chess.

One of the most startling discoveries about the Indus civilization is the absence of weapons. The only ones that have been found were probably used for spearing fish. There is no indication that the Indus had armies or used force to control or protect the vast territory. No city appears to have been destroyed by war or fire, and there is no evidence that people died violent deaths.

What Happened to Indus Cities?

For most of its thousand-year history, men and women seem to have been conservative and reluctant to change their ways. Mohenjo-Daro contains no less than ten nearly identical cities, each one built on top of the last. When a building fell down or was torn down, residents built a similar structure in its place.

But sometime between 1900 and 1700 B.C.E., life in the Indus cities appears to have changed dramatically. Houses are smaller, and the drainage is shoddy. Streets were no longer laid out in the careful grid pattern so characteristic of earlier building. Excavations suggest many people started moving from the countryside into the cities, crowding into buildings and perhaps overwhelming the urban centers. Unburied skeletons found on the top layer of Mohenjo-Daro probably belonged to people who died from disease and were thrown into abandoned alleyways in run-down sections of the city. If so, they attest to the breakdown of city services.

What caused the great influx of people into urban centers and the destruction of the Indus way of life? For one thing, trade in the region seems to have decreased after 1900 B.C.E. Maybe the climate changed because people had cut down so many trees to bake the bricks. Sometime around 1700 B.C.E. great floods and other geologic changes occurred in the Indus and related river systems. One river seems to have dried up entirely, and the Indus River changed its course and could no longer support the rich farmland that had made city life possible. Towns that had been on the sea coast were no longer ports, further disrupting trade. Without surplus grain, it was impossible to support artisans, and traders lost their economic base. Many people were forced back into subsistence farming, and a once-proud civilization lost its political and economic control.

A gate and drains at Harappa

Whatever the causes, urban centers crumbled and eventually the civilization itself was forgotten. Or was it? Did such things as goddess worship, reverence for trees, water, snakes, lotuses, yoga, Shiva, and bulls, as well as a fascination with ritual purity, die with the Indus cities, or will these things re-emerge in later times? As we continue through the human drama, be looking for practices in India that might have originated in the Indus valley.

SETTLEMENTS ALONG
THE YELLOW RIVER

Setting the Stage

Chinese civilization is at least 3,600 and perhaps over 4,000 years old. Very early agricultural settlements existed along the Yellow River, but scholars disagree on when the Chinese people first built towns and cities. Some scholars say cities had developed by about 2200 B.C.E., while others think it was closer to 1700 B.C.E. In any event, China has had an unbroken history for more than 3,500 years.

For most of their history, the Chinese have called their land *Chung Kuo*, meaning the Middle Kingdom or Center of the World. This name reflects the Chinese view of their place in the world. (Because most Chinese now refer to their country as China, we shall also use that term, although from time to time we will also use Middle Kingdom.)

Natural barriers kept the Chinese separated from all but the heartiest foreign traders, scholars, and adventurers from south or west Asia, although nomadic groups could invade from the north. To the east lay the Pacific Ocean, the largest body of water in the world, occupying almost half of the world's total surface area. To the south, tropical forests and mountain ranges isolated the Chinese from their neighbors. To the west stretch the formidable mountain ranges of Sinkiang and Tibet and the Himalayan Mountains, the highest mountains in the world. The Gobi Desert is in the northwest.

In the 1920s in north China, archaeologists discovered a fossilized human skull and numerous bones. Peking Man, the name they gave the skull, was probably about 500,000 years old. (Unfortunately the fossil disappeared in 1941 in the confusion of World War II, so scholars are unable to test it with the most recent dating methods in order to determine its exact age.) Archaeologists have recently discovered ten thousand year-old farming communities on the hillsides above the Yellow River. These farmers grew millet (a cereal grass), herded dogs, sheep, and pigs, and probably knew how to make silk from silkworm cocoons. The first urban centers grew from these communities.

Why Was the Loess So Important?

Men and women settled in the valley of the Yellow River in part because of the excellent soil called loess, that is light and can be cultivated without large animals. In north China the loess is many feet deep, but because it is powdery, winds blow it easily. In addition, during heavy rains the loess erodes and flows into riverbeds, where it collects along the bottom, raising the level of the rivers and causing floods. As in Sumer and the Nile and Indus valleys, the flooding river deposited rich mud as it receded, keeping the soil fertile. Farmers produced a lot of food from tiny loess plots, so dense populations lived in relatively small areas for long periods of time.

Long grass also grew in the loess soil. Bundles of dried grass made an excellent fuel for cooking, burning very quickly and producing a very hot fire. This kind of cooking fuel led women to chop vegetables and meat into tiny pieces, which they cooked quickly in these flash fires.

The Yellow River, where Chinese civilization started, got its name because the eroding loess made the river a muddy yellow color. The river was also called "China's Sorrow" because it flooded so often, even changing its course by as much as 400 miles, causing great suffering and hardships. People who lived along the Yellow River, like people in Mesopotamia, had to cooperate to build irrigation projects to control flooding and irrigate the land.

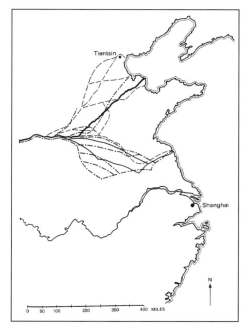

Changes in the course of the Yellow River

What Values Do the Sage Rulers Exemplify?

The Chinese tell of several legendary sages, wise rulers who united and ruled their country sometime in the third millennium B.C.E. Although these sages may never have actually lived, and stories about them were created much later in Chinese history, they are very important and serve as models for how legitimate Chinese leaders should rule. In fact, the Chinese consider stories about these early sages much more important than creation stories.

Divine Farmer

One ancient sage is supposed to have invented baskets for hunting and fishing, domesticated animals, and taught people to get married. Another was the divine farmer who invented agriculture, taught about herbs, and created markets and trade. A third, named Huang Di, defeated the nomads, invented the compass, created a government, built roads, and coined money. Huang Di's wife taught people how to produce silk from cocoons, while the emperor's chief minister developed the first written Chinese language.

Three sage-rulers, Yao, Shun, and Yu, were said to have come after Huang Di, sometime around 2300 B.C.E. Yao and Shun were models of virtue and wisdom, who surrounded themselves with moral advisors and chose virtuous men to rule when they died. Yao was so just that he refused to make his own son, whom he considered incompetent, his successor. Instead he designated Shun—who was poor but had the qualities associated with a good ruler. These qualities included being gentle but firm, outspoken but respectful, straightforward but warm, and hard but just. By not making his own son the next ruler, Yao established the precedent that a ruler must be worthy and good and that an able minister might be selected to succeed the emperor.

Tradition gives Shun credit for inventing the brush used for writing Chinese characters, but Shun's chief virtue was that he was a kind and obedient son. Even though his father and stepmother treated him badly and even tried to kill him, Shun respected his parents. The Chinese trace reverence for ancestors back to sage-ruler Shun. Following Yao's example, Shun made his most distinguished and virtuous minister, Yu, the next ruler.

Yu's fame comes from his heroic work in saving the Chinese people from a great flood. Yu worked thirteen years to channel the flooding water into canals and dig holes in the mountains so it could run to the ocean more easily. "But for Yu," the Chinese say, "we'd all be fishes." Unlike Noah, a hero of a nomadic people who, after the flood, founded a new land in a new location, Yu returned to his native village to continue ruling where he had always ruled. Yu's example teaches the importance of place in Chinese civilization. It reinforced the concept of Chung Kuo, the Middle Kingdom. The Chinese did not celebrate a restless search for new frontiers or the belief that happiness lay just around the corner; they emphasized coming to terms with life in the place where one was already living.

The Mandate of T'ian

Despite Yao's example, dynastic families have ruled during most of Chinese history. Chinese historians claim Yu founded the Xia dynasty, the first Chinese dynasty, around 2205 B.C.E. Because Yu's son was honorable, Yu passed the rule to him, setting the precedent that as long as members of the ruler's family were righteous, they should rule. After centuries of virtuous rule, however, the Xia kings became corrupt. The last Xia ruler was so cruel and unjust that a member of the nobility organized a rebellion, overthrew him, and founded the Shang dynasty sometime between 1766 and 1557 B.C.E. The Shang ruled to 1100 B.C.E.

The explanation of how the Shang got control reflects the great importance Chinese people placed on having moral leaders. They did not think military might alone was enough to give a ruler legitimacy. A new ruler might use soldiers to seize power—that is, he might "win the kingdom from horseback"—but he could not rule effectively with military might alone. Early in their history the Chinese developed the concept of the Mandate of T'ian as the basis on which a leader and his government claimed legitimacy. T'ian, sometimes translated Heaven, represented the natural order in the universe and the basic morality in the world. T'ian blessed leaders who were moral and virtuous and conferred legitimacy on a ruler by giving him a mandate or order to rule. Although the ruler was called the "Son of T'ian," having the Mandate did not mean a ruler had divine blood or was a god. If he became corrupt, T'ian removed its mandate, and the people had the responsibility to overthrow the government.

The people's obligation to depose an immoral or unjust ruler was an important part of the Mandate of T'ian. If people revolted and successfully overthrew the government, that proved it had lost the mandate. If, on the other hand, the ruler and his forces put down a revolt, that indicated he still had the mandate. (The Chinese trace this concept of moral rule all the way back to Yao, and even the Communist Revolution of 1949 claimed that virtuous men and women have the responsibility to overthrow corrupt governments.)

The Importance of Written Chinese

Chinese historians maintain that the Xia was the first Chinese dynasty, and lasted from about 2300 B.C.E. until 1700 B.C.E., when the Shang took over. Thus far, archaeologists have found no satisfactory evidence that the Xia Dynasty existed. Some scholars even doubted the existence of the Shang Dynasty until the discovery of the so-called dragon or oracle bones in the 1920s. Chinese druggists had long prized ancient tortoise shells and oxen and deer shoulder bones because their customers believed that eating a little bit of ground-up bone would cure various ailments. Curiosity seekers, who knew the bones and shells were very old, collected them. No one paid much attention to the markings on the shells until scholars realized they were similar to characters in the Chinese language.

Historians concluded out that rulers had used the bones for divination, determining the future by asking the spirits to indicate answers to questions. They wrote questions on the bones such as "Will the crops prosper?" or "Should I invade the province of Wu?" or "Should I send 3,000 or 5,000 troops against Lu?" Priests then heated the bones, causing them to crack, and determined answers to the questions from the direction of the cracks. These oracle bones proved that by 1700 B.C.E. the Chinese had already developed a unique and sophisticated style of writing. Because creating a written language takes generations, the bones suggest Chinese writing must predate the Shang and perhaps the Xia Dynasty really had existed.

Chinese is written with characters that are both pictorial and ideographs, not with an alphabet based on sounds. For example, the characters for water and mountain written together represent landscape. The characters for sun and moon written together mean bright. Since the Chinese originally wrote on bamboo strips, they wrote vertically, not horizontally. Many characters on the oracle bones are essentially the same as some contemporary Chinese ones.

Their written language has been extremely important in Chinese history. For one thing, only a few diligent scholars could learn the many unique characters, so the Chinese developed a small but very powerful group of scholars. Most important, however, written Chinese helped bring the country together and keep it unified. Although there are numerous Chinese dialects, the written character for any word is the same all over China. (Think about our number system where 5 can be read many ways in different languages, including "Five" or "Cinq" or "Panch.") Because some ideographs also convey values, the language helped promote unified beliefs as well. For example, the character for good is a mother with child, while the character for trouble is three women under one roof.

Mountains

Water

Landscape

Woman; Feminine

Child

Good

Chinese characters

It is difficult to overestimate the importance of the Chinese language. Learning to read and write Chinese became the criteria for being Chinese, and the language has been the core of Chinese culture throughout its history. Calligraphy became an important art and possesses a beauty that languages based on alphabets seldom have. The quality of one's writing reveals the writer's personality and training. In addition, because a character often has several meanings, it is well-suited to poets who often want their words to have a wide range of interpretations.

Ongoing Reverence For Ancestors

During the formative period of Chinese civilization, reverence for ancestors seems to have been a crucial ingredient in Chinese life. Many people believed that spirits of dead family members continued to influence what happened. Ancestors were also believed to act as intermediaries between this world and the spirit world, and their spirits could also influence various deities.

People kept ancestral alters in their homes and performed sacrifices and acts of remembrance, hoping that their ancestors would bring good fortune to living family members. Bad luck might mean one's ancestors were angry or felt neglected. Ancestor reverence was so important that their major legendary heroes, such as the sage emperors Yao, Shun, and Yu, were held up as models because of their respect for their parents.

Whether complex urban life developed in China in the third millennium B.C.E. or not until after 1700 B.C.E. it is clear that agricultural communities existed along the Yellow River for a very long time. The importance of the rich, powdery soil called loess, the central and unifying role of written Chinese, and ongoing influence of one's ancestors were well established by the early part of the second millennium. Isolated from other parts of the world and encountering only pastoralists on their borders, it is hardly surprising that the Chinese developed the idea of the Middle Kingdom and had a strong belief in their uniqueness and superiority. What happens to their sense of importance and uniqueness when they meet large numbers of other peoples will be an important theme in the human drama.

SCENE FIVE

MANUFACTURERS AND TRADERS IN THE AEGEAN

Setting the Stage

Cities and complex societies first developed in river valleys. By 3500 B.C.E. there were large urban centers in Mesopotamia and by 3200 B.C.E. a unified and sophisticated civilization existed along the Nile. People were carrying out urban planning and creating centralized plumbing in the Indus River valley by 2500 B.C.E., and significant settlements, if not cities, existed in the Yellow River valley as early as 2000 B.C.E. Floods threatened all four areas, but by cooperating with one another, people transformed potentially destructive rivers into sources of surplus and an abundant material life.

Cities also developed on the island of Crete in about 2000 B.C.E., even though it has no major river. Crete borders the Aegean Sea, which is in the eastern end of the Mediterranean Sea. The Aegean is surrounded by the Peloponnese, (the southern tip of the Greek main-

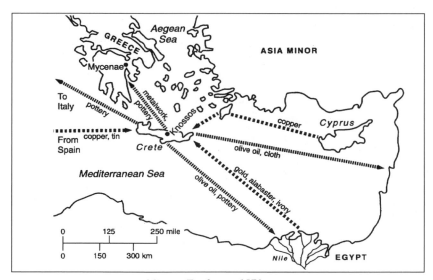

Minoan Trade, ca. 1570 B.C.E.

land), the western coastline of Anatolia (Asia Minor), as well as the island of Crete. By 2500 B.C.E. Cretans were trading with Phoenicians, who came from the east coast of the Mediterranean and established a significant trading network throughout the Mediterranean, with people living in Asia Minor and on islands in the Aegean, and, perhaps most importantly, with Egyptians. By 2000 B.C.E. maritime trade made it possible for Crete to build cities. Historians call Crete's complex society the Minoan civilization after King Minos, a legendary leader.

Transforming Nature into Commodities

Crete—only about 200 miles from the African coast, 120 miles from Asia Minor, and 60 miles from the Peloponnese—was in an ideal place for trade. Although the mild climate was good for agriculture, the island was mountainous and rocky. Sheep and goats could graze in the lowlands, and large trees provided excellent wood for boats, but the soil was not rich enough to produce large amounts of wheat or other grains. It was best suited for growing grapes and olives, but people cannot survive on these alone. Without trade, Crete could not have produced enough surplus to support cities.

But neighboring areas such as Egypt were producing large amounts of surplus grain, so adventurous Minoans became artisans and traders. They transformed dirt into beautifully decorated pottery, which they often filled with oil crushed from olives. They also used olive oil for soap, and burning a wick in a bowl of oil was a good source of light. Grapes became wine, which they used in rituals and celebrations and also mixed in the drinking water. A little wine seemed to prevent the water from making people sick. They did not realize that alcohol killed some germs in the water.

Trade encouraged Minoans to cooperate, and the more they cooperated, the more profit and surplus they made. At first individuals ventured out in small vessels to swap goods for things they needed. Gradually they organized and centrally controlled trade. It takes several years before grape plants or olive trees produce fruit, so supporting farmers during this period also required cooperation and central planning. One production center for wine and olive oil may have been the palace of Knossos. Its ground floor had a maze of rooms and chambers that may have been storehouses and offices from which overseers supervised manufacturing activities.

Interaction Leads to Innovation

What made it possible for the Minoans to develop their complex society? Toynbee's theory of challenge and response does not seem to fit Crete, because, initially, there was little incentive for people to work together. But McNeill's theory of interaction fits well. Crete was on the major sea-routes of the ancient Mediterranean world, and foreign traders and travelers often came to the island, bringing new ideas and novel methods for doing things.

Its strong navy gave Crete hegemony (influence or authority) over the Peloponnese and the western coastline of Anatolia, and rulers must have demanded tribute—the payment or tax that inferiors must give to superiors—from these areas. Knossos and other Minoan cities had no fortified walls, and few weapons have been uncovered. It stands to reason that if the Minoans controlled the seas, they also controlled who could approach their cities. If the Minoans made jewelry, not war, it is appropriate that the single individual whose name survives from ancient Crete was Daedalus, a talented artisan.

Traders who came and went did not try to conquer the island. When a ship landed on Crete, men and women not only exchanged goods, but also ideas. Then the ship sailed away, giving individuals time to think about what they had seen and heard, adopting what they could use and ignoring the rest. They also learned what outsiders might want to buy and adapted what they made accordingly. Many Minoans appear to have been comfortable but not rich, and there is no evidence that they kept slaves. Judging from frescoes, women played a prominent position in Minoan

A Cretan Pot

The Cretan Snake Goddess

culture, participating in sports along with men and enjoying festivals and spectacles.

Many historians believe the Minoans worshiped goddesses of fertility pictured with snakes and birds. Several figurines show a goddess with a dove or owl and with snakes wound around her arms. Snakes were also associated with goddess worship in earlier settlements in Anatolia. Because they shed their skins, snakes are excellent symbols of death and rebirth. Birds live on land and in the air, so they often symbolize both the heavens and Earth.

Did Theseus Really Slay the Minotaur?

There are many unanswered questions about Minoan culture. For centuries scholars did not even know the civilization had existed. Myths were the only clues to life on Crete, and most historians thought they were not really true. Excavations now suggest that the myth about how Theseus, a Greek hero who fought the Minotaur (a beast with a bull's head and a man's body) in a labyrinth (a maze), might reflect events that actually happened. According to the myth, King Minos, the Cretan ruler, lived in a great palace where he kept a ferocious Minotaur hidden in the basement. Every nine years, the king demanded that young men be sent from the mainland, probably as hostages to guarantee tribute payment. Most of the youths, who had to enter the labyrinth and battle the Minotaur, died. In the myth, Ariadne, King Minos' lovely daughter, helped Theseus escape from the labyrinth after he had killed the Minotaur. This might stand as a metaphor for the end of Cretan hegemony

The palace at Knossos was called a labyrinth, which meant "house of the double ax," and it was filled with double axes. The maze of rooms in the basement of the palace may well have confused frightened captives, who carried home terror-filled tales about a dreaded labyrinth. Eventually labyrinth came to mean a maze.

It is reasonable to conclude that the bull somehow represented the king, who may have worn a bull's mask during certain rituals to symbolize that he had the power and potency of a bull. That would explain the origin of the Minotaur. Perhaps the bull was ritually slain —either by dancers who broke his neck, or by priests who stabbed it—so that its power would be transferred to the king or people. (Similar rituals occurred in ancient west Asia and in India and may continue in an all-but-forgotten form even today in bullfights in Spain). Numerous frescoes (paintings) on the palace walls picture young men and women turning sumersaults through a bull's horns in what must have been ritual games or sacrifices.

Bull jumping

What Happened to the Minoans?

Judging from the elegance of the palace at Knossus, Minoan civilization reached its height around 1600 B.C.E. The Minoans had hegemony over the whole Aegean Sea and could demand tribute from settlements on the mainland. By 1400 B.C.E., however, Minoan power had ended, and Knossos lay in ruins. Scholars are still debating what happened. The palace appears to have been destroyed by earthquake and fire about 1500 B.C.E., rebuilt and then destroyed again, perhaps 100 years later. Evidence of plunder also suggests Minoan authority had weakened. By 1400 B.C.E. the center of civilization in the Aegean shifted north to the Greek mainland, particularly cities such as Mycenae.

But Crete was not the only civilization undergoing dramatic changes in the early centuries of the second millennium B.C.E. All four river valley societies also experienced significant changes starting about 1700 B.C.E. At that time Indo-European nomads began to migrate out of the Eurasian steppes, and Semitic nomads coming from Arabia pushed into Mesopotamia and Egypt. These waves of migrations and invasions continued for hundreds of years, changing the face and future of human life in the Eastern Hemisphere. The story of the interaction between the nomadic and the settled communities is the focus of the next act of the human drama.

ACT TWO – SURPLUS, SPECIALIZATION AND CITIES

Setting the Scene

1. What does civilized mean? Ask several adults the same question. Compare their answers. Use civilized in a sentence to describe a certain way of life. Use civilized or uncivilized in a sentence to make a judgment about a certain way of life.
2. What are the characteristics of a civilization? Ask several adults the same question. Compare their answers.
3. Explain the importance of surplus and specialization in city life.
4. In what ways must people in cities cooperate?
5. Why did people build the first cities in river valleys? Why did people build cities near rivers that flooded?
6. Explain what Toynbee meant by "challenge and response." What is an example of a challenge people recently have had to meet? What response(s) have they made?
7. Why does McNeill think contact with strangers is so important? Give an example of something that people in the United States have adapted from some other country. How important has contact with strangers been in United States history?

SCENE ONE
City-States in Mesopotamia

1. Identify some of the important features of the geography of Mesopotamia. How did the people take advantage of these features? What challenges did the geography present? In what ways did people meet these challenges?
2. What does sovereignty mean? What is a state? What is a city-state?
3. What can we tell about daily life and worldviews by the layout of a city?
4. What is a ziggurat? What role did the ziggurat play in Sumerian life?
5. Why was Sumer's economy called a temple (ziggurat) economy? Who were in the temple? What jobs did the temple servants have?
6. What does legitimacy mean? What gave the temple servants legitimacy? What gave the king legitimacy? What kind of legitimacy does your teacher have? What gives the President of the United States legitimacy?

SCENE TWO
Permanence and Peace Along the Nile

1. Identify some of the important features of the geography of the Nile Valley. How did people take advantage of these features? Why was Egypt called the Gift of the Nile? Why was ancient Egypt more peaceful than Sumer?
2. What type of government did the Egyptians have? What gave the pharaoh legitimacy?
3. Explain the structure of Egyptian society. What jobs did people have? Who had the most prestige?
4. What is a bureaucracy? What jobs did the Egyptian bureaucrats have and how could people enter the bureaucracy?
5. Why did the Egyptians build pyramids? What can we infer about Egyptian society from looking at its monumental buildings?
6. Why did the Egyptians invent embalming?
7. Look at some paintings and statues Egyptians created in the third millennium B.C.E. What do these works of art suggest about how people lived and what they believed?
8. Compare life in Sumer with life along the Nile.

SCENE THREE
City Planning in the Indus Valley

1. Identify some of the important features of the geography of the Indus Valley. How did people take advantage of these features? What challenges did the geography present? How did people meet those challenges?
2. Why is it particularly difficult for historians to figure out what everyday life in the Indus Valley was like?
3. What evidence is there that some kind of central control existed in the Indus civilization? Who might the rulers have been? What might their source of legitimacy have been?
4. What evidence is there that Indus cities were carefully planned? Who do you think was responsible for the uniform town planning? What is unique about these cities?
5. Explain the role of trade in the Indus civilization. What might have hurt trade in the later years of the civilization? Why did the Indus civilization collapse?
6. Briefly explain what the following things might reveal about what Indus people believed: the many drains, the "Great Bath" on the citadel, the seal with an image of a man in a tiger skin seemingly practicing yoga, and goddess figurines, and ritual purity.
7. Why do you think there were few weapons and no evidence of warfare in

the Indus civilization?

8. Compare life in the Indus Valley with life in Sumer and along the Nile.

SCENE FOUR
Settlements along the Yellow River

1. Identify some of the important features of the geography in the Yellow River Valley. How did people take advantages of those features? What challenges did geography offer? How might geography have contributed to making the Chinese think of their country as the Middle Kingdom?
2. What is the loess? What importance does it have in Chinese history?
3. What can you infer about Chinese life and what the Chinese people think is important from the things that the legendary sages and sage rulers did? How do these stories compare to stories we tell about some of the early leaders in the United States such as Abraham Lincoln and George Washington?
4. What is the Mandate of T'ian? How did the Chinese know that a ruler had lost the Mandate of T'ian?
5. Chinese characters do not represent sounds as our alphabet does. What are the advantages and disadvantages to their system of writing? How did written Chinese help unify the Middle Kingdom?
6. What role did one's ancestors play in Chinese life? What responsibility did people have toward their ancestors?
7. Write an essay with the following statement as your thesis: "The fertile loess, the written language, and reverence for ancestors were very important to the Chinese people." In your essay explain how or why each of those things was important in the Middle Kingdom.
8. Compare life along the Yellow River with life in any of the other river valley civilizations.

SCENE FIVE
Manufactures and Traders in the Aegean

1. Identify some of the important features of the geography of the Aegean. How did people take advantage of these features? What challenges did the geography present? How did people meet those challenges?
2. In what ways does McNeill's theory about the importance of interaction with outsiders fit the Minoan civilization?
3. What does hegemony mean? What evidence is there that the Minoans had hegemony over people in lands bordering the Aegean Sea?
4. Why are Goddess figures often associated with snakes and birds?
5. Who ruled Crete? What might have been the basis of his legitimacy?
6. List the facts about the Minoan civilization that you can infer from the story of Theseus slaying the Minotaur. How can you be sure the things

you listed really happened?

7. How did the way of life in ancient Crete compare with early life in a river valley?

8. What happened to the Minoan civilization?

Summing Up

1. Compare how people adapted to geographic conditions in these five civilizations. What challenges did geography present? How did the people respond to these challenges?

2. Identify the various sources historians have used to find out about these early civilizations. What are the advantages and disadvantages of each?

3. Imagine that a historian who lived in the end of third millennium B.C.E. came back to life and asked you about life today. What might surprise him or her about what you reported?

4. Compare the different kinds of legitimacy rulers in these early civilizations had.

5. What group do you think was the most important in these early civilizations: Priests and Priestesses? Political rulers? Traders? Farmers? Others? Why?

6. If you could go back in time, in which of these areas would you have wanted to live and when? What job would you want to have had? Would you rather have been a woman or a man? Why?

6. Using the information from this act, write an essay that answers the question: Why did people in the early civilizations cooperate with strangers?

ACT THREE

Nomadic Migrations and Invasions (second millennium B.C.E.)

SETTING THE STAGE

By 2000 B.C.E. impressive cities flourished in four areas, and there were significant farming communities in many other parts of Eurasia, especially the Yellow River Valley. At the same time, pastoralists were tending their herds and flocks in the Eurasian steppes and Arabian peninsula.

Fully nomadic pastoral nomadism developed as pastoralists began to ride horses. Pastoralists usually stay in certain areas, except when they take their animals to new grazing land, but pastoral nomads are constantly on the move. Although some herders on the steppes had learned to ride horseback as early as 4000 B.C.E., pastoral nomadism did not become a significant way of life until late in the second millennium B.C.E. Riding horseback allowed pastoral nomads to raise more animals and support much larger populations. By the start of the first millennium B.C.E., Indo-European pastoral nomads were living in the steppes of inner Asia and Semitic pastoral nomads were living in the Arabian Desert.

While most of the evidence about early urban centers comes from bits and pieces of long-buried cities, much of our information about second millennium B.C.E. pastoral nomads comes from myths and stories passed down orally or from written accounts by settled people who often disparaged them.

Cold Eurasian 'core'
(Below 0° F in January)

Cool peripheral zone

Developing centres
of urban life

Approximate maximal limit
of Inner Asian cultural area

How Pastoral Nomads Lived

Pastoral nomads survived by consuming meat and milk from their herds and the animals they hunted. They roasted most of their meat and boiled only a small percentage, because boiled food cooks slowly and requires more fuel and pots.

Pastoral nomadic groups thought of themselves as blood brothers, committed to live and die for their tribe. Their society was patriarchal, and men owned the herds. These cowboys of the ancient world loved riding and racing horses, hunting, wrestling, and archery.

Warfare was even more important for pastoral nomads than it had been for the earlier pastoralists, in part because increasing population created more competition for land on which to graze their herds and flocks. Pastoral nomads had to be ready to fight at a moment's notice. In addition, men often had to fight off wild animals. Absolute loyalty, obedience, and bravery were of the utmost importance. In the heat of battle there could be only one leader, and he set the standard of courage and superior strength.

A first-century B.C.E. Chinese historian described the Xiongnu, a large pastoral nomadic group, in the following way:

> The Xiongnu live in the Northern Barbarian lands and wander, following their herds, moving from place to place. . . searching for water and pastures. They have no cities, no permanent dwellings and no cultivated fields. . . . Their children ride on the backs of sheep and shoot [arrows] at birds and rats. . . . According to their custom, during times of peace they follow their herds and hunt animals and birds to sustain life; in crisis everyone uses their unique tactics for an attack and invasion. . . . When it is profitable they advance; when it is unprofitable they withdraw, never being ashamed of retreat. . . . From their rulers on down everyone eats meat, wears animal hides and puts on felt and furs.

Hunting provided training for fighting. In large hunts hundreds and later even thousands of men fanned out to encircle a vast area. They then gradually moved toward the center, forcing the animals that were in front of them into a smaller and smaller area until they could easily be killed. These hunts were similar to military campaigns in which commanders had to keep track of a great many men.

Pastoral nomads lived close to nature, and many worshiped deities that represented the natural forces of the universe, such as fire, sky, wind, and storm. Volcanoes, thunder, and lightning filled them with much more awe than crops emerging from the earth. They celebrated gods that reflected their militaristic, patriarchal, pastoral, mobile society, and they did not settle in one place long enough to worship the earth. Instead, the feminine deities they revered included dawn, night, and speech.

Women in pastoral nomadic communities must have been well respected. Most of them internalized nomadic values, such as strength, aggressiveness, and courage. They shared the hardships of nomadic life with the men and were hearty enough to survive harsh conditions. Women probably fought alongside men when outsiders threatened their communities, but they did not accompany them when they attacked other groups. Women helped set up the tents, kept them in good repair, and performed other domestic chores.

Who Wants to Be Like Those People?

For the vast majority of human history, nomads and settled peoples have lived side by side, having little or nothing to do with one another. Neither group had much interest in nor respect for the other. Nomads had no desire to settle and farm. Urban dwellers, for their part, considered nomads to be like animals. People in the Aegean region used the term "barbarian" when talking about non-Greek speakers whose language sounded to them like babble. The Chinese referred to their nomadic neighbors by a similar term that meant anyone who did not speak their language.

The following is how a Chinese historian described what the Chinese thought of their nomadic neighbors.

> As for customs, food, clothing, and language, the barbarians are entirely different from the Middle Kingdom. They live in the cold wilderness of the far north. They follow the grazing fields, herding their flocks and hunting game to maintain their lives. Mountains, valleys and the great desert separate them from us. The barrier, which lies between the center and the alien outside, was made by Heaven and Earth. Therefore, the sage rulers considered them beasts, neither establishing contacts nor subjugating them. . . . Their land is impossible to cultivate and it is impossi-

ble to rule them as subjects. Therefore, they are always to be considered as outsiders and never as intimates. Our administration and teaching has never reached their people. . . . Punish them when they come and guard against them when they retreat. Receive them when they offer tribute as a sign of admiration for our righteousness. Restrain them continually and make it appear that all the blame is on their side. This is the proper policy of sage rulers [Yao, Shun, and Yu] toward the barbarian.

Pastoral nomads did not want to lose their unique way of life and become dependent on the Chinese. No doubt they tried to follow the advice of a Chinese official who told them they must retain their own clothing and food if they wished to remain strong and independent. To illustrate his point, the official:

> . . . wearing the silk and cloth of the Chinese, rushed on horseback among the bushes and thorns, letting his coat and trousers be entirely torn to pieces to prove that the material was inferior to garments made of wool and pelts. He also rejected all Chinese foods to demonstrate that they were not as good and desirable as milk and curds.

Contacts Between Urban Dwellers and Pastoral Nomads

In spite of very different lifestyles, settled and nomadic people did interact. Urban dwellers had tools, weapons, and especially surplus food, which the nomads often desperately needed just to survive. Nomads frequently had access to the minerals and timber settled people needed for their buildings, ships, and tools. Most important, nomads had horses. People in urban centers were usually willing to exchange grain, cloth, tools, and weapons for horses, hides, wool, and minerals. Peaceful exchanges took place, sometime in the form of tribute or gifts.

Nomadic groups usually needed what settled people had more than urban dwellers needed their animals. In fact, grain from agricultural

An emaciated herdsman

communities was often essential to nomads' survival. As a result, when settled people refused to exchange goods, nomads were forced to raid.

Mounted warriors had a significant military advantage over their settled neighbors. It was relatively easy for nomads to launch an attack on an urban center and take what pleased them. Nomads could swoop down, plunder a city, and flee. They attacked without warning, and surprise gave them a distinct advantage. Even if they were pushed back, they merely retreated into what, to the settled people, appeared to be vast wastelands.

By and large these raids did not significantly change the way either group lived, mainly because nomads usually withdrew to their own grasslands once they got what they wanted. However, during several periods in the human drama, large numbers of nomads throughout Eurasia invaded and stayed in settled areas. The first period of intense invasions occurred in the second millennium B.C.E., starting about 1800 B.C.E. and continuing for almost a thousand years. The second period was in the first millennium C.E., starting around 300 and continuing to around 800. The third significant wave originated at the beginning of the second millennia, starting about 1100 and continuing into the 1400s. Nomadic invasions also took place periodically in the Americas.

Was There a Chariot Revolution?

Around 1700 B.C.E., Indo-European pastoral nomads began long marches out of the inner Asian steppes, and Semitic nomads from Arabia pushed into Mesopotamia and Egypt. Historians sometimes call the thousand-year period from about 1700 to 800 B.C.E. the Chariot Revolution in part because chariots may have contributed to the increase of pastoral nomadism and helped nomads invade and conquer settled areas. These invasions radically changed the lives of both invaders and city dwellers and altered human life in the Eastern Hemisphere forever.

Historians debate the role the chariot played during this first wave of invasions. People in Mesopotamia had developed a solid wheel made from the cross-section of a tree trunk. They used it on a four-wheel oxcart, but the slow, cumbersome cart was best for transporting goods to market, not for warfare. Pastoralists bred horses, even though initially they had no carts and few rode on horseback. They used the horse mainly for milk and meat. In those early centuries, because they did not know how to harness the horse to pull a load without choking it to death, the horse's speed and strength were of little use. For the same reasons horses were relatively useless for farming. Besides, they were too expensive for farmers to keep because they required extensive pasturelands.

Gradually, through the interaction of the nomadic herder and settled artisan, somewhere in northern Mesopotamia someone invented a wheel with spokes that met at a center axle. Then came a two-wheeled cart and the chariot. Spoked wheels were lighter and stronger than solid ones, and the two-wheeled chariot put most of the cart's weight on the wheels, not on the horse's neck. Then someone figured out that a horse harnessed with only a small strap under its neck could pull the new mobile chariot—even with a driver and archer aboard—up to 30 miles per hour.

Chariots created a demand for horses, may have contributed to the growth of pastoral nomadism, because nomads now had even greater incentive to raise horses to trade. The demand for horses also increased contacts between settled communities and nomads, stimulating migrations and invasions.

The chariot gave some nomads enormous military advantages, tempting them to invade. Archers, shooting from swiftly moving char-

An early war chariot

iots, could escape quickly. Warriors in chariots could see more of the battlefield and send signals to their troops. Chariots were a sign of status, even luxury.

Although pastoral nomads used chariots, their actual military value varied. It was difficult to shoot a bow accurately from a moving chariot, especially in a hilly countryside. City walls were a good defense against chariots, which were more practical in flat areas, such as the Gangetic plain in India, as well as vital to Chinese warfare. But during the Trojan War, Greek soldiers used their chariots rather like taxis, riding in them to the battlefield and then standing in them as they taunted their Trojan opponents. When they were ready to fight, they got down out of their chariots and fought, often one on one.

How Important Was Iron?

Other technological innovations may have stimulated nomadic invasions. During this period Indo-Europeans also developed iron weapons. Although iron was a common metal, it had been relatively useless in warfare because weapons made of melted ore were brittle and shattered easily. Bronze weapons, made by combining copper and tin, were strong but expensive. A rare piece of a meteorite could be shaped into a weapon, though more often communities worshiped these precious stones. Once people discovered that if they heated iron on a fiery bed of charcoal, it became very strong and could be shaped, they began to make iron weapons.

Historians are not sure who discovered how to smelt iron ore into a useful metal or whether it played a significant role in stimulating nomadic invasions. The practice may have originated in the area between the Caspian and Black seas. The Hittites, in west Asia, initially used iron primarily for ornaments. The Assyrians were the first to use iron for weapons. Soon iron technology spread to other peoples in west Asia. Iron swords and spears were superior and could change the balance of power. Iron also led to improved chariots that could withstand the rigors of speedy travel across rough terrain.

Pushes and Pulls from Steppes to City

Although the chariot and iron played a role in the invasions, no doubt it was a combination of geographic, demographic, and technological factors that encouraged pastoral nomads to leave their own grazing areas in the steppes and invade settled communities. Numerous attractions of urban life probably helped pull them into settled areas as well.

Geographic factors include changes in climate. Prolonged droughts could have made it difficult for pastoral nomads to find adequate water or grass for their animals, forcing them to move to more fertile land to keep their flocks and herds alive or to find food for their themselves when their animals died. Periodically, overgrazing might have meant the steppe could no longer support their animals, and they coveted greener pastures that belonged to farmers.

Demographic factors include changes in population. If their numbers increased, as we know they did after horseback riding became common, nomads might have had difficulty getting enough food. If the population of other nomadic groups farther north increased as well, and those people forced them to move out of their traditional grazing lands, the displaced groups might have had to move to land nearer settled areas or even invade those areas.

Sometimes an individual leader pushed his group to invade. A charismatic leader (one who can inspire people to follow him), capable of uniting a number of nomadic tribes, would have a powerful fighting force. Perhaps the lure of cities, with granaries filled with food, tempted nomads. They had little respect for urban dwellers, but that did not stop them from wanting their goods.

Sensing a growing weakness in the settled areas may have encouraged nomads to invade. Nomadic groups were always along the borders, and their spies knew what was going on in the urban areas. When nomads were hired to defend the borders, they knew that the settled people's defenses were weakening. In addition, when settled areas were fighting among themselves, nomadic leaders could easily conquer an area.

The map on the next page shows the main paths of Indo-European and Semitic migrations and invasions. Instead of traveling as one unified mass, Indo-European nomads migrated as hundreds of separate groups. Hittites plundered Anatolia, Aryans invaded the Indian subcontinent, Kassites settled in Babylonia, Achaeans and later Dorians came into the Greek peninsula, and Latins went into the Italian

Peninsula. Semitic groups who came out of the Arabian Desert included the Hyksos who conquered Egypt, Chaldaeans who went into Mesopotamia, and the Apiru (which may have been another name for the Hebrews) who went first into Mesopotamia and then to Egypt. The many changes caused by these invasions are the focus of this act of the human drama.

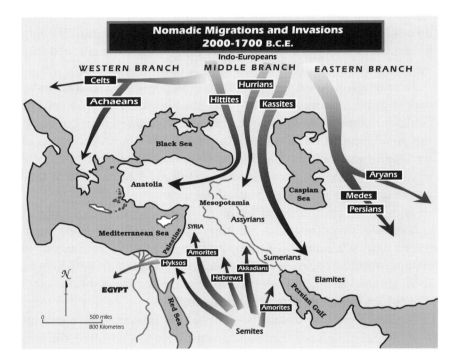

SCENE
ONE

NOMADIC INVASIONS
IN WEST ASIA

Setting the Stage

By 2300 B.C.E. urban life had been thriving in Mesopotamia for about a thousand years. All that time pastoralists from Inner Asia and the Arabian Desert were a potential threat to the prosperous Sumerian city-states situated along the Euphrates and Tigris rivers. The Fertile Crescent, the area in west Asia that extends from the Mediterranean Sea to the Persian Gulf, seemed to invite invaders, because no mountains, sea, desert, or cataracts stood in the way.

For centuries Indo-European and Semitic herders had periodically exchanged goods with people in the Sumerian city-states, but most of the time these groups had little other contact. But after 2300 B.C.E., that delicate relationship changed as invading nomads tried to extend their power into west Asia. Akkadians came first, followed by Babylonians, Hittites, Kassites, and Assyrians. Victorious invading groups usually only controlled an area for as long as the initial leader survived but sometimes their rule lasted for several generations.

Invading nomadic groups usually conquered and maintained control by force. Some historians refer to these early conquests as empires, but they are also called kingdoms. In trying to determine the difference between kingdoms and empires, it might be helpful to think of a spectrum of political units. At one end of that spectrum is a village led by a chief or elder. Then comes the city-state ruled by a priestess, priest, council, or king. As the city-state absorbs more land, it becomes a kingdom that a king rules. Finally, on the opposite end of the spectrum, is an empire, a very large area of diverse people and cultures, united under a central government ruled by a single person called an emperor (or another term meaning emperor).

It is sometimes difficult to distinguish between a kingdom and an empire. In deciding what to call an area, we should consider how

much land the government controls, how diverse the people in the
area are, and how long the rulers maintain control. We should also
keep in mind that our values may influence which areas we designate
kingdoms and which we call empires. For now, it is probably more
accurate to refer to these early states in Mesopotamia as kingdoms.

The Pattern of Invasion and Conquest

The pastoral nomads who invaded Mesopotamia in the centuries
between 2300 B.C.E. and 1000 B.C.E. followed a fairly consistent pattern of invasion and conquest. First they moved into a relatively
unsettled area north of the existing urban centers. Once they had
established a power base, they attacked and slowly expanded their
control until they had united several cities into a kingdom.

The Akkadians were Semitic nomads from the Arabian Desert who
settled in a sparsely populated area just north of Sumer around 2500
B.C.E. They created a power base, built the city called Akkad, and
became known as Akkadians. In 2334 B.C.E. an Akkadian leader
named Sargon led his men against the neighboring cities and gradually claimed he controlled the whole area from the Persian Gulf to the
Mediterranean Sea. Soldiers held Sargon's kingdom together, but
these troops survived by plundering the very people they had conquered and were supposed to be defending. Because this practice
angered people in the countryside, his kingdom fell apart after his
death, and individual cities again exerted their own sovereignty.

Sargon may have given people in Mesopotamia a taste for creating
kingdoms because after his death, various Sumerian city-states tried
to conquer one another. For a brief period around 2200 B.C.E. the city
of Ur dominated the other cities. Ur's rule ended when the Amorites,
another group of Semitic nomads, threatened.

Following the same pattern, the Amorites settled north of Akkad
and built a city they called Babylon, and they were called Babylonians. Once the Babylonians had created a power base, they defeated
Akkad, Ur, and other city-states and created the Babylonian kingdom
(empire), which stretched from the Persian Gulf to the Mediterranean
Sea. Their government was a hereditary monarchy and Hammurabi,
the most famous Babylonian king, ruled from 1792 to 1750 B.C.E.

Mythology Reflects the Tension between
Settled People and Nomads

Tension between settled people and pastoral nomads was a constant reality in west Asia, but it is difficult to know exactly what happened. By and large historians must use stories and myths to try to piece together the long history of invasions and assimilation that took place across the area during the second millennium B.C.E.

Relations between nomad and settled peoples was an important theme in the epic *Gilgamesh*, written down about 1900 B.C.E. It tells about Enkidu, the hairy one who ran with the animals and did not even know he was human. That was probably the way settled people described steppe nomads. After a priestess "humanized" Enkidu, he went to the city of Uruk and challenged its king Gilgamesh. The fight between Gilgamesh and Enkidu ended in a draw, and they become lifelong friends, undertaking numerous adventures together, including the conquest of the Cedar Forest to the west (that probably referred to present-day Lebanon). If Gilgamesh represents settled people and Enkidu represents pastoral nomads, then this story suggests that nomadic herdsmen and settled rulers became friends. It is interesting to speculate why people in Mesopotamia wanted to present this picture and to what extent it was true.

Hymns to the gods and goddesses also reveal possible relations between nomads and settled people. Nomadic warriors, we noted, worshiped forces of nature such as fire, volcanoes, storms, thunder, and lightning. Their deities were also associated with warfare, which was so common in these hunting, fighting societies. Early Sumerian gods and goddesses, on the other hand, were associated with the land, and thought to be loyal to the agricultural people who had worshiped them long before pastoral nomads invaded.

When nomads conquered an area in Mesopotamia and decided to settle down, they had to establish their legitimacy in the eyes of the people they had conquered. Because the ritual marriage had been the way Sumerian rulers had symbolized their legitimacy, invaders tried to use the same ritual to gain legitimacy. The invading hero that the local goddess chose as her consort would become the legitimate king. But stories from that time suggest she was reluctant to choose an invader. In the Sumerian hymn about the courtship of Goddess Innana

and Dumuzi (the shepherd), Inanna makes it clear whom she prefers.
She states:

> The man of my heart works the hoe.
> The farmer! He is the man of my heart!
> He gathers the grain in great heaps. . . .
> The shepherd! I will not marry the shepherd!
> His clothes are coarse; his wool is rough.
> I will marry the farmer.

Inanna finally chooses Dumuzi, and everyone joyously celebrates
their marriage. Perhaps the poet made the goddess initially reluctant
to accept Dumuzi so that Mesopotamians would find the poem more
believable. They, too, were having trouble accepting the authority of
the herding people who had conquered them.

Power Shifts from the Ziggurat to the Palace

As invaders grew more powerful, they became increasingly belliger-
ent toward the old gods and goddesses. Aggression and war were
becoming more important than fertility and farming, and the goddess'
blessing no longer conferred legitimacy. This change is also reflected
in *Gilgamesh*.

King Gilgamesh and his friend Enkidu insulted Ishtar, the patron
goddess of Uruk, identified as the goddess of love, fruitfulness, and
war. (Note that by 1900 B.C.E., when the Babylonians wrote down this
epic, they identified Ishtar with war as well as fertility.) Ishtar wanted
to marry Gilgamesh and offered herself to him. "What should I gain
by taking you as wife?" he asked her. When she tried to list the blessings that would come to him should they become lovers, Gilgamesh
stated all the awful things she does to people, and then he shouted:

> We outgrow our naivéte [innocence]
> In thinking goddesses
> Return our love.
> I am tired of your promises. . . .

King Gilgamesh no longer needed the ritual marriage to ensure his
legitimacy, and he rejected the goddess. After all, gods and goddesses

had not prevented invaders from conquering their cities or driving them from their temples, and the temple servants had not been able to recommend charms or rituals to prevent disaster. *Gilgamesh* may well reflect the historic transition from divine to earthly leadership — from priests to kings — that was taking place in Mesopotamia as people sought other kinds of protection and security. It may also suggest why temple courtesans, who had been involved in the sacred marriage rituals, lost status. The king and his army replaced religious leaders, and warfare rather than rituals ensured the community's safety.

Warfare: The Key to Defense and Expansion

Military power had always been important in the Sumerian city-states, and war became even more significant after 2300 B.C.E. Neighboring cities often fought over water rights or one another's land, so each city had to be ready to defend itself against its neighbors. Without natural barriers, cities needed strong armies as protection from pastoral nomads intent on plunder or conquest, so city leaders mobilized more soldiers. Men organized for war could also fight floods. Although a strong army could not prevent the river from rising, effective centralized control could quickly and efficiently supervise repairs on dikes and other flood prevention projects.

Pastoral nomads who invaded Mesopotamia brought their militaristic values with them, which contributed to the increased emphasis on fighting. Nomads with a fighting spirit kept coming into the area, and even when they settled down, these invaders did not quickly lose their warrior values. For example, Gilgamesh had gone soft before Enkidu challenged him, but together they went on a military campaign against the Cedar Forest.

By the end of the third millennium B.C.E., both literature and religious beliefs reflected the importance of war. In the Babylonian creation story Marduk, their primary god, killed the goddess, tore her apart, and created the world out of pieces of her dead body. Gone was the idea of creation coming from a goddess of fertility. In its place, warfare and power were the source of creation. Priests and poets no longer described a triple goddess whose power extended over the natural cycles of birth, life, and death. Increasingly she was identified as a goddess of war, all-devouring in her power, the destroyer of foreign lands that cowered at her cry.

Law: The Key to Internal Order

Rulers in Mesopotamia relied on the army to control conquered areas and defend against new challengers. But Sargon's experience had demonstrated that military might alone was not adequate to hold a kingdom together. People resented soldiers telling them what to do. Once in control, leaders had to figure out some alternative to brute force to encourage diverse people within the community to live harmoniously with one another and settle their differences peacefully.

In small communities people often relied on their families to protect them. When a family member was wronged, others in the family sought out the offender and punished or killed him or even his whole family. People felt safe because they knew their family was protecting them, and wrongdoers avoided those with powerful families and friends. Villages, where many people were related, could use this same method to keep order.

However, family feuds might go on for generations, and in a kingdom with a large number of people, this kind of vengeful justice was destructive. In order to get people to give up these established ways of seeking revenge or compensation for a wrong, the society had to have another system for defending property and punishing wrong-doers. In larger towns and cities, Mesopotamian leaders turned to law to established property rights and settle disputes.

The development of a legal tradition in Mesopotamia was one of its most outstanding contributions, and the idea of rule by law soon spread throughout west Asia. Public knowledge of what was legal and what was not meant everyone knew what punishments to expect for violations of the law. Moreover, establishing guilt or innocence by calling witnesses and trying to present the facts of the case gave average people protection from capricious decisions imposed by those more powerful.

The application of law served to regulate both criminal and civil activities. Criminal law dealt with killing or physically harming others, as well as theft and other illegal ways of obtaining property. Civil cases involved marriage and divorce, business contracts, property rights, other aspects of financial dealings, and social conduct. Law provided a new way of governing and keeping the peace. (When American political leaders say "We are a government of laws, not of men," they are reminding us of the importance of law.)

HAMMURABI'S LAWS:
AN EYE FOR AN EYE AND A TOOTH FOR A TOOTH

By the time of the Babylonian kingdom in the eighteenth century B.C.E., Mesopotamian rulers were already experimenting with using laws to govern their people and establish internal order in their kingdoms. Excavations have uncovered numerous sets of laws from that period. The most impressive were the 282 laws that King Hammurabi proclaimed in the second year of his rule, about 1790 B.C.E. Hammurabi ordered these laws carved in stone so everyone could see them. They give modern historians many clues about Babylonian life, and many contemporary legal practices can be traced back to them.

Steele with Hammurabi's 242 laws

The first rules have to do with false witness. Lying threatens the system of law and the trust people have for one another and the community, so even an important person like a judge had to obey the laws. Judges who accepted bribes or judged unfairly were put out of office. Laws also protected a person's right to own property. In the case of robbery, the thief had to pay compensation many times over. When people were accused of theft, they had to produce witnesses and contracts that established they had bought the goods, not stolen them.

Hammurabi's laws reflect the importance of the army. Several rules protect the rights of soldiers. In the first place, an individual was not allowed to hire a substitute to fight. If he tried to do so, he would be put to death and the person he hired would get his estate. If a soldier was captured or killed, his land went to his sons. If his son was under-age, the mother received one third of the "field and orchard" so that she could raise him. If a soldier without heirs was mistakenly presumed dead, and his land had been given away, he was to get his land back if he returned from the war.

There were rules governing rental policies, amounts of interest, how a renter must use the land, and types of payments in case of floods. Rules covering the irrigation system were also listed, and a lazy man was not allowed to let the dikes go unrepaired. Rules established liability for doctors, builders, and others whose work might harm people.

Some of the rules reveal the social stratification in Babylon. Instead of being uniform for everyone, laws varied with different people, and so did punishments. If someone stole from a rich man, he must repay him thirtyfold; if he stole from a middle-class person, he repaid him only tenfold. In addition:

> If a nobleman has knocked out the tooth of a man that
> is his equal, his own tooth shall be knocked out. If he
> has knocked out the tooth of a freeman, he shall pay
> one third of a mina of silver. If a man strike the head
> of a man who is his superior, he shall receive sixty
> blows of the ox-hide whip in public. (200–202)

It is possible to get some idea of the role and status of women in Babylonian society from Hammurabi's laws. Several cover what happened to a wife if her husband became a prisoner of war. If there were sufficient goods in her home, she should remain there. If there was not enough for her to live on, she would not be blamed if she entered another's house. She should return to her first husband if he unexpectedly returned from war, but she did not have to go back if he returned after he had deserted.

Laws reveal that women worked in certain occupations outside the home and could own their own business, such as beer-shops. Most marriages were arranged, and rules governed this. In some cases a woman, "if she so hated her husband," could initiate divorce and

> If she has been careful, and was not at fault and her husband had gone forth and greatly deprecated (spoken against) her, that woman has no blame; she shall take her marriage portion and go to her father's house. (142)

Repeated Conquests in West Asia

For centuries after the Babylonians, other nomadic groups invaded west Asia and some followed a similar pattern of invasion and conquest. Indo-European Kassites conquered and plundered the Babylonians in about 1600 B.C.E. but had little interest in building a kingdom. By 1599 B.C.E. the Hittites, a large Indo-European group, had invaded and established a federation in north-central Anatolia by defeating the Kassites. The Hittites proved to be a very powerful force, making use of the new chariot technology and, as iron technology spread through west Asia, of iron weapons as well.

The Assyrians were another group that built up a power base in west Asia. The Assyrians were Semitic nomads who migrated to a small plateau near the Tigris River, about 500 miles north of the Persian Gulf. They named it Assur, after their god. After about 1300 B.C.E. the Assyrians began expanding, gaining control of the Hittites in northern Mesopotamia and eventually the whole Fertile Crescent.

Akkadians, Kassites, Babylonians, Hittites, and Assyrians: over and over again a nomadic group settled in Mesopotamia, built up a power base, conquered the existing center of power, and established its own kingdom. Living with the constant threat of war must have been very difficult for urban people. On the other hand, settling down was changing the nomadic invaders as well. While the invasion of nomadic peoples was a common theme in Mesopotamia, Egypt, a much more protected civilization, is about to experience the same phenomenon.

SCENE TWO

TRANSFORMATIONS IN THE NILE VALLEY

Setting the Stage

During the nineteenth century B.C.E., Egypt enjoyed a period of prosperity and peace, but then things changed dramatically. Leaders in the local communities who resented the pharaoh's power staged revolts against the central government, and the country split apart. The government, busy trying to hold onto its power, allowed monuments, temples, and other buildings to deteriorate. No central bureaucracy supervised repairing irrigation projects, and few people wrote or created art. Egypt became vulnerable to nomadic invasions, and even the cataracts on the Nile River and the surrounding desert could not protect it.

What Did the Hyksos Teach the Egyptians?

Egyptian historians likened the Hyksos invasion in 1786 B.C.E. to a blast from a god. Hyksos, which means king-shepherds or rulers-of-foreign-lands, were Semitic nomads from Arabia who had settled along the northern border of the Nile delta. Mixing with other groups already there, they learned how to use horse-drawn chariots and iron weapons. The Egyptians described how these fierce invaders — fighting nearly naked, wielding axes and carrying huge shields — relentlessly swept into Egypt and controlled it from eighteenth to the sixteenth centuries B.C.E. For the first time in their long history an outside power attacked, conquered, and ruled over the Egyptians.

Hyksos rule brought changes in the Nile valley. For one thing, Egyptians learned that an army was very important. They could no longer rely on the desert and cataracts for protection. In order to free themselves from Hyksos rule, the Egyptians became more warlike and used the horse and chariot. By becoming skilled at war, they drove the Hyksos out of Egypt or made slaves of those who stayed.

Egyptian Power Expands beyond the Nile

For the next 600 years, during the period known as the New Kingdom, many Egyptian pharaohs concentrated on warfare, investing much energy and resources in the military. They began to expand their borders and influence beyond the Nile valley. The three dynasties that ruled from 1575 to 1087 B.C.E. followed a policy of military expansion, fighting the Phoenicians, Philistines, Syrians, and Hebrews, as well as the Nubians who lived south of the first cataract.

Diplomatic and military conquests increased the Pharoahs' power. They realized that a large standing army was not only useful in winning new territory but was an effective way to ensure their power at home, as well. Winning new land helped increased their status. The simplest soldiers shared in the military successes, and spoils of war helped pay for the construction of magnificent buildings.

Egyptian forces expanded south into Nubia, the 900-mile area along the Nile that stretches from the first cataract to the area near Khartoum, the capital of present-day Sudan. They also sent troops, many of whom were Nubian mercenaries, into Syria and Palestine where they fought the Hittites. At the height of their conquests, the Egyptians controlled land from Nubia all the way to the Euphrates River. (See map on page 47)

Queen Hatshepsut

Queen Hatshepsut Promotes Trade

Not all leaders concentrated on war. Queen Hatshepsut, who ruled from 1473 to 1458 B.C.E. and assumed all the pharaoh's titles except "Mighty Bull," was the first woman to rule Egypt in her own right. She proved to be an outstanding leader and oversaw the construction of impressive monuments and the repairing of others that had falling down. Instead of building military fortifications, Hatshepsut promoted trade, especially with Nubia, which created a period of economic prosperity.

In 1482 B.C.E. Tutmose III removed Hatshepsut, took control of Egypt and ordered all Hatshepsut's images and inscriptions destroyed. He returned to a policy of military expansion and exploitation, and proceeded to conquer what had been the southern part of Hammurabi's Empire.

Akhenaten and Monotheism Threaten the Priests

During the New Kingdom period, priests became more powerful as the authority of local governors decreased. Perhaps the uncertainties of war made people turn to religion. Priests began to take advantage of people's fears in order to increase their own importance. They convinced people that they did not have to live virtuous lives to gain salvation. Instead, just repeating certain charms would ensure them a happy afterlife. People paid priests to recite the correct charms, so priests were becoming very wealthy as well as powerful. Their increasing power threatened the pharaohs' authority.

Finally, in 1375 B.C.E., Pharaoh Amenhotep IV attempted to weaken the priests and stop some of their more offensive practices. When they proved too powerful, Amenhotep tried to end priestly power altogether by introducing monotheism, the worship of only one god. He called upon people to worship Aton, an ancient name for the sun. He changed his own name to Akhenaten, meaning "Aton-is-pleased," and his wife Nefertiti's name to Nefer-nefru-Aton, "beautiful-

Akhenaten worshiping Aton

is-the-beauty-of-Aton."

Akhenaten left Thebes and built a new capital dedicated to Aton 250 miles down-river. He taught that Aton was like no other god, had no human or animal shape, but was more like a force. Representations of Aton show a disc like the sun with rays of its power flowing out. Akhenaten claimed Aton was not only an Egyptian god, but also the creator of the whole universe who cared for each person and rewarded those with integrity and purity of heart. This was probably the first expression of monotheism.

Akhenaten's devotional songs to Aton beautifully reflect his concept of a single creator god:

> How manifest are thy works!
> They are hidden from before us,
> O sole god, whose powers no other possesseth.
> Thou didst create the earth according to thy heart
> While thou wast alone:
> Men, all cattle large and small,
> All that are upon the earth, . . .
> The foreign countries, Syria and Kush,
> The land of Egypt;
> Thou settest every man into his place,
> Thou suppliest their necessities. . . .

It is amazing that this young ruler, who was only in his twenties, proclaimed this historic breakthrough in religious thought. However, Akhenaten failed to get the people to accept monotheism. Perhaps his youthful enthusiasm led him to try to force people to accept the idea. In addition, Aton did not promise eternal afterlife, which Egyptians had come to expect, so most people remained faithful to the older gods.

When Akhenaten claimed he was the only person who could contact Aton, and everyone had to approach Aton through him, the priests plotted against him. Akhenaten's successor, young King Tutankhamun, rejected monotheism, moved the capital back to Thebes, and allowed the priests to reclaim their former power.

How Did Egyptian Life Change?

War and military expansion significantly changed Egyptian life. Abundant wealth flowed into the country, and so did new technologies. Farmers adopted a neck yoke for their oxen, used wheeled wagons, and perfected their irrigation system. New breeds of sheep and chickens were introduced, and craftsmen began to use a bellows for forging iron. At the same time some of the new ideas undermined the traditional faith in the gods, and many Egyptians adopted the philosophy of eat, drink, and be merry and began to wonder whether the great pyramids would really be able to protect the dead.

Increased wealth slowly undermined traditional ways. For one thing, not everyone benefited equally from the prosperity and power the empire made possible. Many artisans and peasants were upset because things they had once grown or made could now be gotten more easily by fighting or through trade with conquered areas, so people were less interested in buying their goods. Now that pharaohs had their own standing army, local governors no longer had to furnish soldiers. As a result, they lost much of their authority and became mere courtiers, flattering the pharaoh.

Egypt enjoyed its last period of greatness under pharaohs during the Nineteenth Dynasty (1292–1200 B.C.E.). Ramses II, who ruled for 67 years from 1292 to 1225 B.C.E., made significant military advances in Nubia. Unable to defeat the Hittites, he reluctantly made a treaty of friendship with them in 1278 B.C.E. This nonaggression pact put the states on equal terms and said eternal peace was to prevail. But Egypt's last great military leader was Ramses III, whose greatest victories were against the Hittites.

Although Egypt ruled an impressively large territory, it was not able to gain the loyalty or rule effectively over the lands it had conquered. Egyptians administrators collected the taxes, but Syria and Palestine still largely governed themselves. Rebellions were frequent, and the Egyptians maintained control by force.

Despite their military successes, the Egyptians were never enthusiastic warriors. Warfare had not been a significant part of Egyptian life until after the Hyksos invasion, and empire building proved to be a costly venture for this once-proud civilization. They achieved many of their military victories using Nubian warriors who made up a large part of their armies. More importantly, when they turned their attention to the art of war, they lost their uniqueness as a civilization. As earlier conquerors had learned, living by the sword and chariot meant they had to continue to expand or they could not support the troops nor control their conquests. By expanding its empire, Egypt had become fair game for a series of military adventurers who would seek to conquer that rich land. One of the challenges came from the Nubians.

Conquerors from Nubia

Nubia is the area along the Nile valley from the first cataract to the sixth cataract (from the modern Aswan Dam to where the Blue and White Nile rivers join). The name Nubia may have come from *nub*, the Egyptian word for gold, which Egyptians got from there. Herodotus called it Ethiopia and its people Ethiopians, meaning people with burnt faces, but present-day Ethiopia is southeast of ancient Nubia. The Egyptians referred to present-day Somalia as the Land of Punt. Kush refers to a kingdom established in Nubia.

Nubia, like Egypt, was a gift of the Nile River. Herding and agriculture were possible only on the narrow strips of land on either side of the Nile that were renewed by the river's annual inundation. The most fertile soil in all of Nubia and the best area for farming was between the third and fourth cataracts, where the annual Nile inundation was similar to that in Egypt. Here the yearly flooding brought both water and rich silt deposits, so farmers could grow good crops. Grasses grew on the steppe lands south of the fifth cataract, so herding was possible there.

Few records exist to tell about the early history of Nubia, although a few Egyptian rock inscriptions report military victories or trading expeditions near the first cataract. The Island of Meroë, which lies between the White Nile, Blue Nile, and Atbara rivers, was probably the site of the earliest Nubian agricultural and herding settlements, where the Nubians produced a surplus from hunting, farming, and grazing animals. Nubia was an important center of trade, transferring goods from the Mediterranean world to the interior of Africa and from the interior to the Mediterranean and Red seas. Besides hiring Nubians as mercenaries (hired to fight), Egyptians often forced

Nubian soldiers they had captured to fight for them.

Remains of at least 10 forts built around 1780 B.C.E., most of them clustered around the second and first cataracts, suggest extensive settlements existed in Nubia. If the Egyptians built these forts to protect their southern border, they must have considered Nubia a serious military threat. On the other hand, if these forts were used as trading stations rather than for defense, many goods must have passed between Egypt and Nubia.

After the Egyptians drove the Hyksos out of Egypt, Egyptian rulers re-established trade with Lower Nubia and built a settlement at Napata, the end of two busy caravan routes. Under Ahmos (1580–1558 B.C.E.) and Tutmose (1525–1512 B.C.E.), Egyptians may have created a garrison at Napata to control whoever crossed the Nile as well as trade along the caravan routes. Ramses II had a temple to the god Amun constructed there, and it became a major pilgrimage site.

The Kingdom of Kush Rules Egypt

As Egyptian power weakened during the first centuries of the first millennium B.C.E., Nubians conquered Napata and established the Kingdom of Kush in the rich agricultural lands between the third and fourth cataracts. This kingdom existed from 750 B.C.E. to 350 B.C.E., and Napata was its first capital. As the Kushites got stronger, they began a military campaign against Egypt. Beginning in 751 they captured Thebes and most of upper Egypt and by 730 had established Egypt's 25th Dynasty, which ruled Egypt until 664 B.C.E., when the Assyrians joined the Egyptians and drove the Kushites out.

Moving south after their defeat, the Kushites made Meroë the capital of the Kingdom of Kush. Meroë was farther from Egypt than Napata, so it had less Egyptian influence. Not only did Meroë have rich pasture lands along the rivers that formed the Island of Meroë, but the area got rain as well as the annual inundation and was rich in iron ore and timber for the furnaces in which they smelted iron. Iron was rare in Egypt but plentiful at Meroë, so the Kushites were able to manufacture strong iron weapons and tools. In addition, Meroë linked two major trade routes. The ruling elite included priests, and a middle class, probably made up of merchants, potters, blacksmiths, and other craftsmen. Most people were probably farmers and cattle breeders,

The Lion temple with Queen Amanishakheto

followed by slaves who were prisoners of war. Until the fourth century B.C.E., the kingdom of Kush will play an important role in the ever-expanding web of urban and trading centers in Africa as well as the Mediterranean World, South Asia and China.

The Hebrews Create A Kingdom

The Hebrews offer a dramatic example of a nomadic people's successful conquest during the first millennium B.C.E. Migrating from the Arabian Peninsula sometime between 2,000 and 1,000 B.C.E., the Hebrews followed a pattern of invasion, conquest, and settlement similar to many other Indo-European and Semitic pastoral groups. In the Bible, which records much of their early history, the Hebrews described themselves as a loose federation of twelve tribes. Perhaps around the time that Hammurabi was ruling Babylon, some of them entered Canaan, a complex urban society on the eastern end of the

Mediterranean Sea. Some settled down in Canaan long enough to become mercenaries or workers, but most preferred to continue their semi-nomadic life protected by their god YHWH (what may have been vocalized as Yahweh but was considered too sacred to be spoken).

Genesis, the first book of the Hebrew Bible, tells of the tension between nomadic and settled peoples. For example, the two sons of the first human couple, Adam and Eve, were Cain, the tiller of the soil, and Abel, who herded sheep. These brothers fought, and Cain killed Abel. Their animosity may reflect the conflict between herders and farmers.

EGYPT AND THE EXODUS

By 1700 B.C.E., about the same time the Hyksos invaded Egypt, many Hebrews had migrated into the delta region of the Nile and perhaps the Hyksos welcomed them as fellow Semites. Unfamiliar with how to administer a complex society such as Egypt, the Hyksos may have employed some Hebrews as administrators and advisors. Joseph, a Hebrew who grew to a position of importance in the Egyptian government, may illustrate this alliance.

As Hyksos power waned, "a new king arose over Egypt, who did not know Joseph." (Exodus I:8) Having expelled the Hyksos, the Egyptians must have regarded Hebrews with suspicion, and succeeding Egyptian dynasties enslaved many of them. The Bible offers accounts of the Pharaoh's harsh treatment of the Hebrews, even ordering newborn males killed.

After enduring much persecution, sometime after 1300 B.C.E. Moses led the Hebrews out of Egypt. The Bible explains that YHWH helped them escape from bondage by parting the Red Sea, then closing the waters over the pursuing Egyptian army. The Exodus, the name they gave to their flight out of Egypt, convinced the Hebrews that they had a special relationship with YHWH, and that in times of great crisis, YHWH would intervene on their behalf.

COVENANT AND CONQUEST

The Hebrews wandered for forty years in the desert, finally approaching the borders of Canaan. According to the Bible, YHWH appeared to Moses, gave him the Ten Commandments, and revealed that the Hebrews were his chosen people. The Hebrews entered into a Covenant (an agreement or contract) with their Lord. YHWH promised to protect his chosen people as long as they followed the Ten Commandments, which included directives "to have no other gods before me," not to make any "graven images," not to take the Lord's name in vain, and to keep the Sabbath (the seventh day of the week) holy. These Commandments focus on the relationship between YHWH and his people. Some of the Commandments strengthened the community, such as honoring fathers and mothers, not killing, not committing adultery or stealing, not bearing false witness against one's neighbor, and not coveting (desiring) one's neighbors' possessions. (See Exodus 20) The Hebrews believed that YHWH would lead them to the "land of milk and honey" if they faithfully kept their side of the Covenant.

Moses did not live to see the Promised Land. He appointed Joshua as his successor, and Joshua led the Hebrews in their conquest of Canaan, which was long and fierce. After defeating the urbanized Canaanites, the Hebrews, organized into a loose federation of tribes and, following the familiar patterns of nomadic invasion and conquest, settled down and began to farm. Some began to worship local gods and goddesses and adapt other local customs, which violated their covenant with YHWH. Disagreements erupted over how to keep YHWH's commandments and to what extent they could adopt elements of Canaanite culture. Faced with increasing intertribal disputes, they agreed to appoint judges who would settle arguments.

KING DAVID'S KINGDOM

Like other nomadic invaders, Hebrews grew to realize that tribal organization was not suitable if they wanted to rule a state efficiently, and by the end of the second millennium B.C.E. they reluctantly accepted the idea of kingship under Saul. In 1000 B.C.E., when the Hebrews made war against the Philistines, another group living in Canaan, King Saul was killed. David — the next king — made Jerusalem the capital of his kingdom that stretched from Lebanon to the Red Sea. King David ruled from 1000 to 960 B.C.E.

Jerusalem under King Solomon, David's son, was an impressive

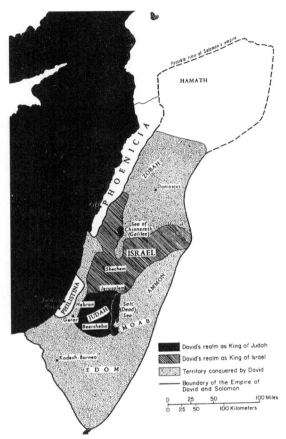

Israel and Judah

city. King Solomon had a large merchant navy built, which monopolized the trade between Egypt and Syria, and he is reported to have entertained the Queen of Sheba, who probably ruled an area in southern Arabia. Like his fellow monarchs in west Asia, he lived in luxury and sponsored extravagant feasts and celebrations. Solomon supervised construction of a great temple that stood at the center of this splendid city. However, his many building projects were expensive, and heavy taxes and corvée caused much unrest. Solomon also seemed to tolerate the worship of deities other than YHWH, adding to people's resentment.

When Solomon died in 930 B.C.E., the Hebrew kingdom was torn by civil war and finally divided into two kingdoms: Israel in the north and Judah in the south. Israel was much larger and more powerful and sophisticated than Judah. Some of the devoutly religious leaders of Israel began to feel that its prosperity encouraged people to stray from the Ten Commandments and violate their Covenant with YHWH. These critics accused people of worshiping local gods and abandoning their old values. Clearly, at the height of their success as a settled people with their own kingdom, some Hebrews wondered if it was worth turning away from the values YHWH had passed down to them in order to have secular (worldly) power and wealth.

Akkadians, Babylonians, Hittites, and Hebrews were just some of the groups that invaded and tried to control west Asia. By the middle of the second millennium B.C.E., law and the military had become well-established. Chariots and iron weapons helped nomadic groups invade and conquer, and enormous changes had taken place in the urban areas they conquered and among the nomadic conquerors. But nomadic invasions and conquest were not limited to west Asia and Egypt. In the next scene we will consider what happens as nomadic warriors enter the Indian subcontinent.

THE ARYANS IN INDIA

Setting the Stage

The Aryans were one of the Indo-European pastoral nomadic groups living in the steppes of southern Russia. They began to move into present-day Iran around 1700 B.C.E., about the same time the Hyksos invaded Egypt and the Babylonians invaded Mesopotamia. Some Aryan tribes continued through the passes in the Hindu Kush Mountains and reached the fertile plain of the Indus River, where they found the decaying Indus cities. Equipped with horse and chariot and driving their herds of cattle, they easily subdued the Indus people they met and destroyed what was left of that sophisticated urban society.

Aryans settled in valleys of the Indus and its tributaries and gradually mixed with people who were already living there. Once they learned iron smelting, they traveled down the Gangetic plain, searching for iron ore to make into axes and other tools and for new land. They slashed and burned forests and began to settle down.

What the Vedas Reveal

The invading Aryans who took over the Indus valley and Gangetic plain left few artifacts. There are no cities to uncover, no graves to expose or pottery to piece together; no bricks or seals remain to reveal to their way of life. The major source of information about the Aryans is a collection of sacred texts known as the Vedas. The four books of the Vedas include hymns to the gods, instructions on how to perform rituals, and some speculation about the meaning of the universe. Because Aryans had no written language when they came into India, they passed the Vedas down orally from generation to generation, by chanting and singing them. The Vedas were so important that historians call the period in India from 1500 to 1000 B.C.E. the Vedic Age.

Although no kings or battles are mentioned in the Vedas, historians can use them to piece together a fairly vivid picture of Aryan life.

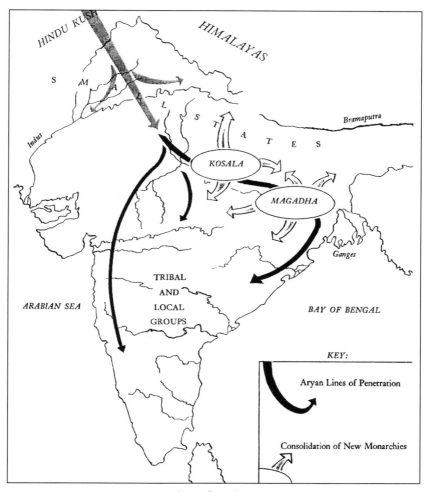

Aryan Invasions

Aryans appear as a fun-loving, vigorous people who enjoyed gambling, horsemanship, and fighting. For example:

> His face is like a thundercloud when the armored
>   warrior goes into the lap of battles. . . .
> With the bow let us win cows, . . . with the bow let
>   us conquer all the corners of the world. . . .
> Standing in the chariot, the skillful charioteer drives

his prize-winning horses forward wherever he
wishes to go. Praise the power of the reigns; the
guides follow the mind that is behind them. . . .
(Rig Veda 6.75.1, 2, 6)

. . . Because of my losing throw of the dice, I have
driven away a devoted wife.
My wife's mother hates me, and my wife pushes me
away; the man in trouble finds no one with sympathy. They all say, 'I find a gambler as useless as an
old horse that someone wants to sell.' . . .
[To the dice:] Grant us your friendship; have pity on
us. Do not bewitch us. . . Lay to rest your anger,
your hatred. Let someone else fall into the trap of
the brown dice. (Rig Veda 10.75.2, 3, 14)

Aryan means the pure or noble ones, and that is probably how they
thought of themselves. The Vedas reveal a hierarchical, male dominated society. Inside the home the man was supreme, and the father
performed rituals and presided over an extended family composed of
his sons and their wives and children. Rajas (chiefs who ruled the
many Aryan groups) called upon male elders for advice, but led their
tribes into battle and had a great deal of power. As tribes merged
together to form larger units, some of the rajas became maharajas
(great chiefs) or kings. One of the strongest Aryan tribes was the Bha-
ratas. Indians sometimes call their country Bharat after this group.

Aryan Gods

Most of the Aryan dieties were associated with nature. The most powerful gods were Varuna, Indra, Agni, and Soma. Varuna was a sky god
who presided over the order in the universe. Indra — the god of
storm, rain, and thunder, and the patron of warriors — was young, virile, and loved to fight. One of Indra's titles was Destroyer of Cities.
He hurled thunderbolts, destroyed armies, and released the mighty
waters. Perhaps "releasing the waters" refers to how the Aryans
destroyed what remained of the elaborate irrigation projects the Indus
people had built.

Agni, god of fire, was another important Aryan deity, since fire was the center of Aryan worship. Fire must have been comforting when the Aryans lived on the steppes. Agni became increasingly important in later Vedic times, linking the three worlds of the heavens, atmosphere, and earth, and came to represent all the gods. Soma, associated with earth, embodied an intoxicating drink of the same name that may have made devotees who drank it during rituals feel immortal.

The Four Varnas

In the first centuries after the Aryans came into the subcontinent, rulers and warriors, known as *kshatriyas*, were probably the most respected and powerful group. Next were the brahmins — priests who were responsible for the rituals and maintaining the cultural tradition. *Kshatriyas*, brahmins, and *vaishyas* — traders, farmers, and craftsmen — were the upper three communities known as *varnas*. They were called "twice born," because they were allowed to wear the sacred thread and participate in special religious rituals and were also promised an afterlife in heaven.

People in the fourth *varna* were called *shudras. Shudras* served the twice-born and did all the dirty work. The original *shudras* were probably non-Aryans who had been living in the Indian subcontinent when the Aryans invaded. The Vedas referred to them as black, without religion or language, and uncivilized. Aryans thought non-Aryans were vastly inferior, made them work as servants and laborers, and had nothing but contempt for their passive ways.

Because *varna* means color, historians think the four *varnas* might reflect differences in skin color. Twice-born Aryans had lighter skin than darker non-Aryan peoples. The sharp distinction between the top three varnas — the twice-born — and the shudras was probably intended to keep the Aryans separated from the people they had conquered. Aryans tried to prohibit social contact and intermarriage, realizing perhaps that they could easily be absorbed into the vastly larger numbers of non-Aryan peoples if they intermarried. However, the prohibition was impossible to enforce, and over the centuries a great deal of intermarriage took place, leading to a blending of Aryan and indigenous people.

Why Did Power Shift from Warriors to Brahmins?

In the early days of the Vedic Age, political and military leaders fought, raided, and ruled. Fathers performed sacrifices and other rituals in the home and only called on priests for special occasions. However, sometime around 1000 B.C.E., as Aryan tribes began to settle down into farming communities and warfare decreased, fighting became less important than growing crops and looking after cattle.

In order to ensure that their harvests were bountiful and that the universe continued, brahmins staged public sacrifices instead of just performing private rites in homes. These public rituals became increasingly elaborate and expensive and soon replaced other forms of worship. The latter books of the Vedas contain detailed instructions on how to conduct sacrifices, some of which involved killing large numbers of animals, especially cattle. Only brahmins had access to the Vedas, so they were the only ones who knew how the sacrifices should be performed or which magic words to speak. Brahmins carefully conducted each sacrifice with exactly the right words and actions, making sure every substance and instrument had been properly purified and blessed.

Performing sacrifices gave brahmins a lot of power, because as long as the sacrifices were done correctly, the gods had to answer prayers and keep the universe going. That meant the community's safety and security rested on the brahmins and their knowledge of the sacrifices and other rituals. Even kings, when they wanted to go to war, had to consult their brahmin advisors and get their blessing. Brahmins also began to teach royal children and serve as "brain trusts" for various kings. In Mesopotamia and Egypt, rulers and warriors gradually became more powerful than priests, but by 900 B.C.E. in India, it was the other way around: Brahmins were becoming the most important group.

One of the most familiar Indian creation stories in the Rig Veda reflects the growing importance of brahmins. In this hymn the Self, in the form of a cosmic man called Purusha, allows himself to be sacrificed. According to the hymn, different parts of Purusha's body become the parts of the world. Brahmins claimed the sacrifice of Purusha showed that they were the most important group because they came from Purusha's head.

> When they divided the Man [Purusha], into how
> many parts did they apportion him? . . . His mouth
> became the Brahmin; his arms were made into the
> warrior, his thighs the People, and from his feet the
> Servants were born. (Rig Veda 10.90.11)

This hymn reflects the brahminic ideal of the four divisions in the society with brahmins at the top, followed by *kshatriyas* (political leaders and warriors), then *vaishya* (artisans and businessmen), and finally *shudras* (laborers). However, this division was always more the ideal than the way society was really organized, in part because people could move up or down in the *varna* system. New groups of skilled warriors could be considered *kshatriyas*, successful traders could gradually be accepted at *vaishyas*, and a few groups even gained brahmin status.

The Role of Women

Women in the Vedic Age in India, as in most nomadic societies, enjoyed quite a bit of freedom. Because marriage ideally took place within the *varna* system, educated men wanted well-educated wives, so twice-born girls were allowed to study sacred texts and learn secular knowledge as well. Young girls could also move outside the home and mingle with boys their own age.

All girls and boys were expected to marry, usually by the time they were 16 or 17 years old. The Vedas reveal that young women, with the approval of their parents, had some choice in selecting their life partners. Married couples were to base their relationships on mutual respect and affection. In one Vedic verse a bride states:

> Become thou my partner, as thou hast passed all the
> seven steps with me [part of the marriage ritual] and
> apart from thee I cannot live. Apart from me do thou
> not live.

Within the family the husband was supreme, and the wife was expected to have sons and serve her husband faithfully. Husbands addressed their wives as "friend," and wives were permitted to attend festivals and participate in local governing assemblies. Widows could remarry and often wed their husband's younger brother to keep the family intact.

The *Mahabharata* Describes Heroic *Vira* in the Epic Age

Two major Indian epics, the *Mahabharata* and the *Ramayana*, reveal what life was like from about 1000 to 500 B.C.E. These epics are so important that historians call this period in India the Epic Age. Although Indians did not write these epics down until hundreds of years later, the *Mahabharata,* especially, reflects values and the way of life that probably existed in the Gangetic plain at the start of the first millennium B.C.E. Being a *vira* — a heroic warrior — was the kshatriya ideal. Aryan mothers prayed for heroic sons, and the *Mahabharata* celebrates battles these warrior heroes fought.

The *Mahabharata*, the story of a great civil war among several Aryan tribes, centers on a dispute among cousins and their allies over who had the legitimate right to rule. When King Dhritarashtra went blind, he gave his crown to his younger brother, Pandu. But no one could agree on who ought to succeed Pandu. Should the crown go to

Draupadi at the gambling match

the sons of the ruling king Pandu, or to the sons of the elder blind king Dhritarashtra? Both groups of cousins had legitimate claims to the throne. The princes attempted to settle the matter by a gambling match; ultimately they fought over the kingdom and involved countless neighboring states and warriors in the battle. Aryan tribes probably fought over similar questions of legitimacy as they vied for power.

The *Mahabharata* tells of tribal groups competing for legitimacy, not conquering new territory nor building vast empires. When the epic ends, almost everyone has been killed; no kingdom of any significance remains. Perhaps the bards who sang these stories wanted to show how destructive tribal warfare could be in order to convince people to find more peaceful ways to choose their rulers.

The *Ramayana* Provides Models
for Doing One's *Dharma*

During the Epic Age, *dharma* became more important. *Dharma* means to uphold, but it is often translated duty, a person's role, or a thing's attributes. Each person and thing has attributes or unique properties. Rain falls, and ice is solid. Birds fly, fish live in water, apple trees produce apples, and fire burns. A good fire is one that burns well. It makes no sense to criticize a fire that burns homes instead of wood. Rain falls on "the just and the unjust;" it cannot worry about what is underneath. Birds do not swim, apple trees should not grow foxes, and wives should not dominate their husbands. No matter what happens, brahmins taught, people should perform their *dharma* and not try to do someone else's *dharma*.

Some aspects of *dharma*, such as gender and *varna*, are set at birth. Some aspects change as a person gets older. A young boy should to be a good son, but as he matures, his roles change and he takes on the *dharma* of a husband, father, and elder in the community. A dutiful daughter becomes a good wife, a loving mother, and a just mother-in-law.

The *Ramayana,* the other important Indian epic, celebrates doing one's *dharma*. The hero, Prince Rama, always tried to do his *dharma*. When he was a young boy, Rama was the perfect son. He was supposed to be an ideal husband to his faithful wife Sita, a loyal brother,

Ravana abducts Sita

and a responsible ruler of the people of Aydohya, his capital. Those in the story who violated their *dharma* caused trouble or got into trouble themselves.

Prince Rama was the eldest of four sons, so he should have become the new king when his father gave up the throne. His stepmother, however, wanted her son Bharata, Rama's younger half-brother, to become king. The King had once promised her any two wishes she desired, and she asked that Rama be banished and Bharata be crowned. The King, bound by *dharma*, had to keep his word, and he ordered Rama's banishment. Rama accepted the decree without question. A son must obey his father.

When his wife Sita heard Rama was to be banished, she begged to accompany him to his forest retreat. "As shadow to substance, so wife to husband," she reminded Rama. "Is not the wife's *dharma* to be by her husband's side?

When Rama's brother Bharata learned what his mother had done, he begged Rama to return and rule. "It is the eldest son's *dharma* to rule," he told Rama. "Please take your rightful place as king." But Rama said his *dharma* was to obey his father, so Bharata, the ideal younger brother, agreed to rule as regent in Rama's place. When the fourteen years of banishment were over, he joyously returned the kingdom to Rama.

Later in the story, Ravana, the evil King of Lanka (probably present-day Sri Lanka), abducted Sita. Rama mustered the aid of a monkey army that built a stone causeway across to Lanka and helped him kill Ravana and defeat his forces. Rama freed Sita and brought her safely back to Aydohya. In order to set a good example, however, before Rama would take Sita back as his wife, he made her go through a fire ordeal to prove that Ravana had never touched her.

Rama, Sita, and Bharata all followed their *dharma*. The *Ramayana* celebrated a man of *dharma* instead of *vira*, those heroic warriors so revered by the Aryan invaders. Performing his *dharma* was what made Rama heroic, not fighting. In this way, brahmins further weakened the status of the *kshatriyas*. Perhaps brahmins also hoped that those who followed their *dharma* would never question their authority.

In the 700 years since they had entered the subcontinent, the Aryans had mixed and merged with the people living there, in spite of the ban on intermarriage. They also built new cities along the Gangetic plain such as Varanasi, an especially sacred city and one of the oldest continuous cities in the world. By the seventh century B.C.E., northern India was divided into seventeen small kingdoms and republics, and these petty states were constantly competing with one another for political power, very like the cousins in the *Mahabharata*. Although larger states might for a time absorb smaller ones, no one area dominated for long, and fighting soon started all over again.

As India became urbanized, people wanted more equality, and they began to resent the brahmins' strict rules, expensive rituals, and haughty attitude. After so many centuries of warfare, people were also searching for ways to reduce the fighting and tame the warrior spirit. These yearnings would soon lead to new and innovative solutions. The thinkers who taught new approaches to these problems will be part of the next act. But first we turn to see how movements of nomadic peoples were affecting life in China.

CHINA UNDER THE SHANG AND ZHOU DYNASTIES

Setting the Stage

Whether or not there was a Xia Dynasty, archaeological evidence including oracle bones demonstrates that a group called the Shang had gained control over a significant part of northern China by about 1750 B.C.E. The Shang were not nomadic newcomers but had settled down on the northern border of China and developed a bronze age culture that included writing and stratification. Taking advantage of military technology they learned from nomadic groups near-by, including the horse and chariot, the Shang began to expand, subduing groups who had settled on the flood plain of the Yellow River. Their dynasty lasted until about 1027 B.C.E.

Because the Shang had already settled within the border of China, their conquest did not disrupt Chinese life the way nomadic invasions in other parts of Eurasia had done. Although Shang leaders governed a relatively small area, they were able to influence many surrounding groups by the high quality of their civilization.

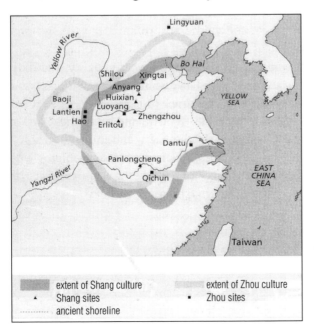

What Was Life Like
When the Shang Dynasty Ruled?

The Shang kingdom consisted of a group of small chiefdoms, each of which had a number of walled cities. Wars occurred frequently among these various chiefdoms, so military might was very important during Shang times, and warriors had the most status. Armies of up to 5,000 men, equipped with bronze weapons, fought one another and made slaves of the prisoners they captured or used them for human sacrifices. The king led his armies into battle, wielding bronze weapons that were a sign of his power and legitimacy.

The horse-drawn chariot gave the Shang military superiority. The chariot became highly valued in Shang life, not only for war, but for impressive hunts and as a status symbol. Grave sites reveal that horses and chariots, and even some soldiers and retainers, were buried along with the lords. Items found in these gravesites indicate the upper class enjoyed many luxuries, which a large artisan class in Shang cities produced.

Shang burial with chariot

The Shang relied not only on military superiority to keep neighboring groups from conquering them, but they also developed a form of sacred rule. Shang rulers ordered the construction of several capital cities that included palaces, temples, and sacrificial altars. Some neighboring groups, to whom these centers must have seemed wondrous, offered their allegiance. Excavations reveal that sacrifices, including human sacrifice, were extremely important.

What Secrets Do the Oracle Bones Reveal?

Shang rulers used reverence for ancestors to help establish their legitimacy The king could contact ancestors through messages on oracle bones, and ancestors could then convey the wishes to the supreme god. The king, aided by a group of priests who served as diviners and helped him understand the ancestors' wishes, had the final authority in interpreting messages revealed by the oracle bones.

Oracle bones are historians' chief source of information about the Shang. Because questions on the bones were written to the ancestors' spirits, scholars believe they contain much reliable information. Perhaps a historian employed by a vain ruler might exaggerate the number of troops the ruler had in an attempt to flatter him, but there would be no reason to overstate the numbers of troops mentioned in questions to the spirits. (If you are writing an application for college, you might exaggerate how many books you had read. But if you went to the trouble to ask the bones whether the English teacher would include *Hamlet* on the final exam, we could assume that you had been studying that play. We could also infer you were in a class that had an exam and that there was a certain amount of concern about its outcome.)

Information gained from the bones helped archaeologists locate and excavate two major urban sites in western China. Remains of these two cities prove that Shang China was as developed materially and artistically as urban centers elsewhere in the world. At the center of Shang cities were palaces and temples. Around these were artisans' homes where they made such things as bronze tools, weapons, and pottery. Peasants lived beyond these in small huts built into the ground around a center hearth. On the outskirts were the graveyards.

During the Shang dynasty, most people were peasant farmers or slaves. They supplied the grain that supported the entire society, and most of what they grew or produced belonged to the government. The Shang also realied heavily on corvée labor supply. It took thousands of workers to build their cities and construct the elaborate tombs.

The Shang made many developments in art, technology, and science as well as religion. Skilled craftsmen created unique bronze weapons and vessels. Their three-legged pots, called *chia*, are among the loveliest bronze works of the ancient world. Various other bronze

| Lower jaw | Forehead | Fang | Snout | Upper jaw or trunk | Beak or fang | Eye | Leg |

The T'ao t'ieh

serving vessels were used for religious ceremonies; some of the most elaborate pieces were altarpieces in temples. Shang art style featured decorations of real and imaginary animals. These elaborate forms evolved into the T'ao-t'ieh image, a monster with only a head, which tries to devour people but injures only itself.

How Did Zhou Aristocrats Act?

By the eleventh century, in about 1027 B.C.E., a large group known as the Zhou defeated the Shang and gained enough power to control much of northern China. The Zhou, probably a mixture of settled people and pastoral nomads from the steppe, had settled in the Wei valley. Zhou kings claimed they successfully overthrew the Shang because Shang rulers had become corrupt and lost the Mandate of T'ian. The concept of the Mandate of T'ian as the sign of a ruler's legitimacy probably began with the Zhou, but in order to increase their legitimacy, they identified the concept with Yao, Shun, and Yu, the early sage-rulers. Zhou writers accused the last Shang ruler of being wasteful and so perverted that he killed people for no reason and even slaughtered pregnant women. Zhou historians claimed T'ian sent the Zhou to overthrow them, take the Mandate, and re-establish virtuous government.

The shift from the Shang to Zhou dynasty did not change much for the average person in China. The Shang kingdom had really been just a loosely knit group of walled cities that dominated the surrounding countryside, not unlike Sumerian city-states nearly two thousand years earlier. During the years from 1027 to about 771 B.C.E., many local leaders switched their allegiance to the Zhou, offering loyalty in exchange for protection.

The Zhou organized society as a hereditary aristocracy composed of those with large landholdings. People were born into the aristocracy; they could not become aristocrats through education or hard work. Still, many aristocrats were educated and had studied music and poetry. They also knew the rites and ceremonies that were supposed to govern all human relationships, what we call rules of etiquette. Zhou historic records suggest aristocrats in early Zhou times followed a code of honor and fought like gentlemen.

Literature Reflects Everyday Life

Although Zhou historians kept careful records of the political life of the rulers, they were not interested in writing about how average people lived. Even so, we can glean from their writings that during this period families started to own their own plots of land, and that when a father died, sons could inherit the land. Glimpses of everyday life are revealed in *The Book of Songs*, an anthology of poems compiled after 600 B.C.E. Many of them were originally folk songs set to music. The poems tell about such things as warfare, courtship and love, feasting, and mourning. Everyday tasks, such as planting and harvesting crops, complaining about excessive taxes, and young women gathering mulberry leaves for the silkworms are described.

The following poem is entitled "In the Seventh Month."

> In the seventh month the Fire ebbs;
> In the ninth I hand out the coats;
> In the days of the First, sharp frosts;,
> In the days of the Second, keen winds. . . . . . .
> In the days of the Third, they plough;
> In the days of the Fourth out I step
> With my wife and children,
> Bringing hampers to the southern acre
> Where the field-hands came to take good cheer. . . . . . .

In the ninth month we make ready the stack-yards,
In the tenth month we bring in the harvest,
Millet for wine, millet for cooking, the early and late,
Paddy and hemp, beans and wheat. . . . (# 154)

Some poems contain complaints against the government concealed as criticism of parents or lovers. Some are love poems. "Of Fair Girls" hints of a courtship near the city wall:

Of fair girls the loveliest
Was to meet me at the corner of the Wall.
But she hides and will not show herself;,
I scratch my head, pace up and down. . . . . . .

She has been in the pastures and brought for me rush-wool,
Very beautiful and rare.
It is not you that are beautiful;
But you were given by a lovely girl. (# 42)

How Was the Zhou Kingdom Organizaged?

The Zhou was supposed to control the whole country, and at its height it probably ruled over 100 lesser territories. Some of the leaders of the smaller areas believed they were distantly related to the Zhou, and that kinship bond provided a basis for loyalty to the central government. This was especially true because families and ancestors were so important.

Although leaders of the smaller areas controlled their own lands, local leaders were tied to the Zhou rulers through rituals, kinship, and the Zhou's military superiority. Zhou kings required lords to rule in the name of the Zhou and supply them with armies whenever necessary. The lords had to visit the Zhou court frequently, bringing the ruler gifts and performing special ceremonies that showed they were inferior to him. Besides leading the armies in times of war, the Zhou ruler conducted religious ceremonies. He was the only one who could perform the sacred ceremonies that people believed maintained the harmony between T'ian and earth.

Zhou rulers depended on the allegiance of these local leaders who provided both armies and revenue. The king granted special titles to the leaders of small states and these titles could be passed down to the sons. By 800 B.C.E., the Zhou kingdom included about two hundred lords with various size territories, but only about twenty-five were big enough to pose threats to the Zhou.

Some historians identify Zhou society as a form of feudalism Although the Zhou surely depended on local leaders or large land-holders to provide soldiers in time of war, and the lords often supplied tax revenues, the Zhou system depended more on kinship ties and ritual relationships that on contracts and formal obligations. Historians suspect that the Zhou maintained only the trappings of centralized rule. As the centuries passed, its leaders became increasingly weak, and wars among local provinces and kingdoms frequently competed for control. The results of these wars is part of the next act in the human drama.

MYCENAEANS AND DORIANS IN GREECE

Setting the Stage

Crete dominated the Aegean world from 2000 to 1400 B.C.E., but like other early urban centers, Minoan civilization disintegrated and eventually fell to invading nomads. Groups of Indo-Europeans began to enter the Balkan Peninsula sometime about 2000 B.C.E., and gradually worked their way down the peninsula. Archaeological evidence sug-

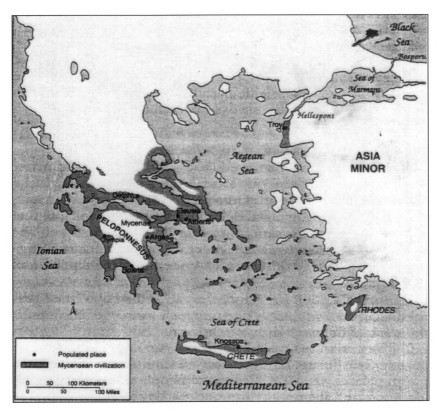

Mycenaean Settlements

gests Mycenae, a thriving urban center from 11400 to 1100 B.C.E., became their main settlement and gave its name to this period, the Mycenaean Age, and to the people, the Mycenaeans. The famous poet Homer, who sang about these Indo-European nomads, called them Achaeans.

Mycenaeans Settle Down

Invading Mycenaeans, like other nomadic groups, had no written language when they came into Greece. Their warrior-dominated society, led by the most battle-tested warriors, was similar to other nomadic communities of the time. For several centuries people in these sparsely scattered communities lived as simple farmers and shepherds and by fighting and piracy. Judging from the number of bones of large game found in their citadels, they hunted as well.

The Mycenaeans built fort-like settlements far enough from the shoreline so as to be safe from possible attack, but close enough to take advantage of the fishing and piracy that the sea offered. Minoan life had centered on the sea and trade, while the Mycenaeans preferred war, piracy, and plunder. Minoans had a large class of artisans skilled in metalwork and crafting fine jewelry, had developed a written language, and worshiped a goddess. Mycenaeans used crude tools, had no written language, and worshiped male gods every bit as virile and powerful as their own kings.

Some of the warrior-conquerors who settled in the Peloponnesus (the southern part of Greece) learned about the dramatically different Minoan way of life on the island of Crete. The Mycenaeans gradually adapted or adopted elements of Minoan culture. Once the Mycenaeans learned Minoan engineering skills, they built fortifications they could defend effectively. Many of their citadels had walls up to ten feet thick. The Lion Gate and the 1,000-foot wall around the citadel at Mycenae, constructed around 1250 B.C.E., suggest that labor was cheap and that kings felt insecure enough to build a strong defensive wall. The Mycenaeans also learned how to work gold. Excavations of tombs reveal gold death masks and breastplates, gold and silver cups, rings, and even sheets of gold.

By 1350 B.C.E. there was little left of Minoan civilization, and for several hundred years the Mycenaeans dominated the Aegean world. It is not clear how much political unity they had; perhaps each area had its own leader or king. Below the leaders were military generals, administrators, charioteers, and leaders of the communities outside the forts. Each area had to remain constantly on guard against hostile neighbors who lived by the same military code.

The Lion Gate at Mycenae

The *Iliad*: A Case Study in Conquest

As the Mycenaeans spread their control and influence in the Mediterranean area, they not only plundered sailing ships but also conquered key cities that controlled trade routes. Troy was one of those cities. The Greek epic the *Iliad*, attributed to Homer, tells the story of the war the Mycenaean heroes — the Achaeans and their neighbors — waged against the cultured city of Troy. Once again literature provides insights for the historian.

Troy was near the Hellespont, the strait known today as the Dardanelles, that leads from the Aegean to Black Sea. The Trojans had probably grown rich by taxing vessels that passed through the Hellespont or by charging fees for the overland haul that sailors made to avoid the dangerous sea currents nearby. King Priam's palace in Troy had "polished colonnades," Homer tells us, "and inside, fifty apartments all of polished stone, one by another . . . and opposite these, within the courtyard, twelve more apartments all of polished stone." (*Iliad* 6.243–48) Achaean warriors from the Peloponnesus must have seemed crude compared to urbane Trojans.

The excuse the Achaeans gave for the siege of Troy was that Paris, an impetuous and irresponsible Trojan prince, had violated the rules of hospitality when he visited Menelaus, king of Sparta. Falling in love with Queen Helen, his host's wife, Paris had eloped with her and taken her back to Troy. King Menelaus appealed to his brother Agamemnon, King of Mycenae, to avenge his wounded honor. Since Menelaus was King of Sparta because he was married to Helen, his crown as well as his honor may have been at stake. Now Agamemnon, perhaps eager to establish Mycenaean influence over the Black Sea trade routes, had an excuse to subdue Troy.

According to the *Iliad*, King Menelaus and King Agamemnon called other warriors from neighboring areas to join in the expedition against Troy. Many Achaeans who fought in the siege of Troy had no personal animosity against Troy or the Trojans. They fought out of a sense of loyalty and to win some of the spoils of war. Even more important, this battle gave them a chance to demonstrate their excellence or *arete*.

Heroic Excellence: *Arete*

Men in this heroic society were often fighting, and *arete* involved courage on the battlefield and physical strength, loyalty, and fearlessness in the face of death. Warriors were expected to fight in the foremost ranks and win great glory for themselves, their family, and clan. When Andromache, the wife of the Trojan prince Hector, pleaded with her husband not to go to his certain death, Hector revealed his understanding of *arete*. He replied that if he did not fight, he would feel shame

> before the Trojans, and the Trojan women with trailing garments,
> if like a coward I were to shrink aside from the fighting;
> and the spirit will not let me, since I have learned to be valiant
> and to fight always among the foremost ranks of the Trojans,
> wining for my own self great glory, and for my father.
> (*Iliad* 6.441–46)

Demonstrating *arete* by fighting bravely was also the way a hero could gain a kind of immortality. Only the gods were immortal, but if a person died fighting heroically, poets might sing about him, and he would live on as long as he was remembered. In the *Iliad*, many of the warriors had to choose whether they wanted to leave the battle-field and have a long, uneventful life but be forgotten, or fight and die young but become immortal through the poets' songs. The heroic answer was to invite death on the battlefield "either to offer glory to some man, or ourselves to gain glory." (*Iliad* 12. 322–28) Sappho, a famous woman poet from Lesbos, captures the kind of immortality Greek heroes sought (and which she claimed for herself):

> The golden Muse gave me
> True riches: when dead
> I shall not be forgotten.

What About the Women?

Even though the *Iliad* is written from the perspective of the invading Achaeans, it reflects a great deal of sympathy for the Trojans, fight-ing to save their city. There are even glimpses in the poem of what women were doing. Their sphere, Homer tells us, included weaving loom and spindle, taking care of the children, and giving orders to servants. He sings of women making robes and weaving tapestries and of a widow who carefully weighs her wool in order to "win a pitiful wage for her children."

But the poets' songs also give us insights into the effect the con-stant fighting had, not only on women but also on the relationship between men and women. The Achaeans were repeatedly attacking settlements, killing the men and carrying off anything of value. Women, taken in war, were expected to do whatever their conquerors wished. Andromache, is a good example of the tragic effect war had on women. Long before the Trojan War, the Achaean hero Achilles had slain Andromache's father and seven brothers, carried off her mother, and ransomed her. In the *Iliad*, Achilles kills Hector, Andromache's husband, and then gives Andromache to his own son as a reward for fighting. Andromache is expected to love and serve him.

In the play *The Trojan Women* by Euripides, set at the end of the Trojan War, Andromache cries out:

> I spit upon the woman who gives in
> And abandons her husband to love another.
> Even animals, lacking language and intelligence,
> Find it hard to switch mates.
> And in Hector I had a man
> Who was all I could wish for in a husband;
> He was wise, agile, courageous,
> Well-born; he cherished us. (940-49)

Hecuba, Hector's mother, advises Andromache to try not to think of Hector and "let your own sweet ways win his [her new husband's] heart towards you." In the next breath, however, Hecuba tells Andromache to hold on to the hope that "your children's children may one day rebuild Troy." (696-701) That hope is destroyed when the Greeks throw her young son to his death. Imagine how Andromache, and the countless other women who suffered as she did, must have felt toward their captors, whom they were expected to serve and satisfy in every way. You can also imagine why the soldiers did not completely trust the women they had won. Perhaps the men projected their fears onto women in general, calling them untrustworthy by nature.

The Trojan horse

The Trojans finally lost, but it took an act of deception to defeat them. After ten indecisive years, the Achaeans pretended to give up and start for home, leaving behind a giant wooden horse. Intrigued, the Trojans dragged the horse inside the city walls. Too late, they discovered it was filled with Achaean soldiers. The rest of the Achaean army was hiding around the first bend of the shore and quickly returned to sack the city. Tradition dates the fall of Troy to about 1200 B.C.E.

But Troy was certainly not the only urban center that fell to the invading Achaeans. This experience of invasion, defeat, and abduction was repeated again and again throughout the second and first millennia B.C.E. In fact, Mycenaean glory was short-lived. Less than a hundred years after the defeat of Troy, new waves of nomadic Indo-European warriors called Dorians began their march into the Aegean world.

Dorians Bring a Dark Age

Indo-European pastoral nomads called Dorians invaded the Balkan Peninsula starting about 1100 B.C.E., burning Mycenaean palaces and living as squatters in the ruins. Writing and record-keeping disappeared, and skills in metalworking and textiles deteriorated. Fine bronze work gave way to the more effective but cruder iron. Because so little evidence remains from this period, historians often call it the Greek Dark Age.

The Dorians conquered the Peloponnesus, and one of their most distinctive settlements was at Sparta. Only Dorians could become citizens of Sparta, and they alone took the name Spartans. The Spartans attempted to stay totally separate from the helots, the people who were already living there. For centuries, Spartans, like Aryans in India, refused to mix and marry with the helots. Perhaps Sparta demonstrates the way nomadic warriors first acted when they conquered settled areas. But unlike the Aryans, Spartans lived like an occupying army in order to insure that they could keep the very large helot population from revolting, and they were always on the alert for possible helot resistance.

To escape from the invading Dorians, many people fled to places like Attica (where Athens is), to islands in the Aegean, to the western coast of Asia Minor, or to more isolated areas of the mainland. Probably only the more enterprising ones survived the ordeal of flight. In his poem *Works and Days*, the Greek poet Hesiod described it was like to live during this Dark Age:

> Then fathers won't get along with their kids anymore,
> Nor guests with hosts, nor partner with partner,
> And brothers won't be friends, the way they used to be.
> Nobody'll honor their parents when they get old
> But they'll curse them and give them a hard time.
> Godless rascals, and never think about paying them back
> For all the trouble it was to raise them.
> They'll start by taking justice into their own hands,
> Sacking each other's cities, no respect at all
> For the man who keeps his oaths, the good man,
> The just man. . . . (212–222)

For more than 300 years, from 1100 to 800 B.C.E., ravaging men broke through city walls as successive waves of Dorian invaders marched into the Greek peninsula. Their military skills and might must have been impressive, but based on other examples of migration and invasion, we can assume that the Dorians not only conquered and destroyed but also mixed and assimilated with the existing people and culture. Out of this mix will come a distinctly Hellenic style of civilization, which we will consider in the next act of the human drama.

ACT THREE – NOMADIC MIGRATIONS AND INVASIONS

Setting the Stage

1. What is the difference between a pastoralist and a pastoral nomad? How important were horses to the later group?
2. What things did the pastoral nomads value? What made their lives exciting? Difficult? Precarious?
3. What did nomads and settled people need from each other? Who needed the other more? How did they get what they wanted?
4. Pretend you are a nomad and explain what you think of farmers. Pretend you are a farmer and explain what you think of nomads.
5. What role did the chariot play in the invasions of pastoral nomads during the second millennium B.C.E.? How was iron used?
6. Discuss the various reasons large groups of nomadic groups might have entered settled areas. Which reasons do you think were most important? Why?

SCENE ONE
Nomadic Invasions in West Asia

1. Why did Mesopotamia experience so many waves of nomadic invasions? What role did geography play?
2. What was the pattern of invasion and conquest in Mesopotamia?
3. What can we infer about the relationship between nomads and settled people in the second millennium B.C.E. from *Gilgamesh* and "The Courtship of Innana and Dumuzi"?
4. Why did power shift from the ziggurat to the palace?
5. Law was an important development in west Asia. What were the people who developed laws trying to accomplish?
6. Are there any similarities between early west Asian law and how you live now? If so, give a few examples. Have you seen any examples of "an eye for an eye or a tooth for a tooth"? Explain.

SCENE TWO
Transformations in the Nile Valley

1. Why were the Hyksos able to conquer such a large society as Egypt?
2. Why did many Egyptians become more militaristic after the Hyksos conquered them?
3. Who was Queen Hatshepsut? What was significant about her rule?
4. Who was Akhenaten? Why did he try to institute the worship of only one god? Why did the priests oppose him?
5. Evaluate this statement using at least three examples: "Empire building destroyed Egypt."
6. Compare the results of the nomadic invasions in Egypt with those in West Asia.
7. Why did Meroë develop into an important center? What was the basis of its wealth and power?
8. What was the relationship between Nubia and Egypt? What does art from Kush suggest about its relationship with Egypt?
9. Identify and explain the importance of the following to the early Hebrews: the Exodus, the Ten Commandments, Chosen People, Covenant.
10. In what ways is the Hebrew experience similar to that of other nomadic groups in west Asia during the second millennium B.C.E.? In what ways was it different?

SCENE THREE
The Aryans in India

1. Where did the Aryans settle? What role did geography play in their lives?
2. What were the Vedas? What do the Vedas reveal about Aryan values and how the Aryans lived?
3. What were the four *varnas*? Who made up the top three *varnas*? Into which *varna* did Aryans put the Indus Valley people? Why?
4. Why did *kshatriyas* have the most power and respect at first? Why did brahmins begin to be more powerful? What does the Rig Veda hymn about the sacrifice of Purusha suggest about the hierarchy at this time?
5. What was the reason for the great war in the *Mahabharata*?
6. What does *dharma* mean? What are some examples of people performing their *dharma* in the *Ramayana*?
7. What does *raja* mean? What does *vira* mean? Was Rama a *vira*? Explain your answer.
8. Would brahmins want people to read and follow the examples in the *Ramayana*? Would *kshatriya*? Do you think average people would have wanted to try to follow those examples? Why or why not?

9. Compare the results of the nomadic invasions in India with those in Egypt and West Asia. How can you account for the differences?

China Under the Shang and Zhou Dynasties

1. What was the first dynasty in China? What is the evidence for your answer?
2. What were the oracle bones? What did historians learn about early China from the oracle bones?
3. Explain the importance of the military to the Shang.
4. What does aristocracy mean? What is a hereditary aristocracy? Would you respect a member of the Zhou aristocracy if you met him or her? Why or why not? Why might Chinese people in more recent times have thought the early Zhou years was an ideal time? Do you think it was ideal for the average person?
5. What was the relationship between the Zhou ruler and the smaller kingdoms over which he was said to rule? How much power did the Zhou ruler have? What was the basis of the power of the local rulers?
6. Compare the results of the nomadic invasions in China with those in India, Egypt, and west Asia. How can you account for the differences?

Mycenaeans and Dorians in Greece

1. The Mycenaeans came into a very sparsely settled area. How did they adapt to the geography there? What kind of society did they establish as they settled down? In what ways was their experience similar to invaders in west Asia, in China?
2. What kind of interaction did the Mycenaean have with the Minoans?
3. What does the *Iliad* tell us about the Mycenaean's attitude toward war? Why did they fight? What did *arete* mean to men in the Heroic Age in Greece?
4. What kind of immortality did the soldiers hope to have? How does this compare with what the Egyptians believed?
5. What does literature about the Trojan War suggest about men and women? about values? about the roles of women? Why might repeated conquests have made men and women distrust each other?
6. Who were the Dorians? How did they treat the helots?
7. What caused the Hellenic "Dark Age?" What were the characteristics of that time?

8. Compare *vira* and *dharma* with Greek heroes and *arete*. In what ways are they similar or different?

9. Compare the results of the nomadic invasions in Hellas with those in China, India, Egypt, and West Asia. How can you account for the differences?

Summing Up

1. Explain the role of new technology during the period of nomadic invasions. How important were things such as the chariot and iron weapons?

2. Look at your list of the possible reasons nomads might invade settled areas. Which reason or reasons do you think were the most important? Why?

3. Explain the importance of literary and religious sources such as the Vedas, the Bible, *Gilgamesh*, and the *Iliad*, as well as the oracle bones, in determining what happened in this period of history. What questions do historians have to think about when they use sources such as these? How can historians determine whether the sources report actual events? How can they be sure their interpretations of these sources are accurate? What do you mean by accurate?

4. Priests who had contact with the gods and goddesses and warriors who controlled the military competed with one another for power during this period. What was the source of legitimacy for each group? What were the reasons that kings and the military became more important in west Asia, while the religious leaders became more important in India? Why was Akhenaten unsuccessful in reducing the priests' role for very long in Egypt? Which of these two groups has more power and prestige in the United States today? Why?

5. If you could go back in time, in which of these areas would you most like to have lived and when? What job would you want to have had? Would you rather have been a woman or a man? Why?

6. Using information from this act, write an essay that answers the following question: "Nomads and Settled: Who conquered whom during the second millennium B.C.E.?"

THE AXIAL AGE
(700 – 500 B.C.E.)

The nomadic invasions of the second millennium B.C.E. changed the way of life of both nomadic invaders and urban dwellers. Invaders gradually settled down in existing villages and towns as well as on forested land they cleared. For the most part, they began to act very much like the people they had conquered. But shifting from a pastoral nomadic way of life in a small homogeneous group to sedentary life in large, diverse cities left many longing for lost freedoms. At the same time, the invaders brought new rulers and ideas, especially superior military technology and tactics. Settled people became more aggressive, so as to defend themselves against further invasions and increase their power base.

As surpluses and trade increased, new cities developed. By the seventh and sixth centuries B.C.E., urban life again flourished in Hellas, Mesopotamia, Egypt, India, and China, but these cities were different from earlier ones. People in each area had to reconcile two very different ways of life. Even though nomads gave up their pastoral ways, nomadic values greatly influenced urban areas, disrupting old values and leaving many people without meaning and direction in their lives.

The clash of settled and nomadic ways of life led to one of the most exciting acts of the entire human drama. It is so important that the eminent philosopher Karl Jaspers has called the period beginning around 600 B.C.E. the Axial Age. An axial idea, like the axle of a wheel, represents the central idea around which society revolves. In the Axial Age philosophers in China, India, west Asia, and Greece suggested new ways to solve the problems they were facing. Great teachers emerged in each of these areas, and their ideas were to have profound effects on the way people thought and what they believed.

Why Was There So Much Speculation?

Why was there so much creative thought in the sixth century? What challenges to human existence brought about these responses, Arnold Toynbee might want to know. In what way, Professor McNeill might want us to ask, did sharing ideas across cultures stimulate change, and how did new technology affect human experience?

One challenge the repeated invasions brought was the almost constant threat of war. There was little or no evidence of warfare in early cities in the Indus, Nile, and Yellow River valleys. But after the nomadic invasions, this was no longer the case. From the eighth century until the end of the third century B.C.E. the Zhou in China could not control the various states that were supposed to be under its authority. In Mesopotamia groups such as the Babylonians and Assyrians used military force to conquer and subdue neighboring areas and create large kingdoms that were held together by force, not by any common loyalties.

Egypt, whose isolation had permitted it to use funds to construct gigantic public buildings, turned its energies to the military in an effort to expand and maintain an empire. And although brahmins in India had acquired higher status than warriors, the subcontinent was divided into numerous small kingdoms that often fought over their common borders. People in each area, faced with constant wars and rumors of wars, felt increasingly insecure and resented the fact that warfare dominated their lives.

Besides the threat of war, many individuals in each of these areas felt uneasy and without direction in their lives. Gods and goddesses in Mesopotamia seemed to bring floods for no reason or get drunk and create deformed people just for sport. They would not, or, worse yet, could not save their devotees from being attacked and killed. In a complicated, interdependent urban environment, constantly threatened by war, sacrifices were fast becoming empty rituals that priests performed in order to get rich rather than to appease or please the gods.

Traders, going from area to area, were skeptical about local practices, and their amused tolerance of diverse beliefs made people uneasy. Experiencing the insecurities of urban existence, people questioned the possibility of any kind of universal order. (Think of when you have allowed plenty of time to get to school, only to have been caught in traffic or been delayed by an accident on the road. Think of when injuries prevented your star athlete from playing in an important game. Think of school violence that might strike at any time.)

What Kinds of Questions Were People Asking?

As business, manufacturing, and trade replaced herding and agriculture, nature gods and agricultural cycles lost their meaning. Nature deities from the steppes personifying storm, thunder, and fire or agricultural deities representing the earth and seasonal cycles were not very significant in a city. Besides, there were too many gods and goddesses, each promising, but not delivering, special protection for its own. Men and women longed for some way to deal with changeable and arbitrary events in their lives.

They also struggled with questions about who should rule and what type of government was best. In Sumer and India, over the centuries, power had shifted between those who could influence the gods and those who controlled the military. In Mesopotamia, leadership went from the temple servants to warriors. In India, on the other hand, the authority shifted from Aryan warriors to brahmin priests who controlled the sacrifices and other rituals. People questioned whether either priests or established rulers were legitimate.

Many subjects in these large kingdoms were growing discontented and even rebellious. Rulers, even when they had legitimacy, were far away, and people had little connection with them. Those rulers were sometimes hostile to local beliefs and customs and made it difficult for local groups to carry on their traditions. People resented high taxes and demands for corvée to construct government buildings. And often there was no protection from either civil war or external threats.

Another problem was the changing status of different groups. Why should hierarchy be determined by birth alone? The number of prosperous merchants was increasing but not their power or prestige. Merchants resented the privileges claimed by both old aristocratic families and religious leaders who jealously guarded their monopoly over the gods. Shouldn't people with more wealth have more status? For their part, established leaders and priests resented merchants demanding power. The lower classes, too, were clamoring for greater participation in society.

The Search for Answers

Insecurity, dissatisfaction, and a desire for change existed all across the hemisphere. From North China to North India, across West Asia to the Peloponnesus, people realized that something was deeply wrong in their lives. In this ferment, a new breed of teacher — people we call philosophers (lovers of wisdom) — began to seek new answers. Many of those philosophers criticized the rampant violence and sacrifices, sports that glorified physical force, and in seemingly pointless wars. They were especially critical of empty rituals performed to ward off the apparent unfairness and capriciousness of the gods. Gods must be more than vending machines that answer your prayers as long as you offer the right sacrifices (that is, put in the right coin).

During the Axial Age philosophers posed many questions, offered new and startling answers, and attempted to attract students. Although many of the challenges and questions were similar from region to region, each philosopher used the terms and values of his culture. In China, Confucius and Laozi will build on earlier Chinese experience of reverence for ancestors and Zhou aristocratic values. In India, Mahavira and Siddhartha Gautama will react to some of the brahmin practices and abuses. In Persia, Zoroaster will use the language and symbols of that war-torn region to call people to battle against evil, while Hebrew prophets, such as Amos and Job, will speak of justice as well as YHWH's mercy. In Greece philosophers and political reformers in Athens, including Solon and Cleisthenes, will build on their faith in human reason.

Though each philosopher was thoroughly rooted in his own culture, they all raised common questions about life — questions we still ask today: Must we use violence to settle disputes? What is the place of power in human life? How can we tame the warrior? What is the nature of the universe? What happens when I die? What is the proper kind of government? How many and what type of rules do people need to govern their lives? Should the state keep out of our lives or intervene in the interest of fairness? What should be the basis for relations among people? How can my concern for you be sincere if you are not part of my family, clan, or people? Is it possible to be loving and just to all people, even those I have not met? Can life ever be fair?

All these questions and many more could be heard daily in the streets of cities such as Varanasi, Memphis, Loyang, Persepolis, Athens and Jerusalem, and the answers people in these areas developed are the focus of this act of the human drama.

THE AXIAL AGE IN WEST ASIA

Setting the Stage

Nomads invaded Mesopotamia and the Fertile Crescent repeatedly throughout the second and into the first millennia B.C.E. No sooner had one group settled down and adjusted to urban life, than another group invaded. The Akkadians started the pattern in 2300 B.C.E. when they established a power base they called Akkad and gradually took over the Sumerian city-states. The Babylonians and Hittites followed the same pattern in the second millennium and, on a smaller scale, so did the Hebrews. After the Hyksos conquered Egypt, the Egyptians built their own empire. Repeatedly invaders established their power base, defeated the existing rulers, and put their own people in charge of their new territory, renaming it after themselves.

Each nomadic group brought a love of hunting and fighting, so warfare continued to be important in Mesopotamia. In addition, rulers discovered that often the best defense was a good offense, so they sent the army to extend their kingdoms. Having soldiers live off the spoils of war was better than paying them with taxes collected from reluctant subjects, and fighting kept the men in good shape and diverted their attention from possible revolts. Good roads connected different areas and allowed leaders to position troops quickly and effectively.

What Made the Assyrians Such Effective Fighters?

Assyrians were one of the groups that had built up a power base in west Asia. In approximixately 900 B.C.E. a Neo-Assyrian kingdom began to conquer land from the Mediterranean coast to Babylon. Driving the Kushites out of Egypt and south of the first cataract, they added Egypt to their kingdom, which lasted until 612 B.C.E.

The Assyrians were skilled warriors, and they also developed a highly efficient military organization. Men drafted into military service were divided into units of 10, 100, and 1,000 so they could be controlled easily. A clear chain of command stretched from the king to the lowest soldier. Soldiers had incentive to prove themselves because good fighters were regularly promoted, but career officers were often moved to new units so they could not develop their own power base. The Assyrians were the first to use cavalry units fight-

Assyrians attacking

ing from horseback. Their mounted messengers and spies traveled quickly, changing to fresh, well-rested horses along the way.

Because the Assyrians relied on force to maintain control, they had to keep their defenses strong and the army loyal. Their officers were

Wounded lion

efficient and willing to be cruel in dealings with the people they controlled. Defeated groups described them as a fierce, brutal, aggressive,
warlike people who forced territories into submission with a combination of terror and resettlement. Their military might was proudly por-
trayed in numerous reliefs showing soldiers wounding and killing
enemy forces and hunting lions.

When the Assyrians conquered an area, they killed off the old leadership and often forced people to move and resettle in other areas.
They captured Babylon in 700 B.C.E., killed many people, looted and
destroyed the city and, as a finishing touch, diverted the Euphrates
River so that it flooded what was left of the city. One Assyrian leader
boasted about the cattle and sheep he had carried away, the boys and
girls he had burned, and how he had dyed the mountains with his
enemy's blood.

The Hebrew Prophets: Monotheism, Ethics, and Law

The Hebrew people, who had split into the kingdoms of Judah and
Israel after King Solomon died in 922 B.C.E., were just one of the
groups the Assyrian attacked.

The people of Judah and Israel watched the growing power of the
Assyrians. Some feared they would not be able to withstand an
Assyrian attack. Others argued that in the covenant they had made
with YHWH, the Lord had promised to protect them as long as they
performed the correct rituals, offered sacrifices and feasts, and obeyed
the Ten Commandments, so YHWH would never allow Assyria to
defeat them. In this setting a group of religious leaders, known as
prophets, emerged.

AMOS

Amos, a prophet who lived in Judah in the eighth century B.C.E., knew
the Assyrian menace firsthand. He wanted to make sure that YHWH
would protect his chosen people from the Assyrians, but he feared the
Israelites were not keeping their side of the Covenant. While other
prophets had worried because Hebrews were worshiping other gods,
Amos was also concerned about justice. When they had lived as pastoralists, the Hebrews had respected tribal patriarchs, not rich people.
Now that they were living in cities surrounded by lots of trade and

wealth, people seemed to respect the wealthy members of the community most.

When Amos went to Israel from Judah in about 750 B.C.E., he was appalled by the luxury of the Israelite leaders. Although they performed lavish sacrifices, no one seemed to care about the poor. Standing in the public square, Amos spoke out. At first he criticized the Egyptians and others in the region, and the crowd cheered. Then he attacked the Assyrians, and everyone applauded even more as he described how YHWH would punish them. But then he said:

> Thus says the Lord:
> "For three transgressions of Israel,
> and for four, I will not revoke the punishment;
> because they sell the righteous for silver,
> and the needy for a pair of shoes -
> they that trample the head of the poor into
> the dust of the earth,
> and turn aside the way of the afflicted. . .
> Behold, I will press you down in your place,
> as a cart full of sheaves presses down. . .
>
> I hate, I despise your feasts,
> and I take no delight in your solemn assemblies.
> Even though you offer me your burnt offerings,
> I will not accept them,
> and the peace offerings of your fatted beasts
> I will not look upon.
> Take away from me the noise of your songs;
> to the melody of your harps I will not listen.
> But let justice roll down like waters,
> and righteousness like an ever-flowing stream."
> (Amos 2:6-7 and 5:21-24)

Amos preached that rituals alone were not enough. They had to be accompanied by righteous actions; otherwise, the Lord despised the sacrifices. Amos preached that the Lord would destroy Israel unless it stopped ignoring the poor.

He went even further, reminding people that laws are intended to

defend the rights of all people and stressing that social justice applies
to rulers as well as average people. Leaders must listen to those who
disagree with them. Calling people back to the Lord, he demanded
justice and the rights of minorities and proposed a moral order as the
basis for society.

Amos predicted the Assyrians would conquer Israel, and the Lord
would be responsible for Israel's defeat. This was a radically new
idea. Gods usually proved their power by defending the people who
worshiped them, not by punishing them. Because YHWH was all-
powerful, Amos said, he would use the Assyrians to punish the
Hebrews if they continued to violate the Covenant and the spirit of his
commandments.

Amos's predictions came true. The Assyrians invaded Israel, and
the northern kingdom fell to Assyria in 722 B.C.E. The lesson was not
lost on people in the southern kingdom of Judah. Religious leaders in
Judah tried to reform their way of life so that YHWH would have no
reason to punish them as well. In spite of their efforts, the Chaldeans,
another Semitic nomadic group following the same pattern of invasion and conquest, conquered Judah in 586 B.C.E. Nebuchadnezzar,
the Chaldean king, sent the Jews into captivity in Babylon. They cried
out:

> How lonely sits the city
>   that was full of people!
> How like a widow has she become,
>   she that was great among the nations!
>   She that was a princess among the provinces
>   has become a vassal. . . .
>
> Is it nothing to you, all you who pass by?
> Look and see
>   if there is any sorrow like my sorrow,
> which was brought upon me,
> which the Lord inflicted
> on the day of his fierce anger.
> (Lamentations I:1, 12)

JOB

By the sixth century B.C.E., the Jewish people were exiles in Babylon, their temple in ruins, their community scattered. Why had the Lord let this happen? How could they find meaning in a seemingly capricious and insecure world? Part of the answer may be found in the story of Job, probably written when the Jews were in captivity in Babylon. It examined suffering and injustice through a folktale in which the Lord and Satan made a wager. Satan saw that Job was a very devout man and bet the Lord that misfortune would make Job lose faith. The Lord bet that no matter what happened, Job would remain faithful.

Job was a devoted elder who kept all the commandments and gave to the poor. Suddenly, he lost all his goods, watched his sons and daughters die, and even experienced great personal pain and disease. Like the people of Judah now in captivity in Babylon, Job cried out, "Why me? Oh Lord? Why am I suffering when I have done no wrong?"

Job believed in a righteous, just, and loving God who had created an orderly universe, made human beings in his own image, and established a special covenant relationship with his people. Job believed that right and wrong behavior brought appropriate rewards and punishments; these were signs of God's dependability. Job felt he had done all that could be expected of him, and the Lord had not rewarded him; instead, God had brought him great misfortune.

Job demanded to know the relationship between ethical living and a happy, blessed life. He would not accept the suggestions his would-be comforters made that some hidden sins in his past accounted for the apparent punishment he was receiving. When Job insisted he was blameless, they suggested that adversity might be a test of faith. Job found that sort of test inappropriate for a god of righteousness. Suffering can have a healing effect on the sufferer, they said, but Job could see no good coming from it.

Job used the metaphor of a trial and legal justice. He repeatedly argued that were he only able to bring his case before the divine court, the Lord would vindicate him of any hint or trace of evildoing and restore all his belongings and his health.

Gradually Job's vision widened, and his question became, "Why do good people suffer?" He wanted to plead not only his own case but his people's cause and, ultimately, humanity's cause as well. How could the Lord, the all-powerful God of righteousness and justice, allow innocent people to suffer?

Job never got a direct answer to his question, but the Lord finally spoke to Job "out of the whirlwind," demanding to know: "Were you there when I laid the foundations of the earth?" (Job 38:4) Experiencing the majesty of the Lord, Job was filled with awe. Realizing the Lord had purposes which he, a mere mortal, could not begin to fathom, Job fell down in absolute devotion saying:

> I know that you can do all things,
> and that no purpose of yours can be thwarted. . . .
> Therefore I have uttered what I did not understand,
> things too wonderful for me to know,
> that I did not know. . . .
> I had heard of you by the hearing of the ear,
> But now my eye sees you;
> therefore I despise myself,
> and repent in dust and ashes.
> (Job 42:2–6)

Amos and Job are two voices of the Axial Age who expressed the ideals of justice and the relationship between doing the right thing and being rewarded for it. While in captivity, the Jews did not lose their faith in the Lord even when God acted in ways beyond human understanding. They held fast to their faith that even though, or perhaps because, they might suffer, the Jewish people had a unique relationship to the Lord and must remain true to their Covenant.

The prophets were expressing an important idea about divinity. Instead of thinking of YHWH as exclusively their god, they had come to believe in monotheism: their God was the only God, and he controlled all that happened. He could send the Assyrians to conquer Judah and Israel, and he could also come to the aid of his chosen people. The prophets also taught that YHWH was just and compassionate, even if humans could not always understand his ways. The concept of one, and only one, ethical and moral God will have an enduring appeal to many people as we continue through the human drama.

Zoroaster: Dualism and War

Zoroaster, who lived on the Iranian plateau from approximately 630 to 550 B.C.E. was another of the important Axial Age religious thinkers who sought to reform the Aryan tradition into which he was born. Aryans, like most Indo-European nomads, worshiped similar gods, and many of their rituals and sacrifices were also similar. Fire was central to their lives, and they kept a sacred flame burning at all times. Like Aryan groups in India, Iranians thought sacrifices were important. Their priests, called magi, sacrificed animals, poured libations (liquid offerings), and drank something similar to soma in their rituals. Magi were also skilled at divination, interpreting dreams, and foretelling events by the position of stars and other signs.

But as the centuries passed, people began to lose faith in sacrifices and the magi. Rituals were not working; they only resulted in drunken priests and wild orgies. Armies still fought, famine threatened, leaders oppressed, floods struck, and disease and death were everywhere.

WHAT KINDS OF CHOICES DID PEOPLE HAVE?

Into this environment Zarathustra, a member of an Iranian warrior clan, was born. (Because he is best known by the Greek spelling of his name, we shall refer to him as Zoroaster.) Cruelty and violence upset this thoughtful, sensitive young man who wandered in the wilderness of the Iranian plateau for 15 years, trying to find a way to end evil and violence.

When Zoroaster was 30 years old, inspiration came to him. Sitting and watching the sun set, he had a vision that day and night represent good and evil, and that the world was created and governed by those two powerful but totally different forces. Good, Ahura Mazda, was represented by light and fire. Evil, Ahriman, was symbolized by darkness. Ahura Mazda had created truth, wisdom, and all that was good. Ahriman had created falsehood, ignorance, and all that was evil. (The existence of two radically different principles, one good and one evil, is called dualism.)

Fire altar

Zoroaster believed that the world was the battlefield where these two forces were in a constant, cosmic struggle. Ultimately, he believed, Ahura Mazda would win the war against Ahriman and utterly defeat evil. That triumph would usher in an ordeal by fire, a final judgment, and the end of the world. For people who had supported the good, the judgment would seem like "passing through warm milk," and they would have a bliss-filled life after death. Those who had sided with evil would experience excruciating agony and be condemned to an after-life of eternal pain. A person's good thoughts, good words, and good deeds lead him to heaven, he taught; bad thoughts, bad words, and bad deeds lead one to hell.

Because all human beings have the free will to choose between good and evil, making the right choice is extremely important. Zoro-aster did not want people to accept ideas blindly. He wanted people to hear his words and make up their minds about what was right. Individuals could choose either Ahura Mazda and goodness, or join Ahriman on the side of evil. Zoroaster assured people that if they chose the good, they could count on a life of eternal bliss in the here-after. If they chose evil, they would be eternally tortured in an afterlife of pain and suffering. Zoroaster continually used the image of a battle, but his call to arms was accompanied by the inspiring message that if people fought against evil, good would win.

Doing good, according to Zoroaster, did not mean performing ritu-als and sacrifices. Forget fasting, he taught: nobody who abstains from food is able to do great deeds of holiness, or great works, or give birth to powerful children. The world survives by eating; by fasting it dies. Instead, join in the crusade against the forces of evil. Be righ-teous, just, chaste, compassionate, charitable, promote education, take care for cattle, and be beneficent — a doer of good deeds. Don't pol-lute the earth. Put the dead on raised platforms in towers of silence, open to the sky, and let vultures pick the bones clean. Keep an eternal flame burning in the temples because fire, the holiest of elements, represents the good and symbolizes the divine spark within.

WHAT DOES ETHICAL DUALISM MEAN?

Zoroaster divided the world into pairs of opposites. It is easy to make lists of opposites, such as hot/cold, in/out, young/old, guilty/innocent, male/female, smart/stupid, right/wrong, and true/false. But Zoroaster went farther. He added an ethical judgment, saying one side was good and the other side was evil. In ethical dualism the pairs of opposites can usually be judged either good or not good, and people must often determine which is which. On the good side are things people think are moral and right, such as truth, honesty, goodness, and kindness. On the evil side are their opposites, such things as lies, dishonesty, evil, and hatred. One should always choose the right, and fight to destroy what is evil and morally wrong.

Zoroaster attempted to spread his insights, but for the first ten years he was not successful. Finally he converted the king of Bactria, a kingdom on the border of present-day Iran and Afghanistan. Once he had royal support, many more people converted. People who followed Zoroaster's teachings became known as Zoroastrians (and in India today they are called Parsi). They date their calendar from his revelations; the year 1 A.R., corresponds to 630 B.C.E.

Both the Hebrew prophets and Zoroaster tried to find meaning in the face of continual warfare and insecurity. Both wrestled with the problem of evil and emphasized that human beings have a responsibility to act justly and be merciful. We will follow how both the idea of monotheism and this dualistic vision are reflected in and influence the worldview of Greeks, Romans, Jews, Christians, and Muslims in the centuries ahead.

SCENE TWO

THE AXIAL AGE IN INDIA

Setting the Stage

Indo-European Aryans migrated into the Indus River valley around 1700 B.C.E. and destroyed what little was left of the Indus civilization. At first the Aryans kept their nomadic ways, but gradually as they moved eastward to the Ganges River valley, they settled down to a farming way of life and built cities and small kingdoms across the entire Gangetic plain. By the sixth century B.C.E. there were about seventeen small kingdoms in northern India. *Rajas* ruled some, and assemblies of elders, similar to the tribal assemblies the nomads had when they lived in the steppes, ruled others. Magadha and Kosala were the two most powerful states. Magadha had mineral resources including iron and controlled commerce and dominated the eastern Gangetic plain. (See map on page 115.)

As populations of the cities increased, new jobs opened up, offering people more opportunities. However, most occupations continued to be hereditary, and young men did what their fathers had done. Brahmins were especially jealous of their knowledge and social position. They did not want their sons and daughters to marry non-brahmins and they tried to prevent non-brahmins from conducting rituals. Brahmins stressed that doing one's *dharma* kept the whole society prosperous and peaceful.

By around 1000 B.C.E. the brahmins were probably the most prestigious group in northern India. The rituals and sacrifices they conducted gave them so much power that the religion most people practiced at that time is often called Brahminism. But many people resented brahmin power. The *rajas* who ruled the powerful states, some of which had several million people, wanted more say in religious and cultural life. Merchants, increasing in number, were also restless because they received little recognition; even though many were becoming wealthy, they were still third in the *varna* hierarchy.

Ascetics Challenge Brahmin Domination

Many considered the rituals brahmins performed extravagant and wasteful, and they did not make people feel more secure. Many people were also revolted by the slaughter of so many animals in the public sacrifices. They wondered whether there might not be some better way to achieve salvation. A number of thoughtful people were already dropping out of society to practice asceticism (renouncing the worldly life) in the forest, hoping to realize the greater reality behind all the rituals.

Asceticism stresses self-denial. An ascetic withdraws from all pleasure of the senses. He or she seeks a reality not related to everyday activities such as eating, sleeping, owning lots of things, and engaging in sex, and hopes the austerities will result in inner peace and tranquility. By 700 B.C.E. individuals were seeking ascetics who had achieved these deeper insights. Later their teachings were recorded in a collection called the Upanishads (which literally means "to sit down near").

One central idea in the Upanishads is that ultimately the whole universe is composed of only one reality identified as Brahman. (Be careful not to confuse Brahman with brahmin, the name for the highest *varna*.) An individual's deepest self, or *atman*, is identical with the universal essence, Brahman. Through meditation or study, ascetics hoped to experience their true identity and realize their oneness with Brahman, which they called *moksha*.

One explanation of Brahman in the Upanishads involves a young man named Svetaketu who had studied the Vedas for twelve years but still did not understand Brahman. When he asked his father to explain what Brahman was, his father told him to bring a seed from a banyan tree (a very large tree).

> "Bring me a banyan fruit."
> "Here it is, sir."
> "Cut it up."
> "I've cut it up, sir."
> "What do you see there?"
> "These quite tiny seeds, sir."
> "Now, take one of them and cut it up."

"I've cut one up, sir."

"What do you see there?"

"Nothing, sir."

Then he told him:

> "This finest essence here, son, that you can't even see—
> look how on account of that finest essence this huge
> banyan tree stands here.

> "Believe me, my son: the finest essence here—that constitutes
> the self of this whole world; that is the truth; that is the
> self. Thou art That, Svetaketu."

(Chandogya Upanishad, 6.12)

Svetaketu's father also asked him to put salt in some water and then taste the water. Although the boy could not see the salt, he could taste it. Again his father likened the salt to Brahman and told Svetaketu; "That is reality. Thou art That."

Brahman, the ultimate reality, never dies, the Upanishads taught, but individuals are born and die again and again. This idea of rebirth is called *samsara* . While *samsara* may well have developed from the repeated sacrifices that symbolized creation, the first written mention of it is in the Upanishads. Gradually nearly everyone accepted the reality of *samsara* : all that lives dies and is reborn.

The Upanishads also taught that *samsara* is linked to *karma*. *Karma* is the measure of how one performs one's *dharma* (duty, role), and *karma* determines what a person will be born in future lives. Someone who does his or her *dharma* builds good *karma*. Those who violate their *dharma*, even without meaning to do so, build bad *karma*. What one intends to do does not count; what counts is how one acts.

Karma helps explain the seeming unfairness of life: why some die young or are born deformed, why good people suffer and why the scoundrel appears to prosper. "It's his *karma*," people say. Good and bad *karma* stay with a person for many lifetimes. It might take repeated lives to offset bad *karma*, so the law of *karma* helps explain the apparent lack of fairness within a single life time without sacrificing the ultimate ideal of justice.

The Upanishads gave people far more sophisticated explanations than the simple cause and effect principles of the Vedic sacrifices. But even though the Upanishads had great depth and insight, few people could read them because they were written in Sanskrit, a language only the upper *varna* understood. There was little way to spread these teachings to average people whose lives often seemed insecure and meaningless and who resented brahmin control and the rigid rules of *dharma* and *karma*. Average people wanted a message they could understand and a faith that anyone, even women and the lower *varnas*, could embrace. Many religious seekers who lived in the sixth century B.C.E. tried to fill these needs. Two of the most important were Mahavira and the Buddha.

Mahavira: *Ahimsa*, Tolerance and the Doctrine of Maybe

Vardhamana Mahavira (540–467 B.C.E.) was born a prince in Magadha. When he was about 30 years old, Mahavira was fed up with his luxurious princely life and decided to become an ascetic. He spoke out against violence and bloody sacrifices and sought an alternate way of thinking and living.

Mahavira taught that everything in existence is alive with a quality he identified as *jiva*. A jiva is something like a soul. No creator god made the *jivas*; instead, billions of *jivas* have always existed. Everything in the universe, including stars, rocks, water, trees, and humans, contain a *jiva*. *Jivas* are caught up in solid matter. The goal of life, Mahavira taught, is to free *jivas* so they can escape the karmic matter that imprisons them. Human beings can free *jivas* from their own bodies by learning to control their senses.

Mahavira agreed that each action builds either good or bad *karma*. But he argued that one's *karma* either helps free *jiva* or further imprisons it in matter. The worst thing a person can do is harm *jivas*. Since *jivas* are present in all creation, one should not harm anything in the world. Non-injury to any living thing is called *ahimsa*.

Ahimsa is one of Mahavira's most important teachings. He preached against the brahminic sacrifices and urged people to become strict vegetarians because of their reverence for all life. But *ahimsa* applies to emotional as well as physical injury. What a person thinks influences how he acts, and violence in thought leads to violence in action. Mahavira taught that violence in thought was an even greater form of violence and that people should strive to develop total self-control and avoid all forms of injury, whether physical or emotional. A person who has absolute control over his senses is a Jina. Mahavira was a Jina, and people who followed him were known as Jains.

HOW CAN A VIRA PRACTICE AHIMSA?

The traditional ideal for an Aryan prince was to be a *vira* — a heroic warrior. Mahavira also wanted to become a *vira*, but the battle he fought was against his own desires, and the victory he sought was over his own senses and ego. To symbolize his battle, people called him *maha* (great) *vira* (hero), Mahavira, a new kind of hero.

Mahavira taught his followers to try to give up attachment not only to worldly things such as material possessions, lying, and having a good time, but attachment to their own opinions, beliefs, and ideas as well. He suggested that giving up things is often easier than parting with one's opinions. Since any individual can only see a very small part of total reality, each person knows only a very small part of truth. What a person thinks is true depends to a large degree on where he or she is standing and what that person has been taught to think is true.

This principle of tolerance for other views is identified as the Doctrine of Maybe. Maybe it looks that way to you from where you are standing, but remember it might look differently to me. A well-known Jain poem tells about six blind men who went to "see" an elephant, each touching a different part of the animal. One thought it was a fan, another said a wall, and the others said a rope, tree, spear, and snake; each one was sure he knew what the elephant looked like. Each was partly right, and all of them were wrong. Because each person has only a bit of the truth, it is important not to kill those who disagree, for they might be partly right, and they can offer another perspective on the larger truth, which none of us can know alone.

Mahavira wanted to be a great warrior, but his battle was very different from the battle Zoroaster discussed. The kind of tolerance illustrated in the story about the six blind and the elephant was radically different from Zoroaster's dualistic outlook or the legalism of the Jews. Mahavira advised that the best way to deal with insecurities and anxieties was not to try to abolish evil, but to control one's own thoughts and feelings.

The Buddha: End Desire and Seek Enlightenment

Siddhartha Gautama, who lived from approximately 563 B.C.E. to about 483 B.C.E., was the second significant voice of India's Axial Age. He became known as the Buddha, the Enlightened One. Like Mahavira, Siddhartha was also born into a princely family. His father ruled a small state near present-day Nepal. Sages told his father that the boy would grow up to be either a great religious leader or a great king. Since he wanted Siddhartha to follow him as king, he decided to shield his son from life's problems. The king ordered that nothing should trouble the young prince. He put Siddhartha in a pleasure palace and gave him everything he wanted. Siddhartha was married to a beautiful young woman who bore him a handsome son. All the while, he had never seen the world beyond the palace.

One day Siddhartha asked his charioteer to take him outside the palace for a ride. As they rode along, he was shocked to see an old man and even more shocked when his charioteer said he too would grow old. Deeply troubled, Siddhartha went out three more times. On these trips he saw a sick man for the first time, and a dead man being carried to the cremation ground, and his charioteer told him he too could get ill and would eventually die. On the fourth trip Siddhartha saw an ascetic with a peaceful expression on his face.

Back in the palace, Siddhartha could think of nothing but his four encounters. How could life have any joy, he pondered, when it ended

Siddhartha sees a sick man

in sickness, old age, and death? Watching the dancing girls that evening, he suddenly had a vision of them all as old hags, their flesh hanging from their withered bodies. Distraught, he decided he must leave the palace and seek answers to the questions that tormented him: How can people go on living when they know they will die? Why do people suffer and die? What causes suffering, and how can it be overcome?

The Buddhist tradition reports that Siddhartha did not say goodbye to his wife and newborn son. Perhaps he feared that if he spoke to them, he would not leave. After silently gazing at them as they slept, he stole out of the palace and rode away in the darkness. Discarding his princely robes and cutting his hair, he became an ascetic. He lived in the forest with five other ascetics for six years, practicing severe self-denial and hoping to get some insight about human suffering.

Extreme asceticism, however, yielded no more answers than he had gotten from his life of ease and pleasure in the palace. If he starved himself to death, he would only be born again and face the same unanswered questions. Finally he sat beneath a bodhi tree, resolved not to move until either he died or he achieved enlightenment. As he meditated, the demon Mara sent three temptations: pleasure, power, and prolonged life. None moved him. Finally, sitting under the tree, he experienced oneness with all existence. He "woke up," that is, he became a Buddha. He called that experience of oneness *nirvana*.

WHAT DID THE BUDDHA TEACH?

At first the Buddha thought that *nirvana* and his other insights could not be taught. Soon, however, he decided they must be taught, and he devoted the rest of his life to teaching people how to live in peace and achieve *nirvana*. The Buddha taught Four Noble Truths. The first is "Life is suffering." Life is out of joint, like an axle loose from a wheel or a bone from the socket. It is a glittering illusion, a sea of impermanence, constantly changing, tempting people into ever-revolving cycles of birth and death. Nothing is the same now as it was an instant before. Amidst this flux we worry about keeping what we have or getting things we do not have.

"Suffering is caused by desire" is the Buddha's second Noble Truth. We suffer because we long for permanence; we want things to stay the way they are. We get attached to material objects and to our own opinions and do not want to let go. The more we try to hold on, to grasp and clutch, the quicker things slip away. Youth, gone; beauty, gone; loved ones, gone. Life — gone. When we fight against impermanence and try to hold on to our egos and desires, we suffer.

"There is a way out of suffering," the Buddha taught as his third Noble Truth. Stop desiring and suffering will cease. Stop hankering after things and life is transformed. Whatever you have is what you want; whatever you are is who you want to be. Ultimately what is real has nothing to do with having and being, with self and ego.

Buddha's fourth Noble Truth offers a way to end suffering and experience *nirvana* by following the Eightfold Path. When one has experienced *nirvana*, he or she will never be born again. The Eightfold Path included:

1: Right Understanding: Know the truth of the Four Noble Truths;
2: Right Purpose: Have the urge to follow the path and reach *nirvana*;
3: Right Speech: Do not lie or slander anyone and do not say things that are unkind;
4: Right Conduct: Do not kill, steal, lie, be unchaste or drink;
5: Right Livelihood: Choose an occupation that serves humanity and does not harm life;
6: Right Effort: Have self-control, especially over your thoughts. Strive for the good;
7: Right Awareness: Have psychological insight into your own motives and deeds. Do not be moved by either joy or sorrow;
8: Right Concentration: Ponder deeply and meditate until you experience *nirvana*.

THE MIDDLE WAY AND COMPASSION FOR EVERYTHING

The Buddha's teaching offered a Middle Way between the brahmins' exhaustive rules and rituals and the extreme asceticism of the Jains and others. The Buddha taught that anyone can have a meaningful existence by following the Middle Way. Eat enough to survive, but do not live to eat. Try to hurt others as little as possible, but recognize that it is impossible to be blameless and hurt nothing. The Buddha also found a middle way between the concerns of life in this world (*samsara*) and the reality of enlightenment (*nirvana*). The first five steps of the Eightfold Path deal with life within society and how one can live an ethical life. Steps six, seven, and eight are concerned with developing one's spiritual side and how, through discipline and meditation, one can gain freedom from this worldly existence and experience *nirvana*.

A central concept of Buddha's life and teaching was *karuna* or compassion. Compassion for people's suffering started Buddha on his spiritual quest in the first place. Compassion moved him to teach and informed his instruction to hurt others as little as possible. The Buddha knew that it was impossible to eliminate things that made people suffer, but he helped people change their attitude toward those things. For example, one day a grieving young mother came to Buddha, cradling her dead baby in her arms. "Please," she implored, "you are a holy man. Bring my baby back to life." The Buddha promised to do so as soon as she brought him a mustard seed from any home where no one had ever died. She was overjoyed to have been asked to perform such a simple task, and she knocked on one door after another. In every household death had come. Resigned, she returned to the Buddha to listen to his teachings.

People should not rely on the rituals brahmins performed, the Buddha preached, or get involved in intricate philosophical arguments. When asked theological questions, he replied with other questions. "If your friend were hit by an arrow and lay wounded before you," he said, "would you first try to establish who had made the arrow, the materials used, the direction of its flight, and the speed at its impact? Wouldn't you first help your friend? My fellow humans are in pain. I strive to minister to their suffering." And he devoted the last forty years of his life to that ministry.

Buddha was a reformer who wanted to correct some of the problems in Indian society, especially the excessive power of the brahmins. He believed in *karma*, but he thought that if a person had not intended to do wrong, then he or she would not build up bad *karma*. In a radical departure for his time, the Buddha did not believe in gods or goddesses. He taught that everyone could seek enlightenment on his or her own, without the help of brahmins, rituals, or deities. Anyone could follow his Eightfold Path and become a Buddha, and he taught in the language spoken by ordinary people, so anyone could understand his teachings. Equally radical was his insistence on complete equality among his followers. "No one is an outcaste by birth," he said, "nor is anyone a brahmin by birth. It is by deeds that a person becomes a brahmin."

Followers of the Buddha joined together in the *sangha*, the community of monks and nuns. Most of the time, they traveled in small groups, spreading the Buddha's teachings and living on donations people gave them. During the rainy seasons, when it was difficult to travel, they often lived together, and their shelters became monasteries. The *sangha* offered women an acceptable alternative to arranged marriage and the burdens and responsibilities of family life.

By the end of the Axial Age, people who lived in the Indian subcontinent tended to agree on certain principles and accepted *dharma*, *karma*, and *samsara* as major core ideas. Most believed in a single, ultimate reality often called Brahman, and worshiped one or more of the major gods. Because any effort to explain Brahman fell short, Indian thinkers tended to be tolerant of the various ways people understood it. They also had come to believe in *moksha* or *nirvana* — the possibility of realizing their true nature and not being born again.

For Mahavira, self-control and *ahimsa* helped release a person from *samsara* or rebirth. For the Buddha, blowing out the flame of desire would set a person free. The ultimate goal of both teachers was freedom from *samsara*. Others looked inward to the deep recesses of the human mind and spirit to find insight into ultimate reality and answers to the perennial questions of meaning, justice, suffering, and evil. In the next act we will consider how, as the years go by, their insights would reshape the Indian worldview, influence other cultures, and lead to many changes in how people live their lives.

SCENE
THREE

THE AXIAL AGE IN CHINA

Setting the Stage

Traditional Chinese historians say that the Zhou dynasty ruled the Middle Kingdom from the twelfth to the third century B.C.E. At its height Zhou kings claimed they controlled a hundred lesser territories and maintained an elaborate administrative system. Many local lords felt loyal to the Zhou, especially those who believed they were related to them. Rulers of small states performed ceremonies that symbolized their allegiance, and, in turn, Zhou rulers granted them favors. Some members of the hereditary nobility worked directly for the Zhou.

Scholars do not agree on the amount of control Zhou rulers had, even in the early centuries, or whether the dynasty should be called feudal rather than a unified state. The Zhou depended on these small states for taxes, weapons, and soldiers. As long as local rulers believed they were getting something back in return for their support, or as long as the lords were too weak to revolt, they met their obligations to the Zhou.

The Era of Warring States

As centuries passed, bonds of loyalty between Zhou leaders and local areas weakened. Because local lords maintained their own armies and had their own economic base, individual lords were tempted to fight with one another over land or even to challenge the Zhou. By 771 B.C.E. the Zhou controlled the Middle Kingdom in name only. Fighting among the various small states erupted so frequently that the years between 441 and 221 B.C.E. are called the Era of Warring States.

Warfare was all the more lethal because soldiers used iron weapons they had learned about from steppe nomads. War was based on raw power and deception; the old gentlemanly ethic of the Zhou aristocracy, when generals did not attack until the opposing army was ready to fight, was dead. Instead, generals were advised: "When an advancing enemy crosses the water, . . . allow half his force to cross and then strike."

Gone as well were the cultured days of the early Zhou, where Chinese historians claim each person knew his place and performed his proper role. The stability and security of those earlier times seemed far more desirable than the uncertainty, turmoil, and increasingly constant warfare of the later Zhou times.

The Art of War

Generals began to use tactics recommended in *The Art of War*, a manual on how to wage successful military campaigns. It was probably written by Sun Tzu in the middle of the fifth century. *The Art of War* begins:

> War is a matter of vital importance to the State; the province of life or death; the road to survival or ruin. It is mandatory that it be thoroughly studied. (I:1)

This manual suggests ways to defeat an enemy without actually fighting. It says never fight unless the matter has been carefully and thoroughly studied; never undertake warfare recklessly. Use spies who constantly gather information, sow dissension, and nurture subversion. "An army without secret agents is exactly like a man without eyes or ears." (XIII:23) Sun Tzu advised:

> Attack the morale of the enemy, weaken its will and plant the seeds of doubt until the enemy's will to resist is broken. Then the battle is won without a fight.
>
> To subdue the enemy without fighting is the acme (height) of skill. Thus, what is of supreme importance in war is to attack the enemy's strategy . . . Next best is to disrupt his alliance. Do not allow your enemies to get together. . . The next best is to attack his army. The worst policy is to attack cities. Attack cities only when there is no alternative. (III:3-7)

Sun Tzu's work became the textbook for the Chinese military from that time forward. It warned rulers that only a government that had the united support of its people could expect to win, and that to win a military campaign, leaders must first ensure the welfare of the people. Because war involves immense financial and psychological burdens, victory should be gained in the shortest possible time, with the least possible cost of life and effort on both sides. He had no illusions about how to win:

> War is based on deception.
> Therefore, when capable, feign incapacity; when active, inactivity.
> When near, make it appear that you are far away; when far away, that you are near. . . .
> Pretend inferiority and encourage his arrogance....
> Attack when he is unprepared; sally our (attack) when he does not expect you. (I:17-24)

During this period of war and violence, people longed for peace and many sought ways to end the fighting. Educated members of the local nobility in several small states tried to get jobs advising local rulers. Some tried to give advice on how to end the fighting. Confucius was one of then.

Confucius: Harmony and Hierarchy

The most famous Chinese teacher of the Axial Age was Kung Fu Tzu known as Confucius. Confucius was born in the state of Lu and lived from about 551 to 479 B.C.E. (just after Zoroaster and at about the same time as the Buddha in India). Confucius taught by answering questions instead of composing long essays on how to govern or how to act. His students collected his short, pithy statements in a book called the *Analects*. The very first statement in the *Analects* reads:

> To learn and at due times to repeat what one has learned, is that not after all a pleasure? That friends should come to one from afar, is that not after all delightful? (*Analects* I.1)

Further, Confucius said:

> I'm a transmitter, not a composer. I really have esteemed the Ancients. . . . I have listened in silence

and noted what was said. I have never grown tired of learning nor wearied of teaching others what I have learnt. (*Analects* VII.1)

Confucius

When Confucius spoke about the ancients, he meant the aristocratic leaders of the early Zhou rather than the legendary sage-rulers. Confucius longed for the early Zhou, around 900 B.C.E., because he believed Zhou leaders at that time had been moral and each person had performed his proper role. He believed fighting could be ended if the present leaders followed the Zhou example. His solution to the turmoil and chaos all around lay in selecting the right people to rule, not in devising new forms of government, dropping out of society, or stockpiling more weapons. Confucius tried very hard to find a prince of even a small kingdom who would hire him and listen to his advice.

REN AND LI MUST FIT EACH RELATIONSHIP

Ren and *li* were two of Confucius's main concepts. *Ren* is humaneness, the appropriate feelings people should have toward one another. The character in Chinese for *ren* is composed of two other characters: man and two. *Ren*, therefore, has to do with people in relationship with others. It suggests the ability to feel empathy for others, to feel compassion. "Do not impose on others what you yourself do not desire," Confucius taught (*Analects* XV.24). People sometimes call this the negative Golden Rule.

The character for *li* is composed of "one who knows the rituals" or "one who performs the food offerings, the sacrifices." It is translated as civility, decorum, etiquette or politeness. *Li* refers to actions that a person performs: being polite, knowing your place, and saying the right thing to both those who are above you and those who are below. *Ren* (appropriate feelings) and *li* (correct actions) belong together because actions without the proper feelings are empty and feelings without the suitable show of respect are discourteous. (For example, if your elderly aunt came into the room, the proper *li* would be stand up and offer her a seat. But as you do this, you must not be thinking, "The old hag; she looks like she died and forgot to lie down." Instead, your mind should be filled with respectful and loving thoughts.)

People are not born knowing how to act and think in each situation. They have to be taught how to feel humanely and act properly because both depend on who had the most status in any given relationship. Status was determined by whether you were male or female, how old you were, the position of your family, and how much education you had. In the Confucian system women were supposed to accept a subordinate position: a girl was subservient to her father, later she was expected to defer to her husband and, after he died, to her oldest son. In every situation, there was an ethical way to behave, but no single abstract standard could be applied to all situations.

Confucius taught five basic relationships: ruler and subject; father and son; husband and wife; elder brother and younger brother; and friend to friend. The first four were unequal relationships. One half of the pair deserved more respect from, and assumed more responsibility for, the other. Only among close friends might the relationship be equal. If each person acted as he or she should, then the relationship, and by extension the family and the whole society, would prosper.

HOW CAN FILIAL PIETY
BRING PEACE AND GOOD GOVERNMENT?

The most important relationships were in the family, Confucius taught, and one learned proper *li* and *ren* by living in a family. It was clear that a child did not deserve as much respect as his or her parents. On the other hand, parents must take responsibility for the care and nurturing of their children. Parents taught *li* and *ren* by their example and through the atmosphere in the home. By their loving concern for their children, they awakened in them a sense of humaneness and love.

Filial piety, which means reverence and respect for one's parents, is perhaps Confucius' most important concept. The essence of filial piety is summed up in the statement:

> Behave in such a way that your father and mother have no anxiety about you except concerning your health. (*Analects* II.6)

Health tends to be out of a person's control. Other actions that might concern one's parents were things Confucius believed a son or daughter could control. A filial son and daughter should make sure one's parents were always proud of them and never had any reason to be anxious. There was no way a child could adequately repay the gift of life and the loving care that he or she had received. However, when one was older and one's parents were old, one could attempt to lessen the debt. Eventually, aging parents became like children to their children, and the relationship was complete. Confucius advised:

> In serving his parents, a son may remonstrate with them, but gently; when he sees that they do not incline to follow his advice, he shows an increased degree of reverence, but does not abandon his purpose; and should they punish him, he does not allow himself to murmur. (IV:18)

Confucius taught that the family was the model for the larger society. "If fathers are fathers and sons are sons, the country will function smoothly," Confucius taught. If you set the family right, you will set the whole country right. For Confucius, the five relationships and filial piety were the key to ending the constant fighting by creating harmony in the society.

LET CHUNZI GOVERN

Confucius said the ideal leader should be a superior man, a *chunzi*. When asked to define chunzi, he gave concrete examples.

> A *chunzi* takes as much trouble to discover what is right as lesser men take to discover what will pay. (*Analects* IV.16)

> The good man does not grieve that other people do
> not recognize his merits. His only anxiety is lest he
> should fail to recognize theirs. (*Analects* I.16)

> The *chunzi* does not preach what he practices till he
> has practiced what he preaches. (*Analects* II.13)

> The demands that a *chunzi* makes are upon himself;
> those that a small man makes are upon others.
> (*Analects* XV.20)

> A gentleman calls attention to the good points in oth-
> ers; he does not call attention to their defects. The
> small man does just the reverse. (*Analects* XII.16)

Although Confucius appreciated the past and claimed he was not suggesting anything new, he introduced the possibility of social mobility (moving up in the hierarchy) within society. Unlike Zhou times when the aristocracy was hereditary, Confucius believed that no one was born a good leader. Instead, all men were born with the potential to become superior men and even a poor farmer's son could grow up to be a leader if he learned to think and act like a *chunzi*. This was a radical idea for his time and a fundamental shift from the idea of an aristocracy of birth.

RULE BY MORAL EXAMPLE, NOT FORCE

Confucius rejected both rule by force and rule by law. After all, *li* and *ren* depended on the relationship. Instead, he said, the people would willingly follow someone who practiced *li* and *ren* and led by moral example.

> Govern the people by regulations and laws, keep
> order among them by punishments, and they will flee
> from you, and lose all self-respect. Lead them with
> virtue and regulate them by the rules of propriety (*li*),
> and they will keep their self-respect and come to you
> of their own accord. (*Analects* II.3)

If you rule by force, Confucius taught, people will follow only as long as they must. If you rule by laws, people will learn ways to evade them, he claimed, pointing to the turmoil all around. Rule instead, he advised, by moral example. Give people self-respect, and they will control themselves.

Confucius was not very interested in spiritual matters. When someone asked him about serving the spirits, he replied, "If we are not yet able to serve man, how can we serve spiritual beings?" When asked about death, he replied: "If we do not yet know about life, how can we know about death?" (*Analects* II.11)

Rulers of small Chinese states in the 6th century did not pay much attention to what Confucius had taught. He was only one of a great many scholars roaming around the Middle Kingdom, each with his own cure for society's ills. Confucius died thinking he had been a failure, for although he advised one ruler for a brief period, his ideas were considered dangerous by some and irrelevant by most, and he was banished from his own state of Lu. In his waning years, he was asked to return to Lu and probably lived there in obscurity with only a few disciples gathered reverently around him. It is perhaps not surprising that he wrote:

> He [the superior man] does not mind not being in office; all that he minds about is whether he has qualities that entitle him to office. He does not mind failing to get recognition; he is too busy doing the things that entitle him to recognition. (*Analects* IV.14)

Daoism: Flowing in Harmony with the Dao

Daoism was a second major school of thought in the Middle Kingdom. Some claim that Laozi, whose name means "the wise old man," founded Daoism at about the same time that Confucius was teaching, but Daoist ideas go back a long way in Chinese history. The *Daodejing (Tao Te Ching),* a collection of Daoist wisdom attributed to Laozi, was probably an anthology of Daoist thought that wise old men put together. Although it seems unlikely that anyone would organize a government around the principles of Daoism, it too was a protest movement during these troubled times that offered ways to tame the warrior and bring peace.

The *Dao*, which was often spelled tao, is the central idea of Daoism. The *Dao* is difficult to define because "Knowers don't speak. Speakers don't know. . . . The name you can name is not the Name." Dao has been translated as "the Way," but it transcends any attempt to define it. The character for Dao in Chinese combines the characters for head and path or movement. It represented the moral path that humans should follow. It also represented the source of all life, the vessel that continually pours forth life and energy without ever being exhausted, and a great universal womb. "Use it. It will not wear out."

YIN-YANG: THE HARMONY OF OPPOSITES

Daoists taught that all life is interdependent, and human beings and nature exist in harmony. Seeming opposites in nature are bonded together in a single whole. Daoists understand the unity of all existence as the harmony of opposites and used *yin-yang* to symbolize this unity and harmony: *Yin* represents dark, cool, receptive, moist, feminine characteristics. *Yang* represents light, hot, assertive, fiery, masculine characteristics. But as the drawing shows, there is a little *yin* in *yang* and a little *yang* in *yin*. The goal is the balance and harmony of those forces that together make up the whole.

Laozi advised people to relax, get in harmony with the Dao, and let its great energy do the work. "Do nothing, and nothing will not be done," he taught. Practice *wu wei*, that is, acting by not acting. (Consider a glass of muddy water from which you would like to drink. Leave the glass alone and the sediment will settle. Stir it in an effort to make it settle, and the water remains muddy.) Don't do anything, and things happen. If you simply relax and don't try to solve a problem, it solves itself.

Yin-yang

Laozi taught that it was useless to try to build institutions to govern men. Once you devise institutions, you are doing something, and the result will be disastrous. Instead, leave people alone and let individuals get in harmony with the *Dao*. Daoists taught people to look within to find the abiding life force of the universe, the *Dao*, and to float with that invisible tide down the ocean of life. "To bear, to rear—don't possess what you produce, don't covet what you create, don't rush what you raise."

Everything people experience, except the *Dao*, is relative. How one views or judges any event depends on one's perspective. (This sounds like Mahavira's Doctrine of Maybe.) Whether the train whistle is loud or soft depends on where one stands. Humans cannot be sure what is real and what is imaginary. Daoists illustrate this point with a story about Chuang-tzu's butterfly dream. One night Chuang-tzu dreamed he was a butterfly, flitting around, enjoying what butterflies enjoy. The butterfly did not know that it was Chuang-tzu. Then Chuang-tzu woke up, and he was Chuang-tzu again. And he began to wonder whether he was Chuang-tzu who had dreamed he was a butterfly, or was a butterfly dreaming he was Chuang-tzu.

IMITATE WATER AND SURVIVE

Creating institutions or rewarding knowledge was dangerous, Daoists taught, because when people compete they eventually fight. No one seems content with what he has, and few people know when they have had enough.

> Of insufficiencies, none is greater than not to know
> what's enough. Of disasters, none is greater than the
> urge to acquire. So the only "enough" that's enough
> is to know what's enough.

Further, if you have nothing, you will have nothing to fight over. The *Daodejing* advised governments to imitate water and "take the lower course." Water was a metaphor for the highest good that, like the *Dao*, flows to low places. But:

> In the world there is nothing more submissive and
> weak than water. Yet for attacking that which is hard
> and strong nothing can surpass it. (78)

If you take the low state, there will be no heights from which to fall or from which you can be deposed. If you refuse to fight, you cannot lose. Numerous chapters in the *Daodejing* offer advice to local lords, reminding leaders that "the large state, by taking the lower position, annexes the small state." (61) "The submissive and weak will overcome the hard and strong." (36) Powerful states invite confrontation and therefore can be defeated, so do not fight. In addition, the strong usually are rigid and more easily broken. Bend, it advised, for "Trees that stand firm will be felled" (76), while the tree that bends with the wind or bows under the weight of the snow survives.

Laozi's work can be read both as a means of surviving in dangerous times and as a guide for how to lead. Laozi's ideal state consisted of a small, self-sufficient town, where one could hear the cock crow and tend to one's own garden. In such a situation, if the leader followed the *Dao*,

> When his work is done, his aim fulfilled,
> They [the people] will say, "We did this ourselves." (17)

Does Legalism Offer the Only Way to Peace?

The third major Chinese school of thought in these troubled times was Legalism. Legalists believed it was stupid to assume that you could leave the responsibility of government to well-meaning but ineffective teachers like Confucius, and it went without saying that Daoist drop-outs were unfit to rule. Power was the order of the day, and the only way to bring stability was to establish a single, all-powerful central authority that dictated what was right and enforced its rules with a strong police force. Anyone who got out of line should be punished, without exception.

In order to support the army on which this system depended, people would have to be taxed heavily. They might complain and even try to revolt, but their uprisings should be quickly put down. Legalists argued that the majority of people were too burdened, ignorant, or selfish to know what was best for them. When a child had a splinter, they pointed out, he screamed and begged you not to take it out. The good parent held the child down, by force if necessary, and removed the splinter so it would not fester and become infected. Likewise, people would scream and protest against taxes and the police, but those were the very things that kept discontent from festering and people from revolting.

Legalists admitted they were offering an extreme solution, but the times called for drastic action. How much longer could the Middle Kingdom survive when men were constantly at war, crops were crushed by armies, and the morale of the people was all but destroyed?

In the last days of what was the Zhou dynasty in name only, people debated the ideas of Confucianism, Daoism, Legalism, and many other schools of thought as they tried to establish a basis for a stable and legitimate government. Each system had its virtues and weaknesses and lively discussions went on for several hundred years as the Chinese tried to figure out what would end the devastating warfare. Which school of thought do you think the Chinese will choose? We will deal with that question in the next act. In the meantime we will examine Greece, another humanistic tradition.

THE AXIAL AGE IN GREECE

Setting the Stage

The heirs to the civilization of the Minoans and Myceneans in the Aegean world did not call themselves Greeks. That was a term Romans used for crafty traders from the east. The people we call Greeks called themselves Hellenes and referred to their land as Hellas. Hellas was comprised of the southern end of the Balkan Peninsula and Ionia — the eastern border of Anatolia — and the adjacent islands; its geographic center was the Aegean Sea. (See map on page 131.) (We shall use the terms Greece and Greeks and the adjective Hellenic.)

Greece emerged from its Dark Age around 750 B.C.E. By that time the Dorians had settled down, mixed with what was left of the Myceneans, and built many cities throughout the land bordering the Aegean. Some adventurous Greeks even emigrated and began to establish colonies along the Black Sea and the Mediterranean coast.

The economic base of the Hellenic world was manufacturing and trade, not agriculture, in part because the poor, rocky soil could not produce enough surplus to support a prosperous and ever-expanding population. In addition, most areas were no more than 50 miles from the sea, and ships could easily carry produce to new settlements.

By 800 B.C.E. many Greeks were engaged in trade. People all around the Mediterranean wanted to buy the relatively cheap iron shields, helmets, and spears, urban artisans made as well as oil, wine, and pottery, which the Greeks also produced. Instead of just bartering, Greeks used minted coins for money, an idea they had borrowed from Lydia in Asia Minor.

Money represents goods and services. Anything — including precious metals, coins, paper, beads, or bones — that people agree on can serve as money. Since gold and silver are scarce, and can be easily shaped into coins, many societies have used these metals for money, and governments in the ancient world tried to control their mining and processing. Thousands of gold or silver coins have been found in areas where ancient civilizations once flourished.

Money facilitates trade. When bartering, traders must find someone with goods they want who wants what they have to sell. With money, traders can sell their goods and then use the money to buy what they want from anyone. As merchants began to use money as their source of wealth, a strong middle class — people who buy and sell goods and deal in money — began to develop.

Humanism: Man Is the Measure of All Things
(and Can Measure All Things)

Geography challenged the Greeks to find ways to survive on the poor, rocky Greek soil. Greeks answered this challenge by turning dirt into pottery and grapes into wine. Perhaps solving this challenge helped give them faith in their ability to control their destiny and contributed to the philosophy called humanism, the belief that human beings are the center of all things and can rely on their own abilities to meet challenges.

Humanism developed in Ionia, on the western shore of Anatolia, in the centuries following the Hellenic Dark Age. Ionia at that time was the most intellectually creative area in the Hellenic world. A great deal of trade passed through it, bringing new ideas that Ionians borrowed and adapted. Beginning in the seventh century B.C.E., men such as Thales, Anaximander, Heraclitus, and Pythagoras expressed faith in human reason and what we later will call science. Rejecting the earlier idea that the universe came from chaos or nothingness and that capricious or irrational gods controlled the forces of nature, Ionian philosophers suggested that the universe followed natural laws, which humans could understand by observation and logical thought. Placing their faith in human reason, they encouraged others to observe the world around them, to think critically, and to make up their own minds.

Many residents of Ionia were descendants of refugees who had fled from the Dorian invaders. They kept memories of their heroic past alive through songs, epic poems, and legends. The poet Homer is believed to have been an Ionian. In his epic poetry, Homer championed *arete*, an individual hero's courage and display of physical strength, loyalty, and fearlessness. But the *Iliad*, the epic attributed to Homer, also seemed to suggest the futility of war. It ends before the Achaeans defeat Troy, and in the last scene the Greek heroine Helen is grieving over the body of a dead Trojan hero.

The Polis: The Political Base of Humanism

Political reforms were an important part of the human-centered outlook in Greece during the Axial Age. After their Dark Age, Greeks began living in city-states, called poleis. A polis was an independent community with a central city and neighboring agricultural "suburbs." Farmers in the suburbs provided food for the city-dwellers and sought protection within the city's walls in times of attack. Most poleis had a high citadel in the center called an acropolis. Ideally, a person could see the acropolis from any part of the city. Although these communities were similar to the earlier Sumerian city-states, this was a new form of political and social life for the Greeks.

We translate polis as city-state because the polis was about the size of a small city but had the sovereignty (final authority) associated with a state. Each polis had a sense of its uniqueness and individuality and was sovereign over its area, making its laws and regulating the lives of its residents. The mountainous terrain contributed to the development of independent city-states, because valleys were isolated from one another, and people in different valleys had little contact — except through trade or war — with one another and little reason to cooperate. Self-governing settlements developed on various islands as well. Each polis jealously maintained its independence and sovereignty.

Invading Dorians lived near other members of their clan, as they had in their nomadic days. Besides spoils of war, leaders rewarded loyalty and bravery with gifts of land, and gradually landowners, rather than warriors, had the most status and power. They were the aristocracy (the best or most respected people). These rich landowners passed their lands to their sons, so very soon they had become a hereditary aristocracy. In early Greece aristocrats controlled a great deal of land, and they hired laborers to farm their land or make products.

By 700 B.C.E. tribal councils, composed of members of the aristocracy, ruled in most of the city-states. Government by a few is called an oligarchy, and most of the poleis were oligarchies. At first only members of the aristocracy were citizens, that is, persons with rights and responsibilities for governing the community. Members of the aristocracy were generally the only ones who could afford to maintain horses and buy expensive armor, so they made up the armies as well.

Arete and the Athlete: Make Competitions, Not War

Constant fighting during the heroic age had provided many opportunities for warriors to prove their *arete*. However although fierce competition existed among the various poleis and threats of war continued, actual fighting occurred less frequently after 800 B.C.E. How could men demonstrate their *arete* and also stay in good physical condition if they seldom went into battle? Nomads used the hunt but few farmers hunted. Gradually Greeks developed athletic competitions among male athletes from many city-states. These Pan-Hellenic games provided a less violent way for poleis to compete and demonstrate their superiority. Additionally, the games involved some of the same skills soldiers use in war, so they kept men ready for battle.

Pan-Hellenic games, held at various sites every four years, were so important that the Greeks used them to mark time. The earliest com-

Olympic footraces

petition was in 776 B.C.E. (the first date in Hellenic history that historians feel is definitely accurate). Olympia, in the northwestern Peloponnesus, was the site of the most important Pan-Hellenic competitions, and each four-year period between one Olympic competition and the next was called an Olympiad. Dates indicated in which Olympiad an event had occurred.

The five-day festival at Olympia was probably the most important event in all of Hellas. The Olympics attracted thousands of people and provided social and cultural, if not political, unity among the city-states. Rich and poor came to Olympia from as far away as North Africa, Sicily, and Ionia, and merchants sold their goods to spectators and participants. The games transformed much of the rivalry among city-states into friendly competition among athletes, and the Olympic truce reduced the incidence of warfare while at the same time reinforcing the ideal of physical excellence.

Arete, Spartan Style:
Military Preparedness and Austerity

By the sixth century B.C.E. Sparta and Athens were the two most powerful city-states in the Hellenic world. They demonstrate two different ways of life. Spartans set an example of military superiority. Athenians excelled in politics and intellectual activities. In both city-states, people gave their loyalty to the polis rather than to their families. Both honored human excellence (*arete*), but they defined it differently.

We have already noted that the Dorians who settled Sparta, like their Aryan cousins in India, tried to keep totally separate from the farmers who had been living there. Sparta used military might to control the helots (non-Spartans) and was perhaps the only place in Greece where Dorian invaders continued to stay completely segregated from the earlier inhabitants.

Lycurgus was a legendary early leader of Sparta. Tradition claims that when people asked him to establish a democracy, he replied, "Begin by setting it up in your own family." Lycurgus is credited with writing a constitution that provided for two kings who shared power, performed the sacrifices, supervised justice, and commanded the army. A senate of older men passed whatever laws were needed, served as a supreme court, and formulated public policy. An assembly, composed of all male citizens over thirty, met when the moon was full to consent to the laws and elect five overseers. Sparta also had a powerful secret police that spied on helots and had the right to kill any helot who might be a threat to the polis.

STRATEGIES TO CREATE BRAVE WARRIORS

The ideal Spartan was a totally dedicated and selflessly brave warrior. Men boasted that their city did not need walls, claiming they were its defense. Elders examined newborn babies, and those that were too weak or deformed to make good soldiers or become mothers of good soldiers were left exposed to die or thrown to their death.

To encourage loyalty to the group rather than to one's family, young Spartan boys left their homes when they were seven years old and lived in barracks. training with other youths until they were thirty. For thirty more years, they shared one meal a day with the other men. Men started serving in the army when they were twenty and remained until they were sixty. A Spartan soldier was to "come home carrying his shield or on it," but he was never to surrender. In fact, to die in battle was considered the highest honor. Only Spartan men who died in battle and women who died in childbirth had their names on their graves.

The goal of Spartan education for boys was to train ideal fighters. Reading and writing were unimportant; laws were shared orally. Spartans considered art and literature worse than a waste of time because they might weaken one's resolve. Health was a virtue, while sickness was a crime. It was acceptable to be cunning as long as one did not get caught. Boys fought and shunned those who showed pain or cowardliness. Most young boys had male lovers but men were also encouraged to marry, and celibacy was a crime. The usual age for marriage was eighteen, even though young men did not live with their wives until they were thirty. Bachelors could not vote, and women made fun of them and even beat them up.

Spartans did not welcome visitors from other city-states who might bring disquieting new ideas. Few Spartans wanted to travel because they did not believe they had anything to learn from the outside world. To limit the number of outsiders who might bring new ideas, Spartans prohibited importing gold and silver and required merchants to use iron currency in all transactions. The iron bars were too heavy to store or use easily as a means of exchange, so not much trade took place. Spartan men had little personal wealth, and they gave each boy only one shirt. (When we say someone lives a Spartan life, we usually mean he or she has few possessions.)

Spartans told about a youth who had befriended a baby fox and raised it secretly as a pet. Because boys were forbidden to have personal possessions and were not supposed to feel sentiment, he told no one about his companion. One day, while playing with his pet, the boy was called to drill. Caught unaware, he quickly hid the animal in his shirt as he stood at attention. In the confusion and noise of the drill procedure, the fox became frightened and began to claw the boy's chest. The lad, true to Spartan values, did not even flinch until he fell over dead, his stomach torn open by the claws of the terrified animal.

WHAT ABOUT SPARTAN WOMEN?

Spartan women were taught to take pride in being mothers of heroes. Elders encouraged young girls to participate in the games so they would develop strong bodies, and they were well-fed so they would give birth to healthy babies. Their education included training in gymnastics and music as well as in household management and child rearing. Hoping the wives of its citizens would have lots of babies, Spartans over-looked extra-marital affairs as long as both partners were healthy Spartans. If a woman were childless, she could get a divorce and marry again in the hopes that she and her new partner would have a son.

Stories reflect the values women were expected to have. Imagine a Spartan woman who, having sent five sons off to war, waits anxiously for news of the battle. She asks a returning soldier how things have gone, and he tells her that all five of her sons have been killed. She replies, "I did not ask about that! How fares the country?" When she hears that Sparta has been victorious, she replies, "Then I accept gladly also the death of my sons." Another mother, we are told, was burying her son when an old woman said to her: "Ah, the bad luck of it. Poor woman." But the mother replied, "No; by heaven, but good luck; for I bore him that he might die for Sparta and this is the very thing that has come to pass for me." (Quotations from Plutarch) We can ponder whether mothers were really this anxious for their sons to die in battle. As Sappho wrote:

> Death is our evil. The gods believe this,
> or else by now they themselves would be dead.

Spartan women had the reputation in the rest of Greece for being strong, beautiful, and outspoken, and they may have fared better than women in other city-states. Since Spartans did not intermarry with helots, Spartan men had little reason to distrust the women they married. That may help explain the higher status and greater independence of Spartan women compared with the rest of Greece. In addition, because their husbands had to spend so much of their lives in the barracks, Spartan women had almost total control of their lives and households.

Arete, Athenian Style:
Direct Democracy by the Citizens

Athens is in Attica on a southeastern edge of the Balkan Peninsula. Athens also emerged from the Dark Age as an oligarchy dominated by a hereditary aristocracy, a group of landowners whose status and wealth came from their land. The aristocrats made up the Council of Elders that passed laws governing the city.

Athens had no helots, so wealthy landowners hired other Athenians to do the farm work. Poor Athenian farmers who had no political rights and little chance to improve their lives soon began to resent working for landowners who had all the political power. Why not, many asked, pack up and emigrate to a new settlement along the Black Sea or the southern coast of the Italian Peninsula where they could get land and have a say in the government? As colonists, they might become the aristocrats.

Merchants also envied the aristocracy. Trade was important in Athens, and the number of rich, urban, self-made businessmen was increasing. They resented the fact that even though they were wealthy, they had little social status or authority. They began to challenge the aristocracy's hereditary claim to political power.

While merchants were getting richer, many farmers were getting poorer and sinking into debt. When they were unable to pay back

Calf-bearer

their loans, they lost their land. A few found work in Athens; many wandered around as unemployed or underemployed laborers. Some even put themselves and their families up as collateral for loans, and when they could not pay back the loans, they became the moneylenders' debt-slaves. These formerly self-sufficient farmers were left with no land, work, or income.

Revolt and even revolution threatened the aristocrats who ruled Athens. In other city-states where similar situations existed, the poor were turning to tyrants. (Although these tyrants ruled with absolute power, their supporters thought they were reformers who would reduce the power of the wealthy landowners.) Fearing Athens would also turn to a popular tyrant, in 591 B.C.E. the Council of Elders asked Solon to make whatever reforms he thought were necessary to prevent trouble. Although Solon had become a rich businessman, his sympathies were with the poor, so each class grudgingly accepted him as the best hope.

What Were Solon's Economic and Political Reforms?

Solon quickly introduced a sweeping set of reforms in an effort to prevent class conflict and make the government more responsive to the will of all citizens. Solon first tried to reduce the gap between rich and poor and give merchants more power. He did not redistribute land, which the poor classes desperately wanted, but he did cancel all public and private debts and overnight wiped out debt-slavery, freeing those who had become slaves because they could not pay back their loans. Solon then established a graduated income tax, taxing the rich more than he taxed the poor. (The United States did not introduce an income tax until 1913.) He also devalued the currency so it would cost less to borrow money.

Solon wrote a constitution in which he reduced the power of the hereditary aristocracy by permitting more men to hold public office. He divided the people into four classes based on wealth, not on birth or one's clan. He kept the ruling council, but allowed anyone in the richest class to become a member. He also created a Council of Four Hundred made up of merchants and other citizens, even some in the poorest class. This council decided which issues should come before the Assembly, composed of all the male citizens. All citizens, even the lowest class, could participate as jurors, 6,000 of whom were selected by lot annually. The citizens' names were placed in a jar and the men whose names were pulled out served as jurors. (We follow a similar way of selecting jurors today.)

These political reforms mainly affected men, because only males had political power and could be Athenian citizens. Solon did not establish a democracy, rule by the people, but men in all classes were represented in major political decisions, and there was some social mobility, that is, people could move from one class to another.

How Did Solon's Reforms Affect Women?

Women were not considered citizens and had no direct say in the government, so politically all women were inferior to men, even men in the lowest class. However, some of Solon's reforms were directed at women. For example, he put a limit on what people could spend for ceremonies and funerals. Because women were responsible for taking care of the dead and were hired as mourners who grieved publicly, this reform reduced those jobs.

Solon made laws about dowries that brides brought when they married. Her dowry helped pay the wife's expenses and neither her

Women weaving

husband nor members of his family could touch it. Solon reduced the size of dowries, including limiting the number of outfits a woman could have to three. Perhaps he hoped that this would help ensure that poorer girls could find husbands, but restricting dowries also reduced what a girl inherited from her family.

Solon wanted to lessen tensions among the various social classes and institute reforms aimed at both men and women. Once he had put his reforms in place, he relinquished power, retired, and devoted himself to writing poetry. Not many leaders voluntarily give up power as Solon did. Perhaps he was attentive to his own counsel: "Mark a man by his end."

Peisistratus Rules as a Tyrant

Although Solon's reforms prevented civil war, he may have heightened tensions among factions (groups with special interests, such as merchants and aristocrats), especially aristocrats on the Plain and merchants on the coast. All classes were still dissatisfied, but the poorest most of all. Landless people and poor farmers soon rallied around Peisistratus — a new leader who promised to redistribute land — who ruled Athens from 560 to 541 B.C.E. He used the military to stay in power, maintaining his own mercenary bodyguard.

Peisistratus redistributed government agricultural lands to the poor. If aristocrats protested too much, he redistributed their land as well, but he did not take land from aristocrats who supported him. He gave government loans to encourage farmers to cultivate olive trees, and he established commercial treaties with numerous other city-states. He promoted new colonies, especially along the Dardanelles, to help siphon off dissatisfied people, and provided public jobs such as building aqueducts, roads, and temples.

To unite all classes in a common culture, Peisistratus promoted the worship of Athena as the city's major deity and supported the Panathenaea, the yearly festival in her honor. He also established the Festival of Dionysus, where rich patrons sponsored tragedies and other plays that all citizens could watch. Athens became a prominent city and a center of cultural activities, attracting people from other city-states to its theatrical and poetic competitions.

Cleisthenes Reorganizes Athenians into Tribes

Cleisthenes, the third of the major Athenian reformers — often called the "father of Athenian democracy" — came to power in 507 B.C.E. To further reduce factions, Cleisthenes reorganized everyone into ten geographic areas he called tribes. Each tribe included members from the various factions: aristocrats who lived on the plains, rich merchants who lived near the shore, and poor farmers from the rocky hillsides. Each tribe held its own festivals.

A Council of 500 determined the agenda for the Assembly, supervised officials, and administered the polis. Each of the newly created tribes selected fifty members by lot to serve on the Council. The Assembly, composed of all citizens over eighteen — probably between 30,000 and 40,000 men — met four times every 36 days. Government officials, except for generals, were selected by lot from all citizens over 30. The Assembly elected ten generals annually and could elect the same general a number of times.

Cleisthenes also introduced the concept of ostracism, using banishment as punishment instead of the death penalty or keeping guilty persons in jail. A quorum (the minimum number of people who must attend a meeting in order to conduct business) of citizens of the Assembly (6,000) could vote to banish any person whom they believed was a danger to the polis. If a majority of the members present wrote his name on a piece of pottery known as an *ostraka*, that person was ostracized and could not return to Athens for ten years. No one, however, could touch his property while he was banished. In the first ten years, Athenians ostracized only ten men, but the principle helped keep citizens responsible.

Why Did Athens Give More Men Political Power?

The reforms of Solon, Peisistratus, and Cleisthenes during the Axial Age greatly expanded the rights of male citizens so Athens became more democratic. Clearly, extending citizen participation in the government helped reduce the possibility of revolts and kept many poor from emigrating to other areas. Another reason for spreading political rights may have been the new military strategy known as the phalanx.

The phalanx was a group of several thousand soldiers, lined shoulder to shoulder, so close that each man's shield helped protect his

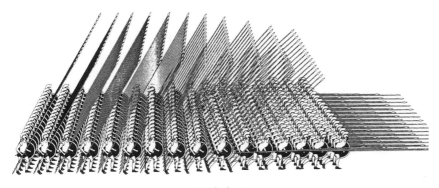

A Phalanx

neighbor. Men marched in tight formation, charging the enemy like a human tank. The phalanx gave foot soldiers an advantage over chariots. Horses could not penetrate it, and arrows were more or less useless against the shields men held. If one man fell, the man behind was trained to fill his place.

Greeks first used the phalanx in 570 B.C.E., drastically changing the nature of warfare, in part because aristocrats no longer had a monopoly in the army. Unlike horses, the iron weapons that phalanx soldiers used were cheap. Soldiers had to pay for their own arms and armor, and now even merchants and small farmers could afford to fight.

In fact, farmers were needed in the phalanx. But why, they must have asked, should we fight for a city-state that denies us political rights? We have little incentive to risk our lives for landowners who have all the power and can even take our land away. One way to encourage the merchants and farmers to fight was to grant them some political power. Political rights give men a stake in society and should make them eager to defend the polis.

Was Athens a Democracy?

Many historians have glorified ancient Athenian democracy, and modern political leaders still refer to the reforms of Solon and Cleisthenes as the birth of democracy. However, we should remember that citizens were a very small minority of all the people who lived in

Attica, and political rights were limited to those citizens. Women, approximately half the population, were never citizens. Slaves had no political rights, and a very large group of merchants and other resident foreigners were also denied citizenship. Athenians saw no contradiction in granting political rights to only a few and building their economy on slavery and thousands of non-citizen merchants and traders.

It will not be long before the Greeks have a chance to take their concept of the citizen-soldier to the battlefield and fight to defend their homeland. By the middle of the first millennium B.C.E., the Hellenic world will be threatened by empire-builders to the east. What happens when Greek citizens encounter subjects of the west Asian Persian Empire is an important part of the next act of the human drama. We might also wonder what will happen to other lofty moral teachings all across the hemisphere as they face the power of the emerging empires. How will men and women adapt and infuse them into their own institutions and how will various political leaders alter aspects of these teachings to suit their own objectives? These questions are part of the focus of the next act of the human drama.

ACT FOUR: THE AXIAL AGE

Setting the Stage

1. In what ways might nomadic invaders have caused people in cities to question their own beliefs and values?
2. How did the process of settling down and adapting to urban life promte former nomadic peoples to questions their own beliefs and values?
3. How do people find meaning and security when there is constant warfare?
4. In what ways was urban life either more or less secure than life as a pastoral nomad or a village farmer? What would make any of these ways of life more secure?
5. Why is this period called the Axial Age? What questions were men and women asking?

SCENE ONE
The Axial Age in West Asia

1. What evidence is there that the Assyrians valued war and the military? What made them good fighters?
2. What role did prophets play in Hebrew society?
3. What questions was Amos trying to answer? What did Amos say about the traditional rituals the Hebrews were performing?
4. What did Amos say the people should do? What should rulers do? What did he say would happen if the Hebrews did not heed his advice?
5. What questions was Job trying to answer? Why did he reject the explanations of his comforters?
6. What insight did Job finally have? Were his questions answered?
7. Who was Zoroaster? What questions was Zoroaster trying to answer?
8. What kind of war does Zoroaster say is going on? What should average people do? How should they act? What does Zoroaster say will happen if people do not heed his advice?
9. What is dualism? What is "ethical dualism"? Give examples from your own life. How widespread is ethical dualism in the United States today? Give some examples.

SCENE TWO
The Axial Age in India

1. What made some people in the subcontinent drop out of society and become ascetics? What questions were they trying to answer?
2. Define Brahman, *samsara*, and *karma*? How do ascetics in the Upanishads use these concepts to answer some of their questions?
3. Who was Mahavira? In what way is he a *maha* (great) *vira* (warrior)? How does he compare to a heroic warrior?
4. What does *ahimsa* mean? What is the Doctrine of Maybe? Why might someone who followed the Doctrine of Maybe probably also practice *ahimsa*? What might Zoroaster say about these two ideas?
5. If a person strictly followed ahinsa in everything he did, would he or she be able to survive? Why or why not?
6. In what way did Siddhartha's Four Encounters change his life? What question was Siddhartha trying to answer?
7. Summarize the Four Noble Truths and the Eightfold Path in your own words. What causes people to suffer? How can their suffering be ended?
8. What did the Buddha mean by the "middle way"?
9. In what ways did Mahavira and the Buddha challenge the authority of the brahmins?
10. Who might be most attracted to Mahavira's teaching? to the Buddha's teaching? Who would probably not be interested in what they had to say?
11. Create a conversation between Zoroaster and either Mahavira or the Buddha.

SCENE THREE
The Axial Age in China

1. What led to the Era of Warring States?
2. What seems to be the underlying philosophy of the *Art of War*? Discuss whether American military leaders follow similar strategies. What might have happened during the Vietnam War had the US military been more familiar with *The Art of War*?
3. Who was Confucius? What questions was Confucius trying to answer? What were the *Analects?*
4. What determines how a person should act (*li* and *ren*) in different relationships? How does right action based on *li* and *ren* differ from the west Asian commitment to Law?
5. What does filial piety mean? How does Confucius say children should

treat their parents? What would happen if students treated their teachers that way? If workers treated their bosses that way? If subjects treated their ruler that way? Pretend you are a good Confucian son or daughter tonight and see how your family reacts. How did they react?

6. How does Confucius think a ruler should act? What is his attitude toward ruling with laws and punishments?

7. Explain *yin/yang*. What is the relationship between *yin* and *yang*? How does this idea differ from dualism and the Zoroastrian idea of a war between good and evil?

8. Pretend you are a good Daoist tonight and report how your family reacts. How do things get accomplished when people follow *wu wei*?

9. How would the Legalists end all the fighting?

10. Write an imaginary conversation in which Daoists or Confucianists or Legalists are discussing what to do about the messy halls in the school and what to do to get the students to keep the school clean. Compare your strategies.

11. Imagine you are a Confucianist and describe Daoism or Legalism. Imagine you are a Daoist and describe Legalism or Confucianism. Imagine you are a Legalist and describe the other two philosophies. Which philosophy do you think will end the constant fight among the warring states? Why?

SCENE FOUR
The Axial Age in Greece

1. Explain the concept of humanism. How might geography have contributed to this idea? Why might people in Ionia have been particularly creative?

2. Imagine going shopping before anyone invented money.

3. What is a polis? Who were the aristocrats in the Greek polise?

4. List the major differences between Sparta and Athens. Why were these two city-states so different? Which fits the Greek ideal and why?

5. What problems was Solon trying to solve? What reforms did he make? Did the reforms solve the problems?

6. What problems was Cleisthenes trying to solve? What reforms did he make? Did the reforms solve the problems?

7. Compare the lives of a Spartan and Athenian woman.

8. Why did the Athenians extend political rights to more Athenian citizens? What was the possible relationship between the military and extending political rights?

9. Imagine a conversation between Solon and Confucius on how best to govern.

Summing Up

1. Select one of the major problems people in the Axial Age were facing and compare the major similarities or differences among the Indian, Chinese, Greek, and west Asian answers to that problem.

2. What evidence is there that people in these areas were in contact with one another and exchanging ideas? Give an example.

3. Several of the Axial Age thinkers made suggestions for how people should act. Compare right action based on law, on *li* and *ren*, and on *dharma*. In what ways are these ideas similar? In what ways are they different?

4. The major thinkers in west Asia, India and the Middle Kingdom all recognize that opposites exist, but they suggest very different ways of dealing with opposites. Compare Zoroaster's idea of a cosmic battle to destroy evil, with the Jain idea of the Doctrine of Maybe and *ahimsa*, with the Chinese idea of *yin/yang* and trying to create a harmony of opposites. Which idea comes closest to the way you think?

5. If you could go back in time, in which of these areas would you have most like to have lived and with whom would you like to have spoken? Write down your conversation.

6. Using the information in this act, write an essay that answers the following question: "How did the Axial Age thinkers propose to end fighting and tame the warrior?"

ACT FIVE

Establishing a Synthesis in the Age of Empires (500 B.C.E. to 500 C.E.)

Pastoral nomads, village farmers, and urban dwellers had very different lifestyles, respected different occupations, had different ways of governing themselves and others, and different reasons for granting their leaders legitimacy. The millennium of invasions by pastoral nomadic groups and the new ideas of the Axial Age thinkers resulted in many clashes in values and also major changes in the way both nomads and settled people lived. As a result of all this interaction and new teachings, a synthesis or merging together of many different beliefs and customs developed in the western Mediterranean, in South Asia and in China during the millennium from 500 B.C.E. to 500 C.E. Traders and travelers contributed to an increasing volume of cross-cultural interaction and change, particularly in the Indian Ocean and along overland trade routes across central Asia. This intense interaction and the contact among a wide variety of cultures ushered in an era of major social change throughout the hemisphere.

Creating Empires

Historians of Greece and Rome call the period from about 500 B.C.E. to 500 C.E. the Classical Age, because people in those areas created very sophisticated cultural traditions, including outstanding art and new technologies, and built up strong forms of political leadership and control. Similar developments were going on in India and China as well, so the term classical need not refer only to cultures in west Asia and the Mediterranean. During this period several strong rulers used their armies to bring very large areas, settled by diverse peoples, under their centralized control, areas correctly identified as empires. In fact, the overarching political characteristic of this period was the creation of empires, so we have identified the era as the Age of Empires.

Empires increase the amount of cross-cultural interaction, because ruling over diverse people brings different groups together. In addition, with the advent of empires people traveled a great deal, serving as ambassadors to other lands, patrolling borders, conquering neighbors, and trading. All of this movement and exposure to other people and cultures led to many changes, whether people welcomed new ideas or resisted them. Which ideas were exchanged, and exactly when and how they traveled, and which emerged independently in more than one place, are some of the questions historians are trying to solve.

Rulers and Ruled

All empires are created by force and use military power to control people. However, as a Chinese proverb says, "One cannot rule from horseback," so after having conquered an area and overthrown the existing rulers, the victors must find ways other than brute force to rule if they want to stay in power.

What do the rulers of an empire expect from the people they control? First and foremost, when they issue a command, they expect the people to obey and not challenge their authority. They look on the people they rule as subjects, not citizens. Subjects cannot expect to have a say in how the government is run, or vote on the amount of taxes or whether to go to war. While the population in general should feel secure, individual subjects have no legal or political rights.

Secondly, rulers expect subjects to support their regime through taxes and corvée. Farmers must share part of what they grow with the government and often must also work on government projects.

Theoretically rulers protect those they rule, so subjects should be willing to serve in the army as well. At the very least, they should not complain if they are drafted.

What about subjects of an empire? What do they want from the ruler? Perhaps most subjects in an empire are only vaguely aware of what goes on in the central government. "Heaven is high and the emperor is far away," the Chinese say. An average subject might agree with the speaker in this ancient Chinese poem said to date from the 24th or 23rd century B.C.E.:

> From break of day
> Till sunset glow
> I toil.
> I dig my well,
> I plow my field,
> And earn my food
> And drink.
> What care I
> Who rules the land
> If I
> Am left in peace?

People want to feel secure. They want to be able to walk safely in the streets and village lanes and be protected from unethical officials who abuse their power. They want to be shielded from civil wars and outside threats. If possible, subjects want rulers to provide this protection without forcing their fathers, sons, husbands, and brothers into military service.

Keeping taxes reasonable is also important. Taxes were usually from one-fourth (low) to one-half (high) of what one grows or produces. If rulers demand too much, farmers are left without enough to feed their own families. Corvée, when people must leave their homes to work on massive building projects that are often in distant parts of the empire, is another form of taxation. If the government requires corvée, subjects should believe the projects are worthwhile. They must think that large temples will please the gods, levees will hold back flooding, and irrigation channels will bring needed water to their fields.

"*The chicken is for this year's taxes. The egg is my estimated for next year.*"

Subjects in an empire know they must obey the rules imposed on them, pay the taxes, and perform corvée, but they want to know what the rules are and how much tax they must pay. Having written laws, enforced equitably by honorable administrators, helps make people willing to submit and give what the rulers demand.

In return perhaps most of all people want to be "left in peace" to live their own lives. Empires are composed of diverse people with different customs, often speaking several languages, and following many kinds of religious beliefs, and people want to practice their own rituals, speak their own languages, and socialize with members of their own communities. Even if the government is not particularly tolerant, it should not bother about local rituals and activities, unless they appear to threaten the government's authority.

Empires vary greatly in how tolerant they are of local customs. Some welcome cultural pluralism, respecting diversity and allowing each group to keep its own culture and practice its own religion, while others insist that everyone adopt a common system of cultural values. Moreover, without some form of strong central government, diverse people with many local hostilities might be constantly fighting one another.

Empire building, cross-cultural interaction, and cultural flowering occurred during the millennium from 500 B.C.E. to 500 C.E. in west Asia, the Indian subcontinent, China, and the Mediterranean World. In order to measure the strength of the empires that developed in these areas, we should find out whether people feel safe, whether they believe their rulers are legitimate, and whether the succession from one ruler to another is orderly and free from violence. Do they think the taxes and corvée are reasonable? Do they know the rules and feel they are enforced fairly? Is the military strong enough to protect the borders? Is the bureaucracy loyal or are individuals just waiting for the chance to overthrow the central government? And finally, do the people identify with the central government, and are they willing to sacrifice for its well-being?

It is no accident that impressive cultural developments took place in this period of strong empires. The government of an empire is usually able to prevent the people it rules from fighting one another. There is usually enough surplus to support artisans, artists, religious leaders, philosophers, and other creative thinkers. The government finances the construction of roads and bridges so troops can travel quickly and leaders can keep in close contact with what is happening all across their empire, and these developments enhance contact among diverse areas and peoples, leading to more exchanges and innovations. The characteristics of empires and the synthesis of ideas that developed in different places during this Age of Empires are the focus of this act of the human drama.

ESTABLISHING A SYNTHESIS IN THE EASTERN MEDITERRANEAN WORLD

Setting the Stage

Two very different civilizations met at the end of the sixth century B.C.E. One was the Persian world of empire, war, luxury, and law. The other was the Hellenic world of the polis, *arete*, democracy, citizenship, and simplicity. Which prevailed? Who ultimately won the struggle between Hellenic and Persian ways of life? What kind of synthesis did men and women work out?

We have already examined several groups that dominated the eastern Mediterranean after 2300 B.C.E., when Sargon first experimented with bringing independent Sumerian city-states under his control. Effective military power is what enabled second-millennium warrior-leaders of different nomadic groups to conquer Mesopotamia and the Fertile Crescent, and they often claimed divine authority and developed lavish ceremonies to awe the people they ruled into obedience. In part because there were no natural barriers, a great deal of trade passed through this area, exposing people to new ideas and different ways of life.

Well-armed and ruthless Assyrians ruled west Asia during the first centuries of the first millennium B.C.E. In 612 B.C.E. the Chaldeans, Medes, and Persians — three groups that Assyria ruled — joined forces, defeated the Assyrians, and divided the land among themselves. The Chaldeans under King Nebuchadnezzar (605–562 B.C.E.) rebuilt Babylon and made it their capital.

After Nebuchadnezzar's death, the Medes and Persians turned against the Chaldeans. Two years later, in 560 B.C.E., Cyrus, the Persian leader, subdued the Medes and took over their territory. Because of its vast extent, which extended from Anatolia to the Indus, the diversity of the peoples it ruled, and the effectiveness of its administration, we can say that by 500 B.C.E. the Persians had created the Persian Empire, also known as the Achaemenid Empire.

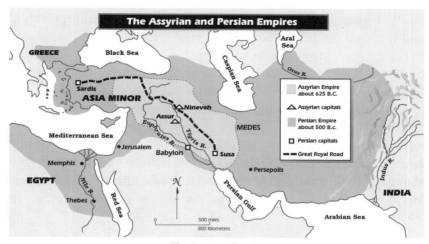

The Persian Empire

Empire Building, Persian Style

Cyrus ruled the Persian Empire from 559 to 530 B.C.E. Like so many rulers in west Asia before him, Cyrus had absolute authority and claimed to have the blessing of the gods. He attempted to rule justly and righteously, and his government established a policy of cultural pluralism, respecting local cultures and permitting people to use their own languages, worship their own patron deities, and practice their own customs rather than trying to make everyone act like Persians. Cyrus released Jews from captivity in Babylon and allowed them to return to Palestine if they wished to do so, although many preferred to stay where they were.

Cyrus instituted a hereditary monarchy, and Darius, king of the Persian Empire from 522 to 486 B.C.E., continued Cyrus's policy of cultural pluralism. To establish an effective way to administer such a large area, Darius divided the empire into twenty administrative units called satrapies, from which the governor — satrap — was responsible for collecting a fixed amount of taxes. Persian nobles living in these satrapies led the army, helped enforce rules, and collected taxes. Some areas were quite independent and, as long as they paid their tribute to the government, could live as they pleased.

The Persian government supported trade by minting coins, building and maintaining a large network of roads, and protecting travelers. Persian troops moved quickly along the 1,600-mile highway from Sardis to Susa; messengers and traders could travel that distance, marked by over one hundred post stations, in a single week.

The Persian Empire had many of the characteristics that make an empire strong. Its leaders claimed to have the support of the gods as well as strong armies. Succession based on heredity resulted in the peaceful transfer of power. The organization of the empire into twenty satrapies, good communication through roads, effective bureaucrats, and the use of spies helped ensure that people paid their taxes and obeyed the laws.

The empire was economically strong, as well. To improve trade, Darius had a canal constructed from the Mediterranean Sea to the Red Sea (along the site of the present-day Suez Canal). The government supervised construction and maintenance of underground water channels that irrigated the land and made farming possible. Trade created prosperous merchants and lower taxes for farmers.

Aware of the vast diversity within their empire, the Persians were tolerant of different faiths. At the same time, the support Persian lead-

Rendering Homage to Emperor Darius

ers gave to Zoroastrianism helped it to spread and its popular appeal helped unify the empire. Gradually an increasing number of people believed that the powers of good were fighting against the powers of evil and that those who chose to support Ahura Mazda would have eternal life but those who fought on the side of evil would burn eternally in hell.

Darius' army conquered much of Anatolia and collected tribute from many of the Hellenic city-states along the Ionian coast. Occasionally one city-state or another attempted to revolt. Persian leaders grew increasingly impatient with these small uprisings and decided to end them once and for all by absorbing the Greek city-states into their empire. The Persians launched war against the Greeks in 490 B.C.E., but Darius' army was driven back at Marathon, north of Athens. His son Xerxes took his father's defeat as a personal challenge and vowed to teach the Greeks a lesson. (If he did not, his wife told him, his subjects would think he was a coward.) But the Persians lost this war in 479 B.C.E., in part because the terrain was too hilly for their land troops, and because they had little incentive to secure what they believed to be a poverty-stricken area on the periphery of their empire. From the Persian perspective, nothing very significant changed as a result of these skirmishes.

After this failed attempt to conquer Greece, Darius' successors used a policy of divide and rule to try to ensure the Greeks remained weak. They encouraged various city-states to fight one another so they would not threaten Persia.

The Persian Wars from the Greek Perspective

Although the average person within the Persian Empire may not have thought that the conflict against the Hellenic city-states was very significant, the Greeks saw the Persian Wars as a turning point in their history. After all, they lived in small independent city-states, and no central authority dictated how they should act. It seemed inconceivable that they could work together to defeat the mighty Persians.

Hellenic city-states along the Ionian coast deeply resented Persians telling them what to do. Paying tribute to an empire really riled them. After all, tribute was what inferior groups paid to a superior power, and Ionian city-states felt inferior to no one. So in 490 B.C.E., after

Athens helped several Ionian poleis try to break free of Persian rule, King Darius led the Persian army to Marathon. The Persians vastly outnumbered the Athenians, the historian Herodotus reported, with only about 10,000 Hellenes against 100,000 Persians. (Might Herodotus have exaggerated the numbers to make the outcome more impressive?)

Surprisingly, the Athenians won, killing 6,400 Persians, Herodotus claimed, while losing only 192 of their own soldiers. In order to get word of the Hellenic victory to Athens before the Persian fleet neared the city, a scout ran there to bring the joyous news of victory. (His 26-mile race is still commemorated by running marathons.)

Darius retreated and died before he could attack Greece again, so his son Xerxes took over the job. According to Herodotus, Xerxes raised 600 ships and massive numbers of men from every part of the empire and set out against the Greeks in 480 B.C.E. His armies crossed the Hellespont on a bridge of ships and then marched down into central Greece, totally destroying the Spartan soldiers who tried to stop him at the pass at Thermopylae.

As the Persians advanced toward Athens, Themistocles, the Athenian general who had built up the Athenian navy, persuaded the Athenians to abandon the city and sail to Salamis. After sacking and burning the deserted city, the Persians took off after the Athenians. Themistocles lured Xerxes' fleet into the bay at Salamis, where the small Hellenic ships outmaneuvered his larger boats, forcing Xerxes to withdraw. The next year the Greeks easily defeated the small force he had left behind, bringing an official end to the Persian Wars in 479 B.C.E.

How can one account for the fact that these small city-states, composed of independent citizens who usually were not able to work together, resisted the mighty Persian Empire? That was the central question Herodotus asked in *The Histories*, and he thought its answer was an important lesson for all people. The Greeks were free men, Herodotus reminded his readers, citizens who had a stake in society and were fighting for their own land, their polis, and their values. *Arete* — bravery in battle and fearlessness in the face of danger — had long been the Hellenic code of excellence, and now *arete* also included loyalty to the polis. This war gave men a chance to prove themselves in both areas. Greece's victory in the Persian Wars proved that free men with a stake in their society would always win against tyrannies, Herodotus proudly wrote.

Herodotus ended his history with a report of a Greek general coming upon Xerxes' tent, with its embroidered hangings and gorgeous decorations. He ordered Xerxes' cook to prepare the sort of meal he was accustomed to serving his former master and told his own servants to prepare an ordinary Spartan dinner. The contrast was remarkable, and, sending for the Greek commanding officers, he told them to look at both. "Gentlemen, I asked you here in order to show you the folly of the Persians, who, living in this style, came to Greece to rob us of our poverty."

The Athenian Golden Moment

All of Greece must have rejoiced at its success against mighty Persia. Athens and Sparta were especially proud. Spartan bravery and skill on the battlefield appeared to justify their strict discipline, and the victory also seemed to support the Athenian commitment to democracy as well as the brilliance of its military leaders. The three decades from 461 to 429 B.C.E., often called the Periclean Age, were particularly remarkable for Athens.

During the Periclean Age, Athens elected Pericles — the city's most important leader — general 32 times. Periclean Athens was a direct, not a representative, democracy. Citizens over 18 met and decided issues by majority rule rather than electing officials to represent and make decisions for them. The Assembly met 40 times a year and could check the accounts of outgoing officials who had only one-year terms, to discourage them from building up a personal power base. The Assembly also oversaw the work of the ten generals.

The Parthenon on the Acropolis

Any citizen might draw a lot for administrative duty, such as supervisor of public works or director of one of the festivals, so all citizens had to be educated and informed and almost all young boys received an elementary education. They learned grammar (reading, writing, and arithmetic), music, and gymnastics. Upper-level education covered government, poetry, ethics, geometry, and rhetoric, including oratory and debating. Public officials, together with jury members, received a salary so any citizen could serve. A trial by a jury of one's peers determined whether a person was guilty or innocent, and the polis punished those the jury found guilty.

During the Periclean Age, Athens developed a strong navy, and even the poorest Athenian could serve because sailors who rowed the ships did not need weapons or armor. Perhaps the development of a navy, as had been true earlier with the phalanx, was another reason for extending political rights to poorer members of the society.

A high degree of social and economic equality existed among the male citizens in Athens during the Periclean Age. There was no wide gap between rich and poor citizens, and, in comparison with today's standards, having time to engage in politics, watch plays, and visit with friends seemed to have been more important to them than wealth, material comfort, or fighting. Prosperous citizens were expected to devote some of their wealth to the polis, sponsoring theatrical productions and competitions among playwrights. During this age poets, playwrights, and artists created some of the greatest works of Greek art and literature.

What Was Life in Athens Like for Women?

Although the Periclean Age may have been a golden moment for men who were citizens, the middle of the fifth century was perhaps the lowest point in the social status of Athenian women. Unlike farming women who worked in the fields with their husbands and sons, Athenian women performed the same jobs as slaves and servants, so their status was not very high. Even upper-class women spent much of their time inside their poorly ventilated, dark homes, running the household, supervising the work of slaves and servants, and having children.

Slaves and lower-class women got out of the house more often.

Slaves went for water and did the shopping. Lower-class women, even from citizen families, often worked outside the home as washer-women, woolworkers, or selling food and cloth they had spun and woven. They also served as midwives or nurses of other people's young children. Because women took no part in the political life of the city, there seemed to be no need to educate them to do anything other than household tasks.

Some women were also prostitutes and *hetaerae*. Hetaerae were female companions or mistresses who entertained men and were often included in men's social gatherings. Some *hetaerae* were highly intelligent and discussed such topics as politics, drama, and philosophy with their male friends. Others were artists' models or ran their own businesses. Perhaps the most famous one was Aspasia, who captured Pericles' affection. This charming, intelligent woman was skilled in politics and a sophisticated conversationalist, and, we are told, Pericles loved Aspasia "with wonderful affection."

While we do not know whether worship of goddesses increases women's power and status, religion often provides options for women. Priestesses serving the Olympian goddesses and performing rituals for the mystery religions were the most respected women in Athens, and participation in religious festivals gave many women a chance to be outside the home. In addition, the Delphic oracle was a woman, and she was perhaps the most influential person in all of Hellas.

Evidence in literature, art, and epitaphs that widowers had carved on their wives' graves suggests women had limited contact with their husbands, who preferred to spend time with other men. Relations between a man and woman was primarily to create children, while affection between men, Greek men maintained, involved the exchange of ideas and genuine companionship and was a higher form of love.

The Growth of Humanism

Most Greeks shared the idea that this world is beautiful, that humans are the most important beings in the universe, and that the human mind can understand existence. Greek art and literature richly illustrate this celebration of human accomplishments. As the famous

Greek dramatists Sophocles wrote in his drama *Antigone*:

> Wonders are many
> And none more wonderful than man. ... (333)

Hellenic art idealized the male body, making gods look like humans and human like gods. Sculptors depicted gods such as Zeus and Apollo as idealized men with perfect proportions and made statues of men that looked like gods. The 5th century sculpture Discus Thrower captured the athlete's balanced, controlled dynamic energy. Hellenic art reached its height with Phidias (500–432 B.C.E.), whose major works include the statue of Athena in the Parthenon and Zeus at Olympia. The Parthenon, the temple to Athena on the acropolis in Athens, is perhaps the most famous of all Athenian buildings. Sculptors carved beautiful friezes on its walls.

Hellenic philosophers believed humans could use their minds to figure out how and why things happened as they did. Ionian Axial Age thinkers had already taught people to search rationally for order

Apollo   *Discus Thrower*

and meaning in the universe. Beginning in the 5th century B.C.E. a new group of philosophers called Sophists (those who are wise) began to argue that it was more important to study how individual people act than to try to unlock the secrets of the universe. Sophists preached against slavery, racial superiority, and the glorification of war. They also taught skills in rhetoric that allowed debaters to win either side of an argument, so some accused them of commercializing the search for truth by teaching people to use their intellect to get ahead.

In spite of their faith in humanism, most Greeks realized that human beings were not free to do anything they wanted to do. Man might be the measure of all things, but he still had to observe the laws of the universe and follow his own fate or else he would come to a tragic end. If an individual thought he was bigger than life and beyond the rules of nature, he was guilty of excessive pride, which the Greeks called hubris.

The Delian League: From *Arete* to Hubris

Greeks realized that although they had stopped the Persians from controlling land bordering the Aegean Sea, they had not really weakened the Persian Empire, so the Athenians invited the other city-states to join a purely defensive organization called the Delian League and support it with either ships or money. The league's objectives were to help free cities that were still under Persian rule, to guard against Persian ships, and to police the Aegean against pirates. The league's

The island of Delos

treasury — money collected from all the league's members — was to be kept at the island of Delos, an important religious center in the middle of the Aegean Sea. Athens had the most ships, so Athenians chaired the league and its generals commanded the fleet.

The Athenian general Pericles used part of the league's treasury to rebuild Athens and pay for the art and architecture that made Periclean Athens so famous. After all, he argued, Athens had taken the brunt of the fighting during the Persian War, when the Persians had sacked the city, and the Athenian general Themistocles had been responsible for the decisive Persian defeat at Salamos. In 454 the Athenians moved the treasury from Delos to Athens, in order, they said, to keep it safe from Persian attack. Athens now controlled the league's entire resources.

Many league members sent money instead of ships, making them dependent on the Athenian fleet for protection. If a polis decided it did not want to continue being a member of the league and tried to withdraw, Athens forced it to stay in and pay its dues. Even if you are not a member, the Athenians argued, we will have to defend you against the Persians, because we cannot allow them to get a foothold anywhere in the Aegean. Logical as that argument sounds, to many city-states those dues began to feel like tribute, and some feared the league was becoming an Athenian Empire.

The Peloponnesian War

Athens's growing naval superiority and arrogance alarmed many city-states. Sparta, whose major strength was its army, felt especially threatened, so Sparta organized its allies into the Peloponnesian League. Relations between Sparta's Peloponnesian League and the Athenian Delian League became increasingly strained, and in 431 B.C.E. the two leagues and their allies started the Peloponnesian War. The war, which lasted from 431 to 404 B.C.E., soon involved all of Greece. Athens and its allies eventually lost, in part because a major plague broke out in the city, killing many Athenians. In addition, Spartan forces defeated an Athenian fleet in Sicily.

The causes of this war and its results are the focus of *The Peloponnesian War* by Thucydides, the second famous Hellenic historian. Thucydides believed the Athenians lost because power had corrupted them. He exposed the amorality of the Athenian position in a fictional debate between Athenian generals and people on the island of Melos. Melos wanted no part in the conflict and had refused to join the Delian League. The generals told the Melians:

> We Athenians will use no fine words; we will not go out of our way to prove at length that we have a right to rule . . . for we both alike know that into discussions of human affairs the question of justice only enters when the pressure of necessity is equal, and the powerful exact what they can and the weak grant what they must. (Book V)

After arguing that might makes right, the Athenians killed all the men on Melos. Elsewhere they installed garrisons to "maintain democracy." What a tragedy, Thucydides wrote, that the same people who had fought for freedom at Marathon should act this way. He hoped his history would teach later generations how power corrupts so they would not make the same mistakes.

The unscrupulous Alcibiades symbolizes much of the erosion of the Athenian spirit. A young and very popular aristocrat, he could easily persuade large crowds, but could just as easily sell himself to whichever side promised him the most power. Moving between both sides in the war, Alcibiades counseled disastrous military campaigns, such as Athens' ill-fated invasion of Syracuse, and fled from the scene when his side seemed to be losing.

Athens never again attained the glory of the Periclean Age, but neither did other city-states. None liked Spartan domination any more than they had liked Athenians bossing them around, and Sparta could not control them. No one polis or group of poleis was able to control Greece; instead city-states kept competing with one another. The Hellenic city-states were no longer the creative force that shaped the lives of Greek citizens; they were also weak and disunited, while the Persian Empire remained strong. We might begin to ask: Who really won the Persian War?

How Did Greek Philosophers Face the Breakup of the Polis?

A number of thoughtful Athenians tried to make sense of the tragedy of the Peloponnesian War. Why had this happened? Was democracy the culprit? Was too much individualism the problem? Were the Sophists undermining traditional beliefs in the state, the gods, and the special powers of the aristocracy by teaching that truth was relative to different groups and times? Three important philosophers of this period, Socrates (460–399 B.C.E.), Plato (429–347 B.C.E.), and Aristotle (384–322 B.C.E.) sought to answer these questions and bring back a belief in absolute truth.

SOCRATES

Socrates, who lived through the Peloponnesian War, apparently wrote nothing himself. Most of what we know about him comes from what his star pupil Plato wrote. From Plato we learn that Socrates wanted his students to question all "truths" including his own teachings. On the other hand, Socrates believed there was a certain absolute truth that each person could know if he or she vigorously applied proper reasoning and did not give up constantly searching for it.

Socrates questioned everything and constantly made the young men who surrounded him examine their own assumptions. He often told his students that the only thing he knew for certain was that he "knew nothing." Unlike most people, however, Socrates knew that he did not know.

Socrates was like a gadfly, irritating others by questioning everything, but his teaching was profoundly moral. Having stripped away false assumptions, he insisted one could discover the deepest truth that is always present in one's own soul, and improving the soul, Socrates was convinced, is the most important human goal. As a teacher, he wanted to serve as a "midwife" whose questions could help people realize that inner truth. After grasping that truth, he taught, people must then live according to its dictates, even if that meant death.

This great teacher had a healthy skepticism about every issue and took nothing for granted. He was especially critical of what he judged to be unthinking mob rule in Athens. Many scholars suggest that

Socrates disliked Athens's more participatory democracy and championed instead an intellectual aristocracy based on talent. His constant questions seemed disrespectful of the gods of the city and heightened popular insecurity. As a result, in 399 B.C.E. the government convicted him of corrupting the youth and condemned him to either ostracism or death. Unable to imagine living anywhere but Athens, he chose death.

PLATO

Plato was devastated by the death of his beloved teacher. Building on Socrates' insights, Plato wrote a number of philosophic dialogues as well as his best known work *The Republic,* in which he provided a script for how to build the perfect society. Plato also sought absolute truth, but unlike the Sophists, whom he hated, Plato argued that the appearance of instability and uncertainty results from people mistakenly thinking that all experience and the nature of the world are impermanent.

Plato founded his own academy where he taught that ultimate truth could only be found in Pure Ideas. Of course, there are such things as trees, people, and love, but, in addition, there are the ideas of these things. Things people experience in everyday life through their senses are largely illusions, Plato wrote; the pure ideas of those things are real. Plato illustrated this idea with the Parable of the Cave. Imagine prisoners inside a cave lit only by a fire. The firelight behind them casts shadows on the cave wall. If people mistake those shadows for real things, they are living a life of illusion. However, people could pierce these illusions, Plato counseled, and realize the Truth by using their powers of reason, by controlling their desires and emotions, and by leading disciplined lives.

Plato, like Socrates, distrusted the growing democracy that seemed to him like mob rule. He argued that instead of democracy, citizens should adopt his version of the ideal government. Plato divided people in his ideal society into three classes: gold, silver, and tin. Each class was to perform specific functions not for its own happiness but for the greater good of the whole society. The gold or guardian class, composed of philosopher-kings who had superior education and knowledge, would make moral decisions that everyone else should follow. Philosopher-kings, modeled on Plato himself, were to be self-less and not marry or own private property. The silver class, the spirited class, would be the armed forces and enforce the guardians' decisions. The tin class, the masses at the bottom of society, would support the other two classes by performing necessary work such as trade, crafts, and farming.

ARISTOTLE

After studying under Plato, Aristotle, the third important Hellenic philosopher, turned away from Plato's search for purely abstract ideas. Instead, Aristotle argued that the material world or matter was co-equal to the world of pure ideas, which he called "forms." Form and matter, according to Aristotle, were two halves of the whole, and together made up the essential reality of the universe. Forms (Plato's Pure Ideas) cause the world to materialize. Each thing that people can touch has within it a Form, something like a soul (in humans) or a seed (in things). Each thing is brought into being by its own seed or Form, which directs its growth and change, its life and destiny. In explaining how institutions change over time, Aristotle stated that the family contained the seed of the state. The family grows into a clan, then a village, a city, and finally a mature state.

Because Aristotle believed the material world was real, he wanted to examine things with his senses, trusting what his eyes and ears could tell him. He spent a great deal of time studying trees, animals, and human relations and trying to classify things into groups of similar plants, animals, and concepts. Aristotle wrote on a vast array of topics, including poetry, natural science, politics, ethics, mathematics, art, and metaphysics. He believed people should take care of their bodies as well as their souls and control their emotions and instincts. Each individual should nurture mind, body, and spirit for balanced growth and development. His famous "golden mean" taught people to avoid excesses in all things in order to integrate the higher aspects of life into a harmonious whole.

Aristotle believed the First Cause — the Prime Mover, the one true god, the conductor of the universal orchestra of beings — stood behind both Forms and the material world. It was responsible for the universe unfolding according to a rational plan. Aristotle's one true god was pure intelligence, without feelings, love, or even compassion for its creatures. He believed the state could help people seek the good inherent in their being and build upon that potential. His *Politics* advocates a mixed government in which the interests of the monarchy, aristocracy, and masses are balanced for the greater good of the whole.

Aristotle taught that the deductive method was the best way to know the truth. The deductive method means starting with a general principle and arguing from it to specific examples. He might state, for example, that all mammals nurse their young and then conclude that whales are mammals but robins and turtles are not. He also reasoned using the syllogism that had major and minor statements followed by a conclusion. For example: All girls are human. Mary is a girl. Therefore, Mary is human.

All three of these philosophers lived during the waning days of the Hellenic city-states and the Athenian experiment with democracy, and each strove to find a suitable philosophy that might save the city's greatness. Each distrusted democracy and the masses and taught that average people need strong leadership and supervision if they are to create the good society.

Macedonia Moves into the Power Vacuum

The Persian Empire continued to dominate the eastern Mediterranean and western Asia during the fourth century B.C.E., and Persia must have been pleased that no city-states posed any significant military threat to its western borders. But perhaps Persia paid too little attention to a seemingly insignificant group of semi-nomadic pastoralists and small farmers in Macedonia, north of Greece, that was building up its power base. How did Macedonia get so powerful?

In 359 B.C.E., 45 years after Sparta won the Peloponnesian War, Philip II became ruler of Macedonia. He was a brilliant soldier, and he trained a highly skilled group of professional soldiers. Macedonians had plenty of land on which to raise horses. Using the cavalry, phalanx, and long spear, as well as sweet words and promises that they would help the Greeks teach Persia a lesson, Philip and the Macedonian troops took control of many Hellenic city-states.

Philip's dream of conquest did not stop at Greece. He wanted to conquer the entire Persian Empire. He carefully taught military and political skills to his son Alexander, who was born in 356 B.C.E., and even employed Aristotle as Alexander's tutor. Aristotle taught young Alexander to love Hellenic things, particularly the *Iliad*, which Alexander is said to have kept under his pillow.

Alexander of Macedonia's Conquests

Philip was mysteriously assassinated in 336 B.C.E., and 20-year-old Alexander assumed the throne. Once in command of the Hellenic city-states, Alexander moved to "liberate" city-states in Asia Minor from Persian control. That accomplished, his Macedonian/Greek army easily conquered Egypt, where priests greeted him as a god. Soon after, his forces routed the Persian army led by King Darius III, who was then killed by his own men. Alexander and his army captured Babylon and Persepolis, Persia's sacred center, where, sitting on the Persian throne, Alexander claimed he ruled the entire Persian Empire. During a drunken brawl among his troops one night, the palace caught fire and burned, symbolizing the end of Persian power and splendor. From then on its subjects would have to send their taxes and tribute to Alexander.

Striving to conquer the world, Alexander led his forces into the Indus Valley and, knowing nothing about China, he thought he was at the edge of the earth. His troops, exhausted from fighting and longing

Alexander and Darius Fight

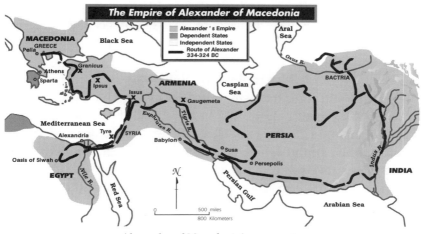

Alexander of Macedonia's conquests

for home, were dismayed to meet travelers in India who had come from even farther east. Fearing Alexander would want them to continue, they threatened mutiny and forced Alexander to turn back. He became sick and died on the return trip to Babylon. He was only 33 years old.

Alexander had a vision of one world in which everyone spoke Greek and Hellenic culture dominated, and his policies helped to increase cross-cultural contacts from Hellas to India. Hoping that marriages among various groups would create one people, he encouraged his men to marry Persian and Indian women and even held a mass marriage in Persia where he and 80 of his officers took Persian wives.

But many Greeks and Macedonians felt Alexander was behaving more like a Persian emperor than either a Macedonian tribal leader or a Hellenic general. Macedonians deeply resented the fact that Alexander treated Persians as equals and even allowed them to join the elite Companions, Alexander's most trusted and loyal troops. They watched with dismay as Alexander began to look and act like a Persian ruler, wearing Persian clothes and a jeweled crown and enjoying elaborate court ceremonies. They hated having to prostrate themselves before him, as Persian subjects were accustomed to doing before their king. That sort of action should be reserved for the gods. Could Alexander believe he was divine? Had he become a Persian ruler? Had the Persian model of leadership triumphed?

The Hellenistic Synthesis

The Hellenistic Age, the name historians have given to the years between Alexander's death in 323 B.C.E. and the founding of the Roman Empire in 27 B.C.E., implies a time when Hellenic ideas and values spread east through Persia to India. Alexander dreamed of one world with a diverse people united by Hellenic ideas and the Greek language. Perhaps Alexander did not realize that he had been influenced by ideas from Persia and India and that his conquests helped spread information about the splendor of the Persian court and the concept of divine kingship westward. What really happened during the Hellenistic Age?

After Alexander's death, the land he had conquered was divided among three of his Macedonian generals. General Antigonus ruled Macedonia and the formerly independent Hellenic city-states. General Ptolemy ruled Egypt, the second kingdom. General Seleucus controlled the heart of what had been the Persian Empire, and from 312 to 250 B.C.E. the Seleucid Empire extended from Asia Minor all the way across the Iranian plateau to the Hindu Kush Mountains.

The Hellenic political ideal was a polis ruled by the direct participation of its citizens. By contrast, the three Macedonian generals who ruled Alexander's lands had been semi-nomadic tribal chiefs, accustomed to following a single person in times of war and a council of elders in peacetime. That is how General Antigonus ruled his Macedonian kingdom. Hellenic city-states became small, relatively insignificant political units within the larger Macedonian kingdom.

Generals Ptolemy and Seleucus and their descendants, who ruled areas that had been under the Persian Empire, followed the Persian style of leadership. Rulers claimed they were divine and their power was absolute. The king appointed Persian nobles and Greeks to serve as administrators or military leaders, and Greek was spoken at court.

HOW DID PEOPLE LIVE?

Members of the upper class became more cosmopolitan, that is, citizens of the whole world or cosmos, and there was a great deal of travel and trade throughout the area. Alexander's conquests and the many highways and caravan routes made trade, the basis of the Hellenistic economy, easier. Traders mixed freely over vast areas, building great fortunes and carrying new ideas as they went. Instead of barter, Hellenic currency, which had evolved from Lydian coinage, and the spread of the Greek language made trading easier.

This period witnessed a dramatic increase in the number and size of cities. Antioch, in Syria, grew by 400 percent. Seleucia on the Tigris River grew from a small village to a prosperous city and Alexandria became the jewel of Hellenistic cities. Adventurous Greeks migrated to these and other cities in western Asia where being Greek gave them high status and they often found good jobs. Many in the upper classes living outside Greece studied Greek ideas, listened to Greek poets and playwrights, trained their bodies and minds after the Hellenic model, and enjoyed the prestige that came with adapting Hellenic culture.

Influences from India were also part of the cosmopolitan Hellenistic world. Think of the similarities between Plato's Parable of the Cave and the Indian idea of illusion and enlightenment when a person turns around or wakes up and realizes what is really real. Plato's *Dialogues* use a conversational format similar to the Indian Upanishads. There are also similarities between Aristotle's Golden Mean and the Buddha's Middle Way as well as Aristotle's First Cause and the Indian idea of Brahman. To what extent these similarities resulted from interaction is a matter of speculation.

Although status came from knowing Greek, Hellenic and other outside influences were a thin veneer on the top of society; most people remained untouched and unassimilated. The majority, perhaps 85 percent of the population, still spoke their own language, not Greek, and followed their ancient religions and long-standing traditions.

Slavery had existed in both the Hellenic world and Persian Empire in the 5th and 4th centuries B.C.E., and slave populations increased during the Hellenistic Age. At this time the majority of slaves were Slavic people who came from the Black Sea area. (The word *slave* first referred to these people.) Slaves were also prisoners of war. Some worked in homes, but most did heavy manual labor on the land, in construction and in mines.

Women usually played no role in the government, and most men in these areas devoted little if any time to political or military service. Making and spending money became important. Diverse peoples in this vast area might disagree about gods and beliefs, but they could all admire rare gems and gold jewelry. Rich merchants hired skilled artists and architects to work on their private residences, not on public buildings, and the best art was in the villas of the rich. Sculpture was increasingly realistic. Wealthy patrons of the arts wanted statues that looked like themselves, not some impossible ideal.

Skepticism, Epicureanism, and Stocism

The cosmopolitan nature of the Hellenistic Age left some people longing for personal meaning in their lives, as evidenced by several new philosophies that developed. One was called Skepticism, which was the idea that nothing could be known absolutely and that people could not be certain about anything. Breaking sharply from Aristotle, Skeptics taught that neither one's senses nor one's reason could lead to truth. They suggested that people should simply give up trying to find eternal truths, abandon making judgments, and seek peace of mind instead.

Epicurus (ca. 342–270 B.C.E.) founded Epicureanism, the second Hellenistic philosophy. He advised people to seek pleasure and avoid pain rather than search for God. Since Epicureans believed there was nothing after death and gods could not help anyone, reason and human experience were the best guides to happiness. For Epicurus, the greatest pleasure was intellectual pursuit within the simple life. (Later, people would focus on their search for happiness and incorrectly identify Epicureans as advising: "Eat, drink, and be merry, for tomorrow we die.")

Zeno (336–264 B.C.E.) led a third movement known as Stoicism. Zeno believed that all things evolved from fire, and, inevitably, all things would be reduced to fire. Then the whole process of creation and destruction would endlessly repeat itself. He taught that the cosmos is one giant machine whose parts are interconnected. Each individual has a part of the divine in his soul, which will be reabsorbed into the divine energy when he dies.

Stoics made no distinctions among people on the basis of race or culture. Humankind was bound in a common community, they taught, and where a person was born was irrelevant. Moreover, distinctions based on wealth or education were equally artificial. Stoics taught that both men and women could find security and peace of mind by controlling their own thoughts. What disturbs people, one Stoic wrote, is not what happens but how they think about those events.

In the Hellenistic Age both men and women struggled to find meaning in the more cosmopolitan world with its hemispheric exchange of ideas. Ideas flowed freely from the Mediterranean to India. Persian values, Hellenic democratic ideas, and Indian insights, particularly Buddhist concepts, all mixed together. Influences from the Roman Republic, which had become more powerful during this time, were also coming into the mix. We shall wait until we examine what has happened in Rome, and the nature of the larger synthesis Rome will create in the Mediterranean world, before we try to determine who finally won the Persian War, after all.

INDIA: A SYNTHESIS OF IDEAS

Setting the Stage

Cultural life in India flourished along the Indus and Ganges rivers after the Axial Age of the sixth century B.C.E. Indian farmers cultivated land throughout the entire Gangetic plain, making the subcontinent one of the most productive regions of the ancient world. Merchants thrived and traded not only with their neighbors but also with others as far away as Persia, Africa, and China.

People in the Indian subcontinent had been in contact with cultures to the west for a long time. Egyptians dyed their cloth with Indian indigo and may even have wrapped mummies in Indian cloth called muslin. King Solomon's temple housed Indian ivory and peacocks. The subcontinent was forced into the Persian world when Darius I (521–486 B.C.E.) made an area west of the Indus River into his twentieth satrapy. Herodotus claimed that this satrapy paid the Persian Empire more tribute than any other, and he emphasized the subcontinent's fabulous wealth, even suggesting that giant ants dug up gold from Indian deserts. During the Hellenistic Age, Persian, Hellenic, and Indian ideas mixed and mingled as travelers and traders took advantage of increased cross-cultural contacts.

Throughout these centuries the Indo-Gangetic plain was never united under one leader; instead by 600 B.C.E. there were seventeen kingdoms, each competing for territory. Religious diversity flourished. Followers of Mahavira and the Buddha spread their message across the Deccan (the plateau in the middle of the subcontinent) and into south India, and missionaries from both faiths sought to convert both kings and common people to their beliefs. These new ideas threatened Brahmanism, the priestly religion of the Vedas, forcing brahmins to reform their practices.

The Mauryan Empire

Magadha, in the eastern part of the Gangetic plain, was one of the most powerful Indian kingdoms. In 322 B.C.E. Chandragupta Maurya, the ruler of Magadha, took advantage of the power vacuum created by Alexander's death and seized the area in western India that Alexander had claimed. Magadhan troops also conquered Kosala, the other strong state, giving Chandragupta control over a significant part of north India. The Mauryan Empire, the territory he ruled, lasted from 322 to 184 B.C.E.

Indians living in the Mauryan Empire left no description of Chandragupta, his rule, or his subjects. Fortunately Megasthenes, a Greek ambassador from the Seleucid kingdom who lived in Pataliputra, the Mauryan capital, reported on what was going on at the court. Much of the information historians have about the Mauryan Empire under Chandragupta comes from what Megasthenes wrote.

Megasthenes was extremely impressed with the grandeur of Pataliputra. A council of elected magistrates ruled the city, administering justice and supervising government relief projects. The city had a nine-mile frontage along the Ganges River; its massive wooden wall had 64 main gates and hundreds of smaller ones. People built two-story homes around central courtyards (not unlike homes in Indus Valley cities). Most buildings were made of wood, and the government took elaborate precautions against fire, putting thousands of water-filled pots along the streets and requiring homeowners to have ladders and pots of water ready. Chandragupta lived in elegant splendor in an impressive palace in the center of the city. Megasthenes wrote that in the Indian royal palace there were wonders with which neither Susa in all its glory, nor magnificent Ecbatana, another Seleucid city, could hope to compete.

Chandragupta's public life was lavish, with much pomp and ceremony. Magnificently dressed in muslin robes with gold thread, he took part in grand parades and royal processions. He enjoyed hunting and watching races and fights between large animals. Fearing assassination, like many of his fellow emperors across the hemisphere, he would not sleep in the same bed twice and made someone sample his food and drink before he ate. Only persons with permits were allowed to enter the palace, and spies watched everything that went on.

Megasthenes wrote that Indians loved finery and beauty and had shoes that made a person taller (suggesting that high heels are not a modern invention). He thought women were well treated. Although husbands controlled their wives, they could be punished for cruelty. Wives retained their dowries as their own property. Husbands could remarry if their wives did not bear children, but widows could also remarry. In the Punjab (the land of five rivers), a province in the northwest, brides still chose their husbands.

Since women could become Buddhist nuns and join the sangha, Buddhism gave women an important alternative to marriage and their *dharma* as wives and mothers. As one nun wrote:

> I am the one
> Who left son and daughter
> Money and grain,
> Cut off my hair, and set out into homelessness. . . .
> I am quenched and cool.

Chandragupta employed well-organized bureaucrats who administered the economic life of his kingdom. Communication was essential, and Chandragupta ordered excellent roads with milestones and rest houses constructed. Taxila was an important trading city on the northwestern corner of the kingdom, and a royal road connected Taxila and Pataliputra. Well-maintained roads enhanced trade and improved contact among all parts of the empire and beyond. A regular postal service also existed.

The *Arthasastra* Provides Instructions for Rulers

Chandragupta maintained a strong army, and his soldiers had very high status and good pay. But even with a strong military force, Chandragupta recognized he would have to be very crafty if he wanted his empire to survive in "the world of the fishes," the amoral world of power politics, where big states conquer smaller ones. In order to survive, little states must use their wits. One of his advisors compiled a manual called the *Arthasastra*. *Artha* means survival and getting ahead, and the *Arthasastra* includes instructions in *artha* for leaders who are relatively weak. If small states want to survive in this amoral world, they have to be cunning. Effective kings never trust anyone

"Before you do something you may regret, I think you should know that I contain six parts of mercury per million."

who has power, including their ministers and assistants, wealthy merchants and brahmins, even their own beautiful queens. Kings need many spies, and they should gather information on powerful people that they can use to blackmail them should the need arise.

The *Arthasastra* also has very practical advice on how to administer a large state. While at court, the king should never keep his petitioners waiting and should always be accessible to his subjects. A good king controls his desires, especially lust, anger, greed, vanity, haughtiness, and exuberance.

The *Arthasastra* also contains "Seven Ways to Greet a Neighboring State." They are:

1. *Saman*: appeasement, sweet talk, soothing words, conciliatory conduct, and such things as nonaggression pacts;
2. *Danda*: power, punishment, violence, being well-armed, and aggression of any kind;
3. *Dana*: a bribe or gift, a donation, an agreement to share the spoils of war;

4. *Bheda*: divide the opposition so as to defeat them, cause a breach in the opposition, sow dissension within the enemy's forces, use treachery, treason;

5. *Maya*: deceit, illusion, fraud, a diplomatic feat (for example, the Japanese mission to Washington offering appeasement as the bombers were preparing to attack Pearl Harbor);

6. *Upeksa*: overlooking, taking no notice, ignoring the enemy until you have decided on the proper course of action;

7. *Indrajala*: military maya, creating an appearance of power when you have none.

These seven strategies can help a small kingdom survive in the cruel world of international politics, a world where big kingdoms conquer little ones. In the *Arthasastra*, if a policy works, it is a good policy; if it does not work, it is a bad policy. In addition, the *Arthasastra* outlines the Mandala theory of foreign relations. According to this theory, one's neighbor is always one's enemy, because there is always the possibility that neighbors will fight over boundaries or things such as water rights. One's neighbor's neighbor, however, is one's friend, because he is the natural enemy of his neighbor. By a similar strategy, one's neighbor's neighbor's neighbor is one's enemy, and so on. (It is

Mandala Diagrams

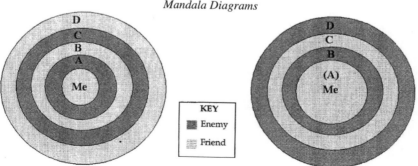

KEY
▓ Enemy
▒ Friend

A is my enemy, **B** is my friend, **C** is my enemy, **D** is my friend

A is absorbed into my circle, so **B** becomes my enemy, **C** becomes my friend, **D** becomes my enemy

instructive to see, even today, how often this Mandala theory applies to relations among nations.)

We can assume that Chandragupta followed some of these instructions as he built up his power base, annexed neighboring kingdoms, and established the Mauryan Empire. However, tradition claims that at the end of his life, he became a Jain monk and traveled to south India, where, practicing absolute *ahimsa*, he starved to death. Perhaps he had had enough of the world of the fishes.

Emperor Ashoka

By the end of Chandragupta's reign in 301 B.C.E. it looked as though India had become another militaristic, land-hungry empire. His son followed much the same pattern, and Chandragupta's grandson Ashoka fought and destroyed his brothers in order to claim the throne in 269 B.C.E. At first Ashoka fought to enlarge his empire, much as Alexander of Macedonia had done, hoping to prove what a great leader he was by conquering the whole Indian subcontinent. He fought a successful but ruthless and bloody war to annex an independent kingdom in western India called Kalinga. The Kalinga War proved to be a turning point in his life. Ashoka stated:

> Eight years after his coronation His Sacred and Gracious Majesty [Ashoka] conquered Kalinga. In that conquest 150,000 persons were carried away captive, 100,000 were killed or maimed and many times that number died. Immediately after the taking of Kalinga, His Sacred Majesty felt remorse. For when an unsubdued country is conquered there occur such things as slaughter, death, and deportation of people. . .

> Even those who escape calamities themselves are deeply afflicted when their friends, acquaintances, companions, and relatives suffer. . . .

> Today, even if the number of people who were killed or who died. . . had been only one one-hundredth or one one-thousandth of what it actually was, this would still be considered serious by His Sacred Majesty. (Rock Edict XIII)

Ashoka pillar

Filled with remorse, Ashoka stopped trying to conquer new territory. From that time on he attempted to rule by moral example rather than military might, stating that the only true conquest was winning people's hearts.

Almost the only source of information about Ashoka comes from inscriptions that he had carved on rocks, pillars, and caves. Historians must build their picture of what happened during Ashoka's reign and what kind of ruler he was largely from these 26 edicts. (These edicts are Ashoka's official pronouncements and may or may not reveal what actually happened.) The edicts are written in the everyday language spoken by the people, rather than the more scholarly Sanskrit, suggesting that many in the Mauryan Empire were literate and that Ashoka wanted even common people to read what he had stated.

Until Ashoka's reign, warrior/administrators and brahmins generally ate meat and drank wine and other alcoholic drinks. Both practices decreased during his rule. Perhaps in recognition of the Buddhist directive to "do as little harm as possible," Ashoka also wanted to protect animals. He gave up hunting, suggesting people go on pilgrimages to holy sites instead, and turned palace banquets into vegetarian feasts. He even began providing health care for sick animals as well as humans. To promote pilgrimages, he ordered rest houses built, banyan trees and groves of mangoes planted, and wells dug for travelers.

WHAT DID ASHOKA MEAN BY DHAMMA?

Ashoka's edicts reveal his philosophy of government. Many contain his message of simplicity, gentleness, and compassion. Ashoka summed up his approach in a single word, *dhamma*. Although dhamma was a Buddhist concept, Ashoka defined it this way:

> Abstention (refraining) from killing animals and cruelty to living beings, kindness in human and family relations, respect for priests and ascetics, and obedience to mother and father and elders. (Rock Edict IV)

Ashoka's dhamma could be accepted by anyone, including Jains, Buddhists, and Hindus, so it helped unify the country. In one edict he also suggested people should have "moderation in spending money and acquiring possessions." Perhaps this advice offended merchants, and that is why it only appears on one edict. During Ashoka's reign the number of merchants and traders grew rapidly and many of them accepted and supported Buddhism.

Ashoka's Empire (250 B.C.E.)

Ashoka worked hard to be a good king, instructing his advisors to call him any time he was needed. Officers of Dhamma traveled all over the country to check on local governors and supervise the day-to-day operations of government. These officers, one edict reads, were to make sure local officials were promoting "welfare and happiness . . . among servants

and masters, Brahmins and rich, the needy and the aged" and were
preventing "wrongful punishment or chastisement." (Rock Edict V)
Tax collectors were to be guided by the Buddhist ideal of compassion.
Officials were to show special consideration to prisoners in "cases
where a man has a large family, has been smitten (struck) by calamity,
or is advanced in years." (Rock Edict V)

HOW DID BUDDHISM ENHANCE ASHOKA'S LEGITIMACY?
Ashoka probably became a Buddhist during his reign. He hosted the
Third Great Council of Buddhism in 240 B.C.E. and sent Buddhist
missionaries to Egypt, North Africa, and northern Greece as well as to
Sri Lanka. Legends about Ashoka claim he also tried to unite and
hold his empire together by building Buddhist stupas.

A stupa is a hemispheric solid mound of dirt or rubble. It was probably originally a burial mound, and similar mounds can still be found
all over Asia. By Ashoka's lifetime the stupa had come to symbolize a
memorial to the Buddha, reminding people of his teachings and
encouraging them on their own spiritual journey leading to *nirvana*.
Several impressive stupas were built at Sanchi.

After his death a legend grew that claimed Ashoka had commis-

Stupa I at Sanchi

sioned the building of 84,000 stupas all over his empire. He then ordered priests, all at the same time, to place a box containing a relic of the Buddha in each one. Even if only a legend, this story suggests that Ashoka may have tried to unite his realm through ritual acts rather than by military might. Having greatly reduced the size and importance of his army, ritual authority had become all the more important.

No matter what Ashoka believed personally, Buddhism was just one of many faiths people in his empire practiced, and he did not try to make anyone become a Buddhist. Ashoka was committed to cultural pluralism and carefully promoted tolerance. He attempted to rule his multiracial, multireligious empire with compassion and tolerance and unify the people with general statements about *dhamma* rather than through specific laws or by imposing uniform beliefs. He advocated tolerance. One of his edicts reads in part:

> The faiths of others all deserve to be honored for one reason or another. By honoring them, one exalts one's own faith and at the same time performs a service to the faith of others. By acting otherwise, one injures one's own faith and also does disservice to that of others. For if a man extols his own faith and disparages another because of devotion to his own and because he wants to glorify it, he seriously injures his own faith. (Rock Edict XII)

During Ashoka's reign Pataliputra become a very great city and a center of art, philosophy, and culture. If we can believe his edicts, his reign is an example of statecraft built on moral leadership and ritual authority rather than force, and he ruled for 41 years.

But by 184 B.C.E., just 50 years after Ashoka's death, his successors were no longer able to hold the empire together. Perhaps his commitment to peace had left the army discontent and restless, undermining the empire's power and unity. The last Mauryan leaders failed to find ways to govern such a pluralistic land, and the empire split again into small kingdoms. Despite the lack of centralized authority, however, the two centuries following Ashoka's death were an intellectually exciting period as Indians created not a unified empire but a synthesis of ideas and beliefs called the Brahminic or Hindu Synthesis, a way of life we called Hinduism.

Hinduism: A Synthesis of Ideas

As Jainism and Buddhism spread and many people accepted these faiths, Brahmanism, the dominant religion of the time, was increasingly threatened. The Buddha had opposed the rigid caste rules that brahmins imposed and Mahavira stressed *ahimsa* at a time when animal sacrifices revolted many people. Although the Upanishads offered a new worldview and seemed to promise *moksha* (salvation) for all, only a few individuals could follow its directives. Buddhism, with texts written in everyday language, promised that anyone could experience *nirvana*. At the same time, merchants were a growing force in Indian life and commerce was thriving. The new middle class wanted more than expensive sacrifices or otherworldly asceticism. Finally, the growing sophistication associated with urban life demanded complex answers for the seemingly capricious world.

Brahmins were worried that they would lose their status, wealth, and privileged place in society if people rejected their rituals and turned to Buddhism and Jainism. They may also have worried that asceticism, discussed in the Upanishads and adopted by both Jainism and Buddhism, could undermine their power. Many brahmins must have concluded that the best way to survive was to incorporate many of the new concepts into their own religious system. Gradually, they began to adapt Buddhist and Jain ideas, much as they had assimilated ideas from the Upanishads. Over the next few centuries the brahmins worked out a synthesis that came to terms with the new reform movements, accepted many popular pre-Aryan religious practices, and retained much of their own system. The result was Hinduism, a total way of life that tries to offer something for everyone regardless of gender, personal qualities, *varna*, or class.

CASTE: A PLACE FOR EVERYONE
AND EVERYONE IN HIS OR HER PLACE

Hinduism rests on the concepts of *karma*, *dharma*, *samsara*, and *moksha*, ideas first discussed in the Upanishads. *Dharma*, one's duty or appropriate role, was the pivotal concept in the Hindu synthesis. Sometime between 200 B.C.E. and 200 C.E. brahmin scholars wrote a series of texts called the *Dharma* Sastras (texts on *dharma*) to explain each person and thing's proper *dharma*. Every person must perform the *dharma* that is appropriate to his or her personality, gender, age, position in the family, and social group. If everything performs its *dharma* — rivers flow and fire burns, teachers teach and children learn — the universe will function smoothly.

The four *varnas* were the ideological framework for the caste system, a distinctive feature of the ideal Indian society and an important aspect of the Hindu synthesis. The four *varnas* were brahmins, warriors, farmer/businessmen, and workers. By this time a fifth major group, the untouchables, at the very bottom of society, had developed. In reality, Indian society was far more complicated than just this five-group classification the brahmins used. Indians were actually born into one of countless smaller groups that they call *jati* and which, thanks to Portuguese missionaries, Europeans identified as castes.

Each person is born into the *jati*/caste of his father and mother, and each *jati* has its appropriate *dharma*, which usually includes an appropriate occupation. Many caste names were and remain occupational, much like our Carpenters, Weavers, and Taylors. If a person was born into the washerman caste, he was expected to grow up to be a washerman and his daughters were to be married to washermen. Each person should perform the job that was appropriate to his or her caste, hoping, perhaps, to build up good *karma* so that in succeeding births he or she would be born into a higher caste.

WHAT WAS THE BASIS FOR RANKING CASTE?

The term untouchable reflects the basis of caste ranking: purity and pollution. Whereas some societies base their social status on wealth and speak of upper and lower classes, and some base theirs on power and speak of the mighty and the weak, in the Hindu synthesis hierarchy was based on ritual purity and pollution.

Purity and pollution are associated with what a person takes in or gives off from his or her body. All foods are ritually ranked, so what an individual eats is important. Grains are considered ritually pure food, but beef, pork, and other animal meat is polluting. Good sights and sounds coming into the body are considered pure, while bad or ugly sights and sounds are polluting.

What comes from the body is also ranked. Reciting sacred hymns, mantras, or sacred texts — that is, giving out good sounds — is ritually pure, but using foul language and improper grammar is polluting. Waste such as sweat, spit, or human excrement is also polluting. Occupations are ranked because purity is identified with people who work with their head, recite scripture, and perform rituals. Pollution is associated with those who perform jobs such as caring for the dead, delivering babies, skinning animals, and carting off waste. These jobs were considered so polluting that the people who performed them were outside the caste system and called outcastes as well as untouchables.

Besides occupation, two other activities separated castes: the exchange of food and whom one married. Because of the fear of pollution, higher castes could give food to lower castes, but they could only accept certain foods from their own or a higher caste. If possible, people were to marry only members of their own caste. A woman might marry someone higher, but a man should never marry a higher-caste woman.

The *dharma* of the upper castes was very strict because they had to maintain their ritual purity. They could not eat meat or drink alcohol, were not expected to work with their hands, and had to perform many prayers, rituals, and ablutions, some of which were very time-consuming. Rules for the lower castes were much less strict. Although they did not have as much status, they also had fewer restrictions and obligations.

The caste system served as an ideal picture of the social system, but in actual Indian society the systems was far more fluid. New groups were constantly moving into the subcontinent, and they usually took on a caste identity appropriate to their power, wealth, and ability to acquire land. Within the social order a caste group could rise if it made a great deal of money or found new agricultural land. After a few generations it could change its caste name to a higher one and find some agreeable brahmin to create a new genealogy for the group. Castes could also fall in the system and over time take on the attributes of a lower caste than their ancestors.

THE FOUR GOALS OF LIFE: SOMETHING FOR EVERYONE

Brahmins, hoping to appeal to a wide variety of people in the rapidly urbanizing country, realized that some are interested in business, some want to rule, or have a good time, or just survive. In developing an ideal system that would appeal to everyone, they began to teach that both men and women should strive for four goals in their lifetime. *Dharma*, one's duty, became the central goal. The three other goals were *artha*, *kama*, and *moksha*.

Artha has to do with survival, power, and wealth. The *Arthasastra* taught leaders how to survive and get ahead. On the personal level, *artha* includes getting rich and becoming important. A person must never violate the rules of *dharma*, but within those rules there is plenty of room to become rich and famous. (Think about how you could apply the "Seven Ways to Greet a Neighboring State" to a personal situation, such as getting your parents to increase your allowance, getting your teacher to put off a test, or convincing the school administration to change a rule. A good daughter could still try to get her parents to extend the curfew.)

The first rule in *artha* is survival. In order to survive, you must know your opposition so you can play on his or her weakness or

PEANUTS reprinted by permission of United Feature Syndicate, Inc.

pride. The underdog must always understand his opponent and hope that the powerful one is too haughty to know much about him. Another good strategy is to try and use another person to help you obtain what you want without getting in the other person's debt.

Even the gods, when forced to resort to cunning, could not violate *dharma*. Once Brahma, Lord of Creation, a familiar story goes, rewarded a devotee by giving him the power to pulverize anyone over whom the devotee held his hand. Elated with his new power, he went around pulverizing everyone he met. Lord Brahma couldn't take away the gift once he had granted it, as that would be against *dharma*, so he had to figure out a way to outsmart this devotee. Brahma sent a beautiful dancing girl who invited the man to her apartment. She put on some soft music, saying, "I bet you are a terrific dancer. Let me teach you some dance steps." Vain and flattered by her words, he imitated her various gestures. "In this one," she said, "you just put your hand over your head like this. . ." and when he did, he was gone.

Kama is the third goal in the Hindu synthesis. *Kama* means pleasure and all kinds of delights. (Be careful not to confuse *kama* with *karma*.) *Kama* includes good food, good drink, joyful games, excitement, and passion. The *Kamasutra*, a textbook in *kama*, includes the 64 arts an ideal wife should master, such as word games, telling stories, home decoration, cooking, music, entertainment, flower arranging, and many other skills. Much beautiful love poetry celebrates *kama*. For example:

> I prefer being bitten by a terrible serpent,
> Long, wanton, tortuous, gleaming like a black lotus,
> To being smitten by her eye.
> Healers are everywhere to cure one of a serpent bite,
> But there is no spell or remedy for me;
> I was struck by the glance of a beautiful woman!

> Sweet maid, you perform a singular feat
> With the archer's bow.
> You pierce hearts without arrows,
> But with strands of your beauty. (#129, #133)

Dharma, *artha*, and *kama* were three of the goals in the Hindu synthesis. Hindus were expected to follow their *dharma*, enjoy *kama*, and excel at *artha*. But what about the people drawn to asceticism? The brahmins offered them a fourth goal: *moksha*. If and when *artha* and *kama* are no longer appealing, and one's sons and daughters are grown and no longer need support, then an individual was ready to seek *moksha*. The Upanishads had taught about *Brahman* (Oneness) and release from *samsara*, and the Buddha had preached about a oneness with all reality he identified as *nirvana*. Brahmins called that experience of oneness *moksha*. *Moksha* brought release from samsara, and *moksha* is the fourth and final goal. A person is ready to seek *moksha* when he asks:

> If wealth which yields all desire is won,
> What then?
> If your foot stands on the head of your foes,
> What then?
> If honored men are drawn to you by riches' force,
> What then?
> If man's mundane body endures for an aeon,
> What then? (#186)

A person who asks "What then?" is seeking something beyond the pleasures of *artha* and *kama* and the rewards of *dharma*. That person is ready to seek *moksha* and literally or psychologically drop out of society. Having achieved *moksha*, one realizes that the world in which he or she lives is really similar to a play in which each person is playing a part (*dharma*). *Moksha* involves recognizing that one's real Self has nothing to do with the part one is playing; one's real Self is identical with the Oneness of the whole universe. Once a person comes to this realization, he or she has broken the chain of *karma*, is released from *samsara*, and will never be born again.

THE FOUR STAGES OF LIFE: FOR EVERYTHING A SEASON
But if everyone drops out, becomes an ascetic, and seeks *moksha*, society cannot function. Rituals and sacrifices were unnecessary for those pursuing *moksha*. So the brahmins proposed an ingenious system called the four life stages. The ideal life of a good Hindu, they

taught, is divided into four stages; two in the first half of life and two in the second half. The first two stages are the student and householder stages. The last two stages are "going to the forest" and the wandering holy man. Each stage has its appropriate goal or goals.

During the first, or student, stage, *dharma* is the only goal. A young man studies, preferably with a teacher, called a *guru*, to whom he should be completely devoted. He serves his *guru* and does exactly what his *guru* says. Young men are to be selfless and put aside any thoughts of pleasure except the desire to please their *gurus*. By and large, young girls are to learn their duties from their mothers.

When a person has finished studying, he or she enters the second, or householder, stage. *Dharma*, *artha*, and *kama* are the appropriate goals for the householder stage for both men and women. Parents select a bride or groom, and the person is married. The young man goes to work, usually performing the occupation associated with his caste. Young girls are usually married to boys in the same caste who have the same occupation as their fathers. During the householder stage of life, people perform their *dharma* for the good of the community. A man must be a good husband and father and do his caste job. A woman is to be a good wife and mother. Both men and women can also seek *artha* and *kama* for their own personal satisfaction. As long as they do not violate *dharma*, the joys of love and the thrills of success are legitimate goals for the householder.

The second half of life is devoted entirely to *moksha*, the fourth goal of life. The third stage is called going to the forest. When a householder's daughters are all safely married and his sons are ready to take on the

Krishna at school

Householders churning butter

family responsibilities, the householder can turn his back on worldly concerns and drop out of society. During this period he meditates or studies in an effort to experience the true nature of life and the oneness of all reality.

If a person experiences *moksha* — oneness with the ultimate — he enters the final stage of life and becomes a wandering holy man, spreading ashes on his body to symbolize that his ego and personality are dead. Holy men who attain release from the concerns of this world wander around, living off the generosity of those who give them alms and offer them shelter. When they die, they are not reborn.

Although women could enter the third stage, very few did. In the Upanishads and especially in Buddhism, women were welcomed into the religious communities, but even there men were reluctant to grant women equality in the religious quest. In the Hindu synthesis brahmins sought to reduce women's role in religious life and counseled them to focus on their roles as wives and mothers. Time enough to be concerned about *moksha* when they were reborn a man.

Although the Hindu synthesis was an idealized description of how life should be lived, it nevertheless offered each individual a wide variety of choices. The four stages of life combined the ideals of living according to *dharma*, *kama*, and *artha* during the first half of life with the ultimate goal of *moksha*. Because of the law of *karma* and reincarnation, each person had countless lifetimes to work out his or her destiny. If an individual wanted to continue pursuing *artha* and *kama*, that was perfectly all right. Many died before they had completed the second stage; many more never wanted to leave the householder stage at all.

The vast majority of Hindus lived as householders, performing

their familiar rituals and trying to survive in an insecure world, and
leaving renunciation for another life. However, the example of the
few who did renounce the worldly life had enormous influence. As an
ideal, renunciation remained at the core of Hindu values, and wandering holy men reminded others that *moksha* was possible. But there
was no need to hurry. Sooner or later, after enough rebirths, the sages
taught, one would yearn for final union with Brahman.

THE BHAGAVAD GITA: PUTTING IT ALL TOGETHER

The work that perhaps best illustrates the inclusive nature of Indian
thought and the way the Hindu synthesis merged brahmin and
Buddhist ideas is the famous sacred text called the *Bhagavad Gita* or
Song of the Lord. Indians had been reciting the *Mahabharata* for centuries; scholar-priests inserted the *Gita* into that epic sometime
between 200 B.C.E. and 200 C.E.

The *Bhagavad Gita* opens as the great battle of the *Mahabharata* is
about to start. Arjuna, a mighty warrior, is preparing to fight his
cousins over who is the legitimate ruler. On the eve of battle Arjuna
asks Lord Krishna, his charioteer, to drive his chariot out to the front
line so he can look over the enemy he must face the next day. Among
his foes, he recognizes his favorite teacher and his beloved grand
uncle and many other relatives and friends. Horrified that he must kill
people he loves, he throws down his bow and arrow and tells Lord
Krishna he will not fight. The *Gita* is the conversation between
Arjuna and Lord Krishna, in which Krishna tries to convince Arjuna
to fight.

Krishna gives Arjuna numerous reasons. "You must fight," he tells
Arjuna, "or it will look like you are a coward, and people will say you
were afraid. You are a prince, and you must do your *dharma* and set a
good example for other people in the kingdom. If the prince refuses to
fight, who else can be counted on to enter the battle? Remember, you
are a warrior, and a warrior's *dharma* is to fight. You will build up
good *karma* if you do, because there is nothing better for a warrior
than to die fighting for a just cause."

Krishna reminds Arjuna of *samsara*. "A person who is born must
die, and a person who dies will be reborn; the wise do not grieve over
that," he says. Dying is like leaving aside worn-out garments, only

instead, one is leaving aside a worn-out body. Krishna reminds Arjuna that the only true essence is Brahman, and Brahman cannot be killed. What dies is not essential. Further, he reminds Arjuna that if he kills his teacher, grand uncle, or cousins in battle, they build good *karma*, so he is really helping them.

Krishna then discusses *moksha*, the ultimate goal of life. If one experiences *moksha*, Krishna reminds Arjuna, he is not reborn. Krishna explains four yogas, or methods to achieve *moksha*. One method is the yoga of meditation. Another is the yoga of knowledge. Both had already been described in the Upanishads, and traditionally only brahmins followed them. But Krishna assures Arjuna that there are two other methods for achieving *moksha* that anyone may follow: the yoga of holy indifference and the yoga of devotion.

The yoga of holy indifference is called *karma* yoga. "You must be indifferent to the fruits of your actions," he tells Arjuna. "You have a right to the deeds, never to the fruits. If you can perform your deeds but be wholly indifferent to the results of your actions, you will not build up any *karma* and you will not be reborn." Fight because you are a warrior, but don't pay any attention to what happens or who wins. "On action alone be thy interest, never on its fruits." (Imagine taking a test and not worrying about the results or playing in a game and not thinking about which team was going to win.)

A fourth method for reaching *moksha* is the yoga of devotion called *bhakti*. "Be devoted to me," Krishna said. "If you perform each act with your mind on me alone," Krishna promises, "you will experience *moksha*. Devotion holds the key."

> Not through sacred lore,
> penances, charity, or sacrificial rites
> can I be seen . . . [but]
> By devotion alone . . . (52–3)
> Acting only for me, intent on me,
> free from attachment,
> hostile to no creature, Arjuna,
> a man of devotion comes to me. (11.52-55)

Arjuna is not convinced by any of these arguments, so Krishna

Krishna reveals himself to Arjuna

finally reveals that he is the supreme god. His revelation is "like the light of a thousand suns in the sky." As Arjuna looks at him, he sees all the world, all the gods, the universe, totality. Filled with awe, Arjuna agrees to fight.

The four ends of life, the four stages of life, *karma* yoga, and the yoga of devotion formed the basis of the Hindu synthesis. A good Hindu does not have to drop out of society or become a Buddhist; he or she can enjoy the pleasures of *artha* and *kama*, perform his or her *dharma* and eventually seek *moksha*. And *karma* yoga and the yoga of devotion make it possible for anyone to perform one's *dharma* and still realize *moksha*.

Waves of new invaders came into the Indian subcontinent in the centuries after the Mauryans lost control, and great wealth, complex urban life, and mature systems of thought were all highly developed in India during this time. People were free to follow Buddhism, Jainism, and Hinduism, and each religion had complex texts and beliefs. Despite this diversity, the basic ideas of Indian thought — that the world is ultimately one, that *karma*, *dharma*, and *samsara* are realities in the world, and that nirvana or *moksha* is possible — remained constant. These values were far different from those that informed the Chinese synthesis to which we now turn.

SCENE
THREE

CHINA DEFINES ITSELF
AS THE PEOPLE OF HAN

Setting the Stage

During the Era of Warring States from 481 to 221 B.C.E., people in China vigorously debated which school of thought could end the chaos and violence that had been going on for over 300 years. Boundaries kept shifting so local leaders ended up serving different lords, and few felt any loyalty to the Zhou. As Zhou control weakened, fighting among the areas they had controlled increased. In addition, continued threats of nomadic invasions from the northwest helped convince the Chinese that military might advocated by the Legalists was probably the only way to bring an end to the era of warring states. Only the most idealistic people supported more peaceful Daoist or Confucian solutions.

The Rise of the Qin

As military tactics changed, mounted riders replaced chariot warfare. The state of Qin, located in the western part of China, where people raised lots of horses, made the switch to cavalry very effectively. Qin rulers in 256 B.C.E. defeated their rivals and created the first united Chinese empire. The Qin scorned feudal chivalry and honor and instead employed strategies advocated by Sun Tzu. Their goal was not social harmony, but to enrich their state and strengthen the military.

Following Legalist philosophy, the Qin established a rigid set of rules and severe punishments that applied to everyone, such as cutting off a nose, branding the head, tattooing the face, taking out ribs or boiling a person alive. The Qin gave warriors the greatest status.

As the Qin conquered new land, they increased food production through irrigation and flood control projects. Li Ping, who died about 240 B.C.E., organized a remarkable system on the Min River (in present-day Szechuan where the system still exists) that divided the Min into two streams, one for flood control and the other for irrigation.

Qin irrigation on the Min River

Boats traveled on the one used for flood control. The other branched
into numerous small canals channeled flooding water into an intricate
network of irrigation ditches. People called this *yin* approach to flood
control the "sea-on-land." (A *yang* approach would mean keeping the
dikes high and building dams to hold back the water.)

Legalism Under Qin Shih Huang Di

In 247 B.C.E. a 13-year-old boy succeeded his father as the leader of
the Qin. At first he had trouble establishing his legitimacy. When
palace guards accused his mother of plotting against him, he had her
placed under house arrest. After that he was reluctant to trust anyone.
Gradually, ruthlessly, one by one, "like a silkworm devouring a mulberry leaf," he conquered all the other states in the Yellow River valley. By 221 B.C.E. he was the supreme ruler of the Chinese people.

Searching for a title that reflected his great power, he finally
decided on Shih Huang Di. Shih means first, and Huang means
sovereign. Di meant Lord and was associated with the divine ancestors to whom sacrifices were directed. The ancient sage ruler Huang
Di had had the same title, so perhaps Qin Shih Huang Di hoped his
name would link him to past greatness and give legitimacy to his

reign. He predicted that his kingdom would last ten thousand ages. We usually call him simply the First Emperor.

The First Emperor followed Legalist-militarist policies. He ruled the country with absolute authority and military might, issuing decrees and backing them up with powerful armies over which he had absolute control. No one was to question his word; his edicts were law.

When Shih Huang Di came to power, only aristocrats from a few clans owned land and enjoyed power. To make his position stronger, the First Emperor ordered his men to kill the aristocrats or take away their land. Those who were not killed were forced to live in the capital, so they had no power base. In their place, he divided the empire into 36 provinces and appointed a civil governor, a military commander, and an inspector to control each province. Hopefully, this three-way balance of power would prevent any one person from building up power and challenging him. In addition, families were grouped together, and all were responsible for one another and would be punished if anyone broke a law. People had to report their neighbors' wrongdoings or suffer the same punishments if a crime were discovered.

To ensure that his officials administered the empire effectively, Shih Huang Di ordered numerous reforms. Roads were built and all cart and wagon axles had to have the same width so it would be easier to travel along deeply rutted roads. To promote trade and make it easier for his officials to collect tax payments, which were all made in kind (goods, not money), he standardized weights and measures. By issuing an edict that simplified some of the Chinese characters and standardized how Chinese was written, he improved communication.

Shih Huang Di had no love for Confucian scholars, and he knew they fundamentally disagreed with how he was ruling. He ordered his ministers to gather up all the Confucian classics and burn all but one copy of each one. Those single copies he intended to keep in the royal library. He also ordered 460 Confucian scholars put to death. Later Chinese historians claimed some were buried alive while others were buried up to their necks and then decapitated.

CONNECTING THE WALL AND MAKING A CLAY ARMY

When threatened by the Xiongnu, a nomadic confederacy on the northern border, Shih Huang Di sent 300,000 soldiers to drive the nomads beyond the Gobi Desert. During the Era of Warring States, various areas had attempted to discourage nomadic invaders by building walls around their borders, and now Shih Huang Di forced tens of thousands of laborers to connect some of those walls by constructing additional earthen walls and signal towers where none existed. So many died from exhaustion and exposure to harsh weather conditions while working on the wall that some later historians called it the longest cemetery in the world.

Signal towers on Shih Huang Di's wall

This wall was north of the so-called Great Wall that was built centuries later, and in many areas it was little more than a series of signal towers, sometimes connected by mud embankments. Although the wall was not completely successful in keeping nomads out, it did mark the boundary between settled and nomadic areas, and it may have discouraged unwanted interaction and invasions.

Perhaps Shih Huang Di's most impressive project was his tomb and the life-size clay army stationed nearby. Modern Chinese archaeologists have located the site of the subterranean palace in which he intended to spend eternity, but they have not started to excavate it. Tradition claims it is a replica of the whole of China with the coun-

Terra cotta soldiers guard the First Emperor's tomb

try's streams reproduced in quicksilver and somehow made to flow into a miniature ocean.

Six-thousand terracotta soldiers guard the tomb. They carry real weapons and many terracotta horses, four abreast, pull real chariots, each attended by 12 footmen. These clay guards, horses, chariots, retainers, and footmen were buried 15 to 20 feet underground and then covered by a roof. The clay army is certainly one of the wonders of the ancient world.

Legalism, backed by military might, was an effective way of establishing control over China, but people hated the First Emperor. He knew that heavy taxation, corvée, military service, and ruthless tactics created many enemies, and he feared they were plotting to overthrow him. Spies continually tried to find dissenters, and he even put on a disguise and mingled in the markets, asking people what they though about the First Emperor and life under the Qin. He seldom let his ministers know in which bed he intended to sleep, and when he traveled, anyone who revealed his whereabouts was instantly killed.

Shih Huang Di was obsessed with searching for immortality. Besides his elaborate tomb, on which workers labored for thirty-six years, Shih Huang Di sought some way to become immortal. Having been told one of the Immortals would exchange an elixir of immortality for young men and maidens and craftsmen, he sent 3,000 people on a voyage to find that Immortal. They sailed away never to return (and tradition claims they settled Japan). The First Emperor never found a magic drink. Instead, he died during a mid-summer tour in 210, when he was fifty years old. His retainers feared there would be widespread rioting if people heard he was dead, so they secretly brought his body back to the capital next to a wagon-load of fish, hoping its smell disguised the odor of the decaying monarch.

The Han Synthesis

Once people found out the First Emperor was dead, civil war broke out, and within four years Qin rule was over. The dynasty that was to have continued for thousands of years was the shortest in Chinese history, only lasting from 221 to 206 B.C.E. In 206 B.C.E. Liu Bang brought an end to the fighting, claimed he had the Mandate of T'ian, and established the Han dynasty. Making Chang'an his capital, he and his successors tried to govern "by the brush," that is, by letting scholars instead of soldiers rule. Historians divide the Han Empire, which lasted from 206 B.C.E. to 220 C.E., into the Early and Later Han.

Emperor Liu Bang and other Early Han emperors created a synthesis of philosophies drawn from the Legalists, Confucianists, and Daoists as well as earlier Chinese traditions. That synthesis became the basis of the way of life for the Chinese, who call themselves not Chinese, after the Qin (originally spelled Ch'in) dynasty, but the people of Han.

What Shall We Keep from the Legalists?

Despite the harshness and brutality of Legalism under the Qin, some Qin innovations made it easier for the Han to rule, and much of the Han political strategy and organization came from the Legalists. For one thing, Han rulers continued to exert absolute control over the country.

In addition, because the First Emperor had "broken the eggs," the Han could now "make the omelet." Most of the old landed aristocracy were dead and in their place there was supposed to be an effectively organized bureaucracy, with built-in checks and balances, all directed from the center. In fact, areas far from the capital were difficult to control, so Emperor Liu Bang appointed some of his own relatives and friends as the civil and military leaders in those areas and gave them significant power and land.

The policy of appointing his relatives and giving them land was a compromise between the earlier Zhou system based on a hereditary landed aristocracy, many of whom the Qin had killed, and the highly centralized Qin rule. Local officials had a certain amount of autonomy as long as they collected taxes, supervised public works projects, and kept order. Each official submitted reports and statistics to the emperor so he would know what was going on throughout his realm. The emperor also sent out censors who served as spies and reported any signs of a local official building up his own power base.

The Han kept the standard axle width that made transportation easier, standard measurements that helped trade, and language reforms that facilitated communication throughout the empire. They maintained and improved the communications systems by ordering the construction of four major highways that radiated out from Chang'an. The large-scale corvée labor system also continued building canals and flood control projects. Men were expected to work about one month a year on government projects. The Han also established six ministries: Appointments, responsible for filling government posts; Revenue, to collect taxes; Ceremonies, to facilitate and supervise all public occasions; Punishments; War; and Public Works, which supervised irrigation projects and maintained the defensive wall and the canals.

Making Confucian Values Official

Han leaders furned to Confucian philosophy to support their rule. Although the First Emperor had ordered most copies of the Confucian classics burned, some scholars had outsmarted him by memorizing the texts. Now that he was gone, they could recite the texts from memory to officials who wrote them down.

Elderly scholar discussing Confucian classics
as his daughter translates for the bureaucrat

Confucius had taught that the emperor's authority over the country, like a father's authority in the home, should not be questioned. There could be only one father and only one ruler. His word was final, and everyone had to obey him as good sons and daughters would obey their father and mother. As a result, the family served as the model for the organization of the government. Of course, Confucius had also stated that in order to keep the Mandate, the Son of Heaven had to rule justly. A ruler was to act like a powerful but loving father of the country who influenced the people by his virtuous conduct and moral example, not by rules or punishments, delegating rather than absorbing power.

Although the Qin had killed many of the old aristocrats, it did not take long for new officials to begin acquiring their own large estates, which posed a threat to the central government. To counter their growing power and influence, Han rulers began to surround them-selves with Confucian scholars. After all, the Confucian ethic in which the scholars were trained emphasized loyalty to the ruler as well as concern for the common people. In addition, men became scholars by education, not by birth, so depending on scholars who had to pass a test should keep a hereditary aristocracy from developing.

TESTING BUREAUCRATS

In 124 B.C.E., to help create a scholarly elite, the government established an imperial university that would train Confucian scholars. It was open to any male and offered instruction in the five Confucian classics including the *Analects*. Scholars took a written examination to demonstrate they knew the classics, and the emperor was supposed to select his bureaucrats from among those who had passed the examinations. (When you take the SAT, you can thank the people of Han.) These scholar-officials were to administer the country.

Han leaders continued to give most government jobs to family members and others loyal to themselves, rather than to scholars, but the system of examinations was an important symbol and a step toward creating a government bureaucracy based on merit. It also helped create officials who would follow Confucian values. (In the United States, it was common after each election for the new administration to give government jobs to their friends and supporters. Civil service examinations were not introduced in the United States until 1887. American officials got the idea from the British, who had borrowed it from the Chinese.)

The Han tried to at least appear to adopt Confucian attitudes toward laws and punishments. Laws did not take into account relationships between people, so they missed the essence of Confucian situation ethics where no single standard could be applied to everyone. In addition, Confucius had taught that punishments and rules were only needed when one was dealing with uncivilized people, particularly nomads, but that cultured Chinese should imitate the moral examples of their superiors.

Now that most fighting had stopped, soldiers dropped to the lowest position in society. One need only read *The Art of War* to understand how amoral military actions have to be. Confucius had said that good iron is not used for nails and good men do not become soldiers. Humane men and women should solve their differences peacefully. Armies should only be needed against barbarians who solve disputes with the sword.

However much they preached moral authority as the basis of their legitimacy and wrote histories to enshrine Confucian values, the Han continued to use rules, punishments, and military authority. The army played a major role during the dynasty, not only protecting the borders but controlling domestic violence as well. The prevalence of Confucian historians during the Han and later times may help explain why many historians have tended to believe that the army and military force were not important in Chinese history.

THINK FAMILY FIRST

Confucius had emphasized the importance of the family, and during Han times, the family, not the individual, was the central unit of society. People thought of themselves not as individuals but as members of a certain family and clan. Moreover, a family included not only living members but also all the ancestors who continue to care about their family. Filial piety was central and young people learned to respect parents, ancestors, older people, and tradition in the home. (Try answering the question "Who am I?" Do you say "I am a girl" or "I am a boy"? Do you say "I am smart" or "I am fascinating to be with"? How many of you identify yourself as part of an organization, cultural group, or religion saying "I am African American," or "I am a Jew" or "I am a boy scout"? How many say "I am a member of my family"? How many of you think of yourselves primarily as an individual rather than as a member of any group?)

The family served numerous functions. Reverence for ancestors was the main religious expression. Elders kept ancestral altars in their homes and supervised rituals to remember and honor the dead. Sons kept the family line going. In the home young people learned filial piety, one of Confucius' central ideas, and boys and girls learned to act graciously by imitating how family members acted.

Economic security often came from jobs families provided for their members, and both old and young, as well as those who were sick or disabled, counted on their families to take care of them. The family was also the center of a person's social life, and family rituals and celebrations were important sources of entertainment. Learning to obey their parents made it easy for people to be obedient subjects of the state as well. If each member of society graciously fulfilled his or her responsibilities to others in the society, the result, in theory, would be a harmonious land.

When we think of living in a family, we often want things to be just and fair. We expect parents to treat each child fairly, distributing chores and rewards equally. Perhaps you have heard family members say something like, "That's not fair. You didn't make Johnny clean *his* room. Why must I clean mine?" or "You let my brother stay out after 12 o'clock. Why can't I say out, too?" We often complain if things are not fair. The good Confucian family, by contrast, was supposed to strive for harmony rather than justice. Father, after much consideration and thought, said what was to be done, and then everyone else tried to carry out his wish with the least amount of friction or debate. If a member of the family was treated unfairly, he or she tried to swallow the hurt and subsume his wants, working instead to create harmony in the family as a whole. Most rural families were self-supporting, making their own food, clothing and utensils, so getting along as a family was crucial if they were to prosper.

By establishing the family as the center of Confucian values and believing that every child could be molded into a good person, the Han attempted to solve the problem of what might happen when the government became corrupt and the leader lost the Mandate. Leaders did not have to rely on the central government to set cultural and moral standards, so a breakdown of central authority should not threaten traditional values. Reverence for ancestors and keeping alive the memory and deeds of past family members significantly contributed to the country's stability.

Be a Daoist on Weekends

Although the Confucian ethic was very important, people needed some relief from constantly thinking about their duties. Any great society needs to promote art, music, and other creative expressions that give life joy and meaning. To fill this need, Han leaders integrated Daoism in their synthesis. Perhaps it is fair to suggest that within the Han synthesis, people were Confucianists during the week and Daoists on weekends. When all the strict self-control required by Confucianism became too much to bear, Daoism provided an escape. An individual could take time off, relax, and just let things happen.

The Han Synthesis

They could revive their spirits by being close to nature, and if unable to get away to the countryside, at least they could contemplate a landscape painting or read some poetry. Daoist reverence for nature became a central value for the people of Han who were taught to live in harmony with their surroundings and not try to dominate or control nature.

Daoists cautioned rulers not to seek a fight but instead to "take the lower position," to bend so as not to break. A good leader follows the natural energies of the universe and lets the *Dao* empower him, delegating authority and making people feel they have accomplished everything on their own.

Daoist ideas also influenced the Han attitude toward war. War results from greed, when people are not content with what they have.

War leads to suffering, misery, and destruction, the *Daodejing* warned. When resources are used for the military, they cannot be used for the people:

> When the Way [*Dao*] prevails in the empire, fleet-footed horses are relegated to plowing the fields; when the Way does not prevail in the empire, war-horses breed on the border. (#46)

On land where armies have fought, only weeds and brambles grow and famines result. Daoists advised leaders to use warfare only for defensive purposes. The *Daodejing* advised:

> When one is compelled to use them [arms], it is best to do so without relish. There is no glory in victory, and to glorify it despite this is to exalt in the killing of men. (#31)

It stated:

> When numerous people are being slaughtered,
> We should participate in war with sorrow and grief.
> When the battle has been victorious,
> We should treat it as a funeral ceremony. (#31)

In general, the Han dynasty maintained this official attitude toward war. In theory troops were stationed along the Great Wall for defense to keep nomads out, and military campaigns were to be used to maintain control over trade routes rather than to annex more territory. When rulers had to use troops against the people to keep order or put down a revolt, that was a sure sign that the emperor was losing the Mandate. However, as in most systems of legitimacy based on moral principles, the Han maintained a large army for defense and also to increase the territory it controlled.

How Were Women Expected to Act?

Although no history of daily life has survived from Han times, documents that have survived reveal important Chinese values including the idea that you'll be like those with whom you associate. In a book written about 40 B.C.E., there is a description of the mother of the renowned Confucian scholar Mencius.:

> Mencius lost his father when he was only three years old, and his mother had to make a living. Mother Meng placed a great hope on her son.
>
> They lived not far from a cemetery. Mencius often played games with other boys to mimic how people buried the dead and mourned for the dead. Mother Meng decided to move out, believing that this neighborhood was no place to bring up a child.
>
> She found a house near a marketplace. But before long Mencius began to play at hawking goods and haggling prices with neighborhood kids like street peddlers and shopkeepers. Mother Meng decided that the environment was not good for the boy, either.
>
> Again she moved. This time she took care to examine the neighborhood before moving in. Their new home was near a school. There they settled down. The boy began to pattern himself after the pupils in the school. Mother Meng was pleased. . . . Mencius then played games of ancestor sacrifices and practiced the common courtesies between students and teachers. His mother said, "At last, this is the right place for my son!" There they remained.

Ban Zhao (ca. 45–116 C.E.), the sister of one of the most famous Han historians, wrote several works including *Lessons for Women*, a set of practical guidelines for women's everyday lives. She wrote:

> Let a woman modestly yield to others; let her respect others; let her put others first, herself last. Should she do something good, let her not mention it; should she do something bad, let her not deny it. Let her bear disgrace; let her even endure when others speak or do evil to her. Always let her seem to tremble and to fear. . . .
>
> According to the "Rites," it is the rule to begin to

teach children to read at the age of eight years, and by
the age of fifteen years they ought to be ready for cultural training. Only why should it not be that girls'
education as well as boys' be according to this principle? . . .

Let the woman not act contrary to the wishes and
the opinions of parents-in-law about right and wrong;
let her not dispute with them what is straight and
what is crooked. Such docility may be called obedience which sacrifices opinion. Therefore the ancient
book, *A Pattern for Women*, says: 'If a daughter-in-
law who follows the wishes of her parents-in-law is
like an echo and shadow, how could she not be
praised?"

Invented by the Han

Because Han rule brought an end to most internal conflicts and rivalries, more resources were available to support artists and scientists,
and many innovations were developed that soon spread to other areas.
The director of the Han imperial workshops announced in 105 C.E.
that paper, much like what you use today, had been invented to
replace writing on strips of bamboo or on wood or silk. Perhaps it is

Wheelbarrow

not surprising that the Han fostered
the invention of paper since writing
and scholarship was so important to
them. Besides the scholars' interest
in historic records and the
Confucian classics, bureaucrats had
to keep careful records of things
such as tax payments and corvée
service. Historical writing, poetry,
and literature also flourished.

Ships improved after the Chinese invented the sternpost rudder.
Perhaps as early as 200 B.C.E. the
Han had invented a form of horse
collar that also enhanced trans-

portation. Instead of choking the horse, as earlier harnesses had done, this collar had a strap that went around the horse's chest, allowing it to pull heavy loads. They invented the water mill that used running water to turn a grindstone. At the end of the Han time, they invented the wheelbarrow, which they called the wooden ox. And silk, while not invented during the Han, was further refined and became an important item of trade during this period.

The Han paid a great deal of attention to improving crops. One innovation transformed how they planted seeds. Instead of just broadcasting them (throwing seeds onto the land), they divided each field into furrows separated by ridges and then carefully dropped the seeds into the furrows. When peasants weeded the ridges, soil that fell around the new plants supported the stalks. Watering was easier, and by rotating ridges and furrows, what was sown and what lay fallow (unplanted) was also rotated. Peasants improved poor soil by mixing in ashes, manure, dead plants, and human waste (called night soil).

Emperor Wu Di Extends the Han Empire

Emperor Wu Di ruled the Early Han for 53 years from 140 to 87 B.C.E. He wanted to maintain tight control over the country and make his ministers report directly to him. At the same time he was sympathetic to the role Confucianism and Confucian scholars could play. Although he chose his bureaucrats from among those who had passed the examinations, he tried to make sure that scholars whose answers reflected Legalist ideas passed. In this way, Wu Di supported Confucian principles, symbolized by the exam, but manipulated them to suit his own purposes.

Emperor Wu was not opposed to using the military to increase the territory he ruled. He extended the borders of his empire to include what is now Manchuria, North Korea, the northern area of Vietnam, and parts of Central Asia.

Although Confucian values downplayed the role of merchants, trade was important during Han times. In fact, it was during Wu Di's reign that significant traffic and trade began to develop between China and the Mediterranean world along what has come to be called the Silk Roads. Because he was probably most concerned with ensuring that merchants and their goods traveled safely along the emerging

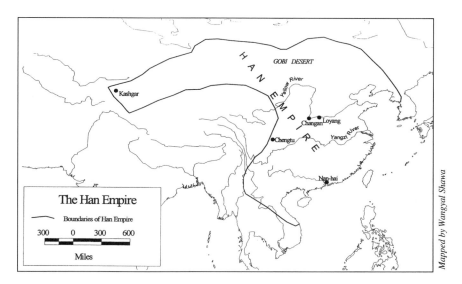

Mapped by Wangyal Shawa

trade routes, Wu Di allowed the people in these areas to maintain their way of life as long as they paid tribute to China.

Local Landlords Gain Power

Keeping local landlords from building up their own power base and threatening the central authority was a constant challenge to Han leaders, as it was to all imperial governments. In order to prevent the build-up of new large estates, the government abolished primogeniture (where the eldest son inherits all his father's property) and required that all sons inherit the same amount of land. It also hoped the scholar-bureaucrats would be a counter-force to the landed nobility.

But scholars were appointed by the emperor, so their jobs were never very secure. They knew they should serve the emperor as good Confucian civil servants who put the emperor's interests above their own. On the other hand, also as good Confucians, they had to think of the interests of their families and clans.

As a result, scholar-officials began buying up land and accumulating large estates so they would have some security to fall back on if they lost their government jobs. Gradually, they became a new class of local landlords. Their estates were often off the tax rolls, which increased the tax burden on small farmers, many of whom had very little land and were struggling just to feed their families on the food they grew. When the local officials tried to force peasants to pay, some sough refuge with a local landlord, asking to live on his estate in exchange for working the land, further reducing the government's income and increasing the landlord's power base.

Why Did the Early Han Lose Control?

Emperor Wu Di tried to find new ways to get funds to run the government besides taxing the peasants. One of his strategies was "leveling." The government bought up food in areas where there was a surplus and resold it in areas where people did not have enough. Wu Di hoped this plan would bring wealth to the government; instead it helped stabilize prices and prevent starvation. (This idea may have inspired an American Secretary of Agriculture under President Franklin Roosevelt to create an "every normal granary" in order to stabilize farm prices in the United States.) Fearing merchants would form monopolies, the government took control of minting copper coins, making salt, and producing iron. Among Wu Di's less successful ideas were having criminals pay for their crimes instead of other punishments and selling government jobs to merchants.

As conditions worsened during the last years before the common era, Wang Mang, an official close to the throne, gained enough support to take over the government and establish his own dynasty and rule from 9 to 23 C.E. Claiming to be a true Confucian who would bring back the stable government of the early Zhou, Wang Mang tried to introduce several significant reforms. In an effort to re-institute the equal field system, he set limits on the amount of land any one family could own and tired to break up large estates, redistributing the excess land to poor peasants. He made slavery illegal, regulated merchants, and tried to adjust officials' salaries depending on the quality of the harvest.

Idealistic as these reforms seemed, they met with a great deal of resistance. Both rich landlords and officials opposed them. In addition, a series of natural disasters — including a major flood on the Yellow River that shifted its course from north to south of the

Shandong Peninsula — caused a great deal of suffering. When desperate peasants rioted in search of food, Wang Mang interpreted their actions as a challenge to his authority and sent the army to put down the unrest. In the general turmoil that ensued, he was killed and the Han dynasty reestablished its control of the country.

For two centuries the Han had ruled a united China, and the Later Han would rule China for an additional 200 years. The Han synthesis, with its centralized control moderated by officials schooled in the Confucian value system and tempered by Daoist attitudes, brought peace and stability to the country, which even Wang Mang's rule did not seriously disrupt. That stability as well as Han influence over territories in Central Asia helped stimulate a great deal of cross cultural exchangest. Before we consider what eventually happed the Later Han and the Roman empires, we shall examine the Roman Empire and cross-cultural contacts that played such an important role during this era.

THE TRIUMPH OF LAW
AND THE MILITARY
IN THE ROMAN EMPIRE

Setting the Stage

The Italian peninsula resembles a 700-mile long boot, bordered by the Adriatic and Mediterranean Seas. Shielded from the rest of Northwest Eurasia by the Alps, a strong of high mountains on its northern border, the peninsula is divided down the middle by the Apennines, a low-lying mountain range that posed little obstacle to exchanges and travel. A few good harbors dot the coastline and the temperature is mild; the rainfall is sufficient for agriculture and the soil is rich and fertile.

The Roman Republic Enters the Drama

The Romans were relative latecomers to the human drama. Sometime after 1500 B.C.E., Latins and other groups moved into the Italian

peninsula and settled along the Tiber River. Etruscans, who lived north of the Tiber River, conquered these Latin farming communities in the early part of the first millennium B.C.E. During the Axial Age, Rome was only a small settlement along the Tiber, ruled by Etruscan kings.

Resenting Etruscan rule, in 509 B.C.E., just before the Greek city-states got involved in the Persian Wars, Roman farmers overthrew the Etruscans and established a republic. A republic is a state where the citizens exercise political power by choosing representatives, who make political decisions on their behalf. The ruler, if there is one, does not have the final authority a king would have; the people do through their representatives.

During the early days of the Republic in the fifth century, Romans concentrated on farming and defending their rich farmland. Farmers in the Tiber River valley gave their primary loyalty to their families where the father's word was law. The family was responsible for educating the children and taking care of sick and elderly members. Romans remembered and respected ancestors as well. They tried to be well-disciplined, down-to-earth, and loyal, and they valued serious-

Roman farmer

ness of purpose, tenacity, training to promote steadiness of character, hard work, and simple tastes.

Land in the Tiber valley was richer than land in the surrounding areas, and no natural barriers isolated it from outsiders who might try to take it by force. Farmers had to be ready and willing to defend not only their own land but their neighbors' land as well. Gradually these independent farmers became citizen-soldiers of their republic.

In emergencies, Romans gave absolute power to one person they called a dictator, but he was expected to relinquish that power as soon as the crisis ended. Cincinnatus, an able soldier and a hard-working farmer, had done just that. When their farms were threatened, Cincinnatus had reluctantly become dictator, but as soon as the emergency was over, he willingly relinquished power and returned to farming. (Cincinnatus was one of George Washington's heroes. When the Revolutionary War was over, Washington tried to retire to Mount Vernon, and he founded the Order of Cincinnatus.)

Why Should Patricians Have All the Power?

Roman society was divided into two main groups: patricians and plebeians. Patricians, the aristocrats who had most of the power, came from old established landowners' families. They were members of the Senate, the governing body that made the important decisions. Plebeians were poorer farmers who had very little political power. They paid high taxes and were often in debt, and they could be sold into debt-slavery if they failed to pay back their loans. There was no mobility between plebeians and patricians: plebeians could never become patricians even if they were rich.

Rich plebeians, like the rising merchant class in Athens at about the same time, wanted more respect and power. For them, the government was a republic in name only because they could not vote, and patricians did not represent their interests. Like poor farmers in Athens, they saw no reason to risk their lives fighting to defend someone else's power. They threatened to refuse to fight and to emigrate and form new settlements where they would be the aristocrats.

Patricians needed the plebeians, so, as aristocrats in Athens had done, the patricians gradually granted plebeians some political rights. In 450 B.C.E. the Romans wrote down and publicly displayed a code of laws they called the Twelve Tables, so everyone knew what he or she was supposed to do. Plebeians got their own Assembly where they made decisions affecting themselves. They elected two officials called Tribunes who attended the Senate and could veto any law the Senate passed. In 440 B.C.E. new laws allowed plebeians and patricians to intermarry. After 367, plebeians could serve in the bureaucracy as magistrates (officials who enforced the laws), and plebeian ex-magistrates were eligible to serve in the Senate. There was also an Assembly of Centuries, composed of citizens with military equipment; men with better equipment had more power.

Is Offense the Best Defense?

Roman citizen-soldiers soon realized that offense was often the best defense, and they gradually increased the area they controlled. Conquering new land brought wealth from the spoils of war and kept men in good condition for both farming and fighting. Merchants favored expansion because it created new trade routes, markets, and more raw materials. Even the average soldier favored conquests that might mean he got new land or, at least, earned glory fighting for his homeland. First Rome dominated the Latin towns south of the Tiber, then it conquered the central part of the peninsula, then Etruscan territory in the north, and finally the Hellenic colonies along the southern coast.

Romans tended to be excellent soldiers, not only because they wanted to protect their own land but also because their devotion to elders in their families had taught them to be obedient and respectful of authority. Roman leaders used several tactics other than open warfare to take over the peninsula. They rewarded people who became their allies with land, spoils, and even citizenship, so some areas did not resist them. Often they did not demand tax or tribute from those areas, but only required them to provide troops, for "mutual defense," should the need arise. They convinced some communities to make defensive alliances with them, assuring Roman legion protection. They weakened some areas by stirring up local trouble and then intervened in order to restore peace and "save" these areas. They also built defenses in the north to keep Gauls, who lived north of the Alps, and other possible invaders out of the peninsula.

Rome Fights Three Wars against Carthage

Having gained control over the entire peninsula by 268 B.C.E., they turned their attention to territories beyond the mainland that might threaten their security. Carthage, a Phoenician settlement on the North Africa coast directly across the Mediterranean Sea from the Italian peninsula, appeared to be Rome's only significant threat in the Western Mediterranean. Carthage was one of a string of colonies the Phoenicians, effective sea-faring traders, had established. Rome fought three wars against Carthage, known as the Punic Wars (because Romans called Phoenician Carthage "Punicus").

By winning the First Punic War (264–241 B.C.E.) Rome gained control over Sicily, Corsica, and Sardinia. During the Second Punic War (218–201 B.C.E.), about the same time that the Han Empire was consolidating its power in China, the Macedonians made an alliance with Carthage, hoping Carthage would defend them against growing Roman power. The Romans, in turn, made alliances with several Hellenic city-states that hoped Rome would liberate them from Macedonian control. When Rome defeated Carthage, Roman legions and soldiers from those Hellenic city-states attacked the Macedonian forces. Macedonia lost and Rome took control of both its Hellenic allies and the Macedonians.

Carthage fought Rome one more time, and the Third Punic War lasted from 149 to 146 B.C.E. This time the Roman forces completely destroyed the city and took control over all of North Africa and Spain. By 146 B.C.E. Rome dominated the Mediterranean world. Perhaps reluctantly and without even realizing it, the Romans were building an empire in very much the same way groups in west Asia had been establishing control for several millennia.

Military Success Transforms the Roman Republic

Rome's military success fundamentally changed the character of both Roman soldiers and the Roman Republic. Early Roman citizen-soldiers had fought to defend their farms. While these "defensive maneuvers" sometimes had taken them far afield, each time they returned to their land, families, and traditional values. Gradually a full-time professional army developed, and many of these soldiers fought not to protect their land but to get spoils. Generals used battles to ensure that their troops remained loyal and to obtain resources with which to feed, reward, arm and pay them, and soldiers became dependent on their generals' skills and leadership.

The new policy of expansion indirectly hurt many Roman farmers. Because Rome gained control over excellent farmland, it could import grain and other goods more cheaply than Roman farmers could produce them, lowering farm prices and making it difficult for Roman farmers to sell their produce. Without markets, farmers went into debt and had to sell their land. But ex-farmers had trouble finding jobs, because returning soldiers often brought back slaves who did farm work. Many ex-farmers migrated to the cities, hoping to find work. As their numbers increased, they made up a growing population of urban, unemployed poor. They had nothing they could call their own except their children, and became known as the proletariat.

The extension of Roman rule brought other changes. Working as magistrates in the newly conquered areas was profitable because provincial officials could keep a portion of the taxes they collected. Senators competed for those jobs, and many were quite wealthy when they returned to Rome after serving in a province. Land was the traditional source of status, security, and well-being, so these ex-officials often used their new wealth to buy more land. Small farmers, many of whom were heavily in debt, were tempted to sell their land, because soldiers and magistrates paid high prices. Soon those farmers used up the money they had gotten for their land and were left without jobs or any kind of security. Many joined the growing urban proletariat.

How Do Reformers Address Unrest and Inequality?

The widening gap between rich landowners and poor proletariat led to a great deal of tension in the city of Rome between 120 and 20 B.C.E. If the government had limited the amount of grain imported into Rome, that would have raised the prices Roman farmers got for their produce and created a market for their goods. The government could also have passed laws that limited the amount of land people could own. Two brothers, Tiberius and Gaius Gracchus, worked for those reforms. When Tiberius was elected tribune, he tried to limit the amount of land any one person could own, but instead of passing his reforms, several senators killed him. His younger brother Gaius, also elected tribune, continued his brother's efforts to help the poor by advocating food subsidies and making land available. However, the large landholders in the Senate feared this might lead to open rebellion against their power and they had Gaius murdered in 121 B.C.E.

To try to pacify the proletariat and divert their attention from their problems, Roman leaders began offering the poor "bread and circuses." They distributed some of the excess imported grain as a dole, or handout, to the poor and put on lavish, often violent, performances in the Coliseum to keep people entertained. Gladiators, trained to carry on public duels to the death, delighted gaping spectators and distracted people from the serious economic inequality.

Still claiming to be a republic with a government that ruled on behalf of the citizens, one leader after another seized control, proclaiming himself dictator because the civil unrest had created a state of emergency. Soldiers returning to Rome were loyal to their generals, who used their troops to get charge of the government.

What Reforms Does Julius Caesar Institute?

In 60 B.C.E. three leaders — Pompey (a powerful general who conquered Syria and Palestine), Julius Caesar (a brilliant general and master politician who was proconsul of Gaul), and Crassus (a Roman financier and politician) — formed the First Triumvirate (rule of three men). They agreed to rule jointly, but Caesar and his army were far away in Gaul. When Crassus was killed trying to occupy Syria, Pompey had himself declared sole dictator and ordered Caesar to return to Rome without his army. When Caesar ignored Pompey's command and crossed the Rubicon River with his army, Pompey fled to Greece, where Caesar's army defeated him in 48 B.C.E. Caesar then declared himself dictator for life.

Caesar had already proven he was a masterful general, and he turned out to be a very able statesman and politician as well and attempted numerous reforms. He weakened the power of the Senate and increased its membership. He extended Roman citizenship to people beyond the Italian peninsula. In place of the lunar calendar the Romans had been using, Caesar instituted the Julian calendar with 365 and 1/4 days. He tried to check the corruption of provincial officers and make them accountable to Rome, and he reformed provincial taxes. To ease the plight of the poor, he used government funds to finance major public works projects that provided jobs for the unemployed, including draining swamps around Rome. His opponents, led by his friend Brutus and the ambitious Gaius Crassus, feared Caesar was getting too popular and too powerful and in 44 B.C.E. they killed him.

Octavian Comes to Power

Caesar had designated Octavian, his grandnephew and adopted son, as his heir. But Mark Antony, another powerful general, tried to prevent Octavian from taking over and envisioned establishing his own power base in the Ptolemic Kingdom of Egypt which was then ruled by Cleopatra VII.

In the face of expanding Roman power, the Egyptian queen tried to

Cleopatra as Goddess Isis

use romantic intrigue rather than armed might to secure her kingdom's independence from the Roman threat. She attempted to link her personal and political future first to Julius Caesar, then Mark Antony. Caesar was smitten with the Egyptian queen and their intimate relationship ensured Egypt's independence for the time being. After Caesar's death, Antony, who had also fallen in love with Cleopatra, began to give land from the Roman Empire to Cleopatra and her children, fathered by himself and Caesar.

Octavian suspected that Antony and Cleopatra were planning to seize control of the whole Roman Empire and rule from Egypt, and many Romans feared Antony was succumbing to the luxuries of the "East." Consequently, Octavian made war on his rivals and defeated them at Actium, a small island near Greece, in 31 B.C.E. Antony then fled to Egypt where he killed himself. In one last effort to save

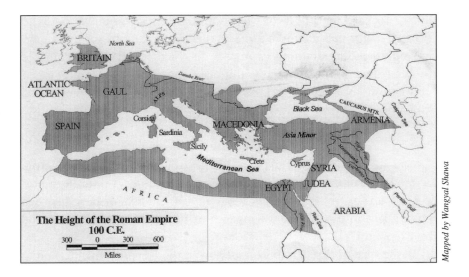

The Height of the Roman Empire
100 C.E.

Mapped by Wangyal Shawa

her kingdom, Cleopatra tried to seduce Octavian. Her charms rebuffed, she also committed suicide.

Octavian then took control of all Rome's territory, claiming he would restore a republic. However, in 27 B.C.E. the Senate named Octavian "Principes" ("first man" from which we get the word prince) and "Augustus" (majestic or exalted one), and he became known as Caesar Augustus or Emperor Augustus. By 27 B.C.E., the Roman Republic had become the Roman Empire. It would soon include most of the land Alexander had conquered except the Iranian plateau, and extend west all the way to the Iberian Peninsula and the British Isles.

The Augustan Synthesis

Caesar Augustus ruled over a vast, centrally controlled, pluralistic empire. Although the Romans retained the appearance of a republic by keeping the Senate, Augustus was an emperor with absolute power over a vast area of very diverse people. He did consult the Senate periodically and treated its members with respect, but he also packed the Senate with his own wealthy friends on whose votes he could count.

Historians call the 200-year period of relative peace during the first two centuries of the Common Era the *Pax Romana*. Greeks claimed to have changed the course of history when their armies defeated the

Emperor Augustus

Persian forces at Marathon, preventing the spread of Persian influences. However, Alexander absorbed much of the Persian model of kingship when he declared himself a god and demanded that his subjects bow down before him. Now the Roman Empire would build on the experience of earlier west Asian empires, taking on some of the same concepts of kingship, while still retaining the heritage of citizenship and law.

LAW AND THE MILITARY

Reliance on the military was a characteristic of both Roman and west Asian societies, in part because there were no natural barriers to protect them. Effective use of the military was certainly one reason for the *Pax Romana*. Half the army consisted of legions composed exclusively of citizens, and half was composed of troops recruited from around the empire. Gradually, colonized soldiers became assimilated to the legions' way of fighting, and soldiers became citizens when they retired. The thoroughly professional Roman army was equipped with the latest weapons and employed expert strategy.

The most favored Roman troops were the Praetorian Guards who guarded the headquarters (the praetorium) of the commander-in-chief. They were Augustus' personal bodyguards (similar to Alexander's Companions). Emperors after Augustus often bought their loyalty by paying them from three to ten times as much as regular legionaries received. Many troops protected the empire's frontiers against the ever-present threat of nomads.

The army helped unite the empire culturally as well. Men from all over the empire could be soldiers, and the common experience of miltary service bound them together. Soldiers tended to lose some of their local customs and loyalties and became romanized. They learned a simplified form of Latin so they could communicate. Roman soldiers spent much of their time protecting merchants, digging canals, and building bridges, aqueducts, and many of the roads, originally constructed so troops could move quickly.

Respect for law was another important characteristic of both Roman and west Asian societies. An efficient bureaucracy strengthens an empire, and Augustus tried to ensure that officials collected taxes fairly and enforced laws impartially. The Twelve Tables the Roman Senate had established 450 years earlier were the basis of the law code of both the republic and empire. It applied in the provinces, although local administrators adapted laws to fit regional conditions and allowed local precedents to influence decisions judges made. For example, governors tended to be lenient with Jewish communities, which did not strictly obey Roman laws.

CREATING LOYALTY TO ROME

In an effort to make people feel loyal to the Roman government, Augustus adopted symbols of west Asian kingship such as a crown, purple cape, throne, and a type of mace. Surrounded by pomp and ceremony, Augustus seemed larger than life, and some subjects called him the "savior of the world" and worshiped him, even though he denied his own divinity. After all, when his uncle Julius Caesar was declared the son of a god, that made Augustus nearly a god. Clearly, Augustus was infusing the Roman tradition of republican leadership with important elements of kingship from Egypt, Persia, and Alexander.

Augustus also cleverly identified himself with the civil religion and had the Senate declare him Protector of Rome. One meaning for the Latin *religio* (religion) is "to bind." Roman worship bound the gods to the people and the people to one another. As the preserver of old virtues, Augustus had 82 temples rebuilt and re-instituted earlier household sacrifices. Worship of Rome spread to the provinces, where people often considered Rome the center of all civilization.

Romans adapted many other cultural traditions, especially from Greece. They took gods and goddesses from the Hellenistic world, gave them Roman names, and added them to the Roman pantheon. For example, Athena became Minerva; Ares became Mars; and Zeus became Jupiter. The Egyptian cult of Isis also grew in popularity, and Romans built a temple to her in Rome. Another particularly popular deity among the women was Goddess Fortuna, who granted good luck to those she blessed. Many Roman soldiers adopted the worship of Mithra, probably originally an Aryan Sun god. Mithraism celebrated warrior virtues such as courage and endurance.

The major factions during Augustus' reign were the urban proletariat, middle class, aristocrats, and residents in the provinces. Augustus sought to balance the factionalism in Rome by offering each group something it wanted. He allowed the middle class to participate in the Senate and serve in the government. To pacify the potentially unruly proletariat, Augustus organized a systematic welfare system that gave each unemployed person grain, most of which was imported from Egypt. He also continued the lavish games and circuses. The welfare system kept the proletariat utterly dependent on the government and the public dole. Some did get temporary jobs on public building projects, but this employment only increased their depen-

The Roman Coliseum

dency on the government. Some become slaves in order to get enough food.

The city of Rome was the empire's epicenter and symbolized both Roman power and cultural achievements. Combining art with engineering, Romans created many remarkably practical achievements. The Coliseum, built about 70 C.E., covered five acres and could seat 50,000; the Circus Maximus, a racetrack and stadium, held 250,000 fans. Romans built massive structures, and their art adorned useful buildings such as public baths numbering over 1,000 in Rome alone.

Alexandria, a major cultural and intellectual center of the Hellenistic world, became a center of trade during Roman times because of its excellent harbor, and this city was second only to Rome in wealth and prestige. The Lighthouse in its port, completed in 270 B.C.E., was dedicated to the goddess Isis. A fire burned night and day in the 400-foot tower of this ancient skyscraper, and historians claimed its light was visible for 100 miles.

Augustus left a prosperous and secure empire of growing wealth and power. The republic was gone, but Roman power extended from west Asia, around the Mediterranean Sea, and into much of western Eurasia. Except for brief uprisings, the Pax Romana brought 200 years of relative peace. During that time trade flourished within and beyond the empire.

The Origin of Christianity

The Roman government tended to be very tolerant toward the diverse groups within the empire and encouraged cultural pluralism. Local rulers appointed by Rome generally favored Hellenism; for example, King Herod (37–4 B.C.E.), a Hellenized Jew, encouraged Greek culture at his court but also rebuilt the Temple of Jerusalem and carefully observed Jewish law. Even so, Roman citizens were expected to honor the emperor above all, give their allegiance to Rome, and worship Roman gods and goddesses.

Palestine at the beginning of the common era exemplifies the mixing of cultures that characterized the cities and towns along the major trading routes of the hemisphere. The area included several Hellenistic cities that were heavily influenced by Greek language, philosophy, and lifestyle. Many Jews living in Palestine felt threatened by the appeal of Hellenistic culture. They also resented living under Roman rule, and as strict monotheists, they strongly resisted efforts to make them worship Roman deities and acknowledge the emperor as supreme.

Some Jewish groups talked openly about breaking away from Roman rule. Many hoped a messiah (an "anointed one") would come to deliver them from Roman control and establish a state like King David's a millennium earlier. Scores of prophets, in the tradition of Amos, were warning Jews against becoming absorbed into the larger cosmopolitan society and urging them to return to the worship of the one true god and more pious lives. When an obscure preacher named Jesus, one of many such teachers of that time, started talking about the Kingdom of God, some Jews wondered if he might possibly be the Messiah.

Jesus was born in Nazareth in approximately 4 B.C.E and grew up in this period of ferment in Palestine. Besides stories about his miraculous birth, when a star appeared in the heavens to guide wise men traveling to honor the babe, almost nothing is known about his personal life. Young Jesus obviously experienced Roman oppression and knew the threat Hellenism posed to Jews. His frequent criticisms of the rich and powerful may have been directed to those Jews who had a fondness for upper class Greek lifestyles and what he saw as their concern with ritual rather than justice and compassion.

Jesus emphasized two commandments, which became the foundation of his message: "Love the Lord your God with all your heart and all your mind" and "Love your neighbor as yourself." He taught love, forgiveness, peace, and nonviolence, symbolized by turning the other cheek. "If anyone wants to sue you and take you coat, give him your cloak as well." (Matthew 5:40) Jesus taught compassion and tempered the Jewish dedication to justice by telling his followers, "Do not judge, so that you may not be judged." (Matthew 7:1) In the Sermon on the Mount, one of his most famous teachings, Jesus said:

You have heard that it was said, "You shall love your neighbor and hate your enemy." But I say to you, Love your enemies and pray for those who persecute you . . . (Matthew 5:43-44)

The teaching style of Jesus relied heavily on parables, short simple stories that covey a message or moral. For example, he told about a shepherd who left his other 99 sheep to find the one that was lost and about a poor widow who was overjoyed when she found one lost coin. He told about a prodigal (wasteful) son who had left home, gotten into trouble, and wasted his inheritance. When he returned home, his father rejoiced and celebrated his return. Jesus used these stories to illustrate God's love and forgiveness.

Jesus urged people to follow a communal life and share their wealth and talents. He spent time with the poor, outcasts, and sinners. In the Sermon on the Mount he taught that the meek would inherit the earth and that the poor would gain the Kingdom of Heaven. Most important, he claimed the end of the world was imminent and that when it came, God would judge both the living and the dead. Good people would be resurrected to live eternally with God, while evil ones would suffer eternal damnation.

Was Jesus the Messiah?

Many Jews, known as Zealots, thought Jesus was the Messiah and expected him to oppose the Roman government. Instead Jesus spoke about a heavenly kingdom where people would dwell with God after they died. Even so, the Roman authorities feared Jesus was stirring unrest and, with support from at least part of the Jewish community, decided to end his teaching. When he was only 33 years old, Jesus traveled to Jerusalem for the Passover celebration and was arrested by Roman authorities, tried for his heretical views, and sentenced to death by crucifixion. However, his death did not end his story. His followers believed Jesus rose from the dead after three days and appeared several times to some of them during the first forty days after his resurrection. At the Pentecost celebration, his followers sensed his presence and with this experience of the Holy Spirit, the Christian community was born.

Early Christians fervently believed Jesus would return to earth within their own lifetime and bring about the end of the world. But as the years passed and Jesus did not return, Christians began to organize. A handful of disciples, many of them women, banded together, called their communities churches, and spread the "Good News" that Jesus had triumphed over death.

In about 70 C.E. several followers wrote down what they could remember or had heard about the life and teachings of Jesus, and these writings, the Gospels, became the first four books of what Christians call the New Testament of the Bible. The Christian Bible includes the Old Testament — the Jewish scriptures or Hebrew Bible — as well as the New Testament that tells about Jesus and the early Christian community, and includes letters of advice to young churches, many written by Paul.

Paul, a Jew from Asia Minor who had never seen Jesus, initially attacked Jews who had become Christians and no longer followed orthodox Jewish beliefs and practices. While traveling on the road to Damascus one day, he experienced a sudden conversion to Christianity. Convinced Jesus had never intended to preach only to Jews, Paul devoted the remainder of his life to teaching Gentiles (non-Jews) about Jesus' resurrection and how they, too, could overcome death.

Paul became the most important early Christian, working tirelessly throughout Asia Minor and Greece to help people organize Christian communities and writing them letters of encouragement. Teaching that Jesus was not only a Jewish messiah but a universal redeemer, whose message applied to everyone, Paul called Jesus "Christ," the Greek word for messiah, and earnestly spread the Good News, organizing missionaries throughout the empire.

Can Christians Build a Following?

Early converts to this new faith came from all social classes. Many impoverished people found comfort in Jesus' message. In Rome Christianity appealed especially to wealthy, high status women. Both Hellenistic and Rome society devalued women, particularly wives. It was common practice to kill newborn baby girls, and daughters were looked on as a liability. Since Christians opposed infanticide and prohibited divorce and incest, as well as polygamy (having several wives), many Roman women readily embraced the new faith. The conversion of pagans by their wives was an important reason for the spread of Christianity. Additionally, many soldiers were attracted to Christianity and spread and actively spread the faith among the legions.

As long as only a few people were attracted by the Christian message, leaders considered the new faith merely a nuisance. Even so, from time to time Roman authorities persecuted Christians who refused to accept the divinity of the emperor, serve in the army, or pay their taxes. Some who would not renounce their faith were put to death. Emperors also used Christians as scapegoats, blaming them for political unrest or natural disasters.

Persecution helped Christianity spread. When Christians were attacked, they forgot their petty jealousies and clung together, protecting and comforting one another. In addition, early martyrs seemed to go to their deaths joyously, smiling serenely as the lions charged. Many non-Christians wondered what special truth these mad martyrs possessed.

Christianity, like Buddhism, was open to all people, and Christian converts had the zeal and enthusiasm new converts often have. They believed they had been promised eternal life in heaven after death, and they were not to worship other gods or participate in other rituals. Some Christians performed miracles, including driving out demons and curing the sick, and exorcism of demons was one of the most sought-after services of the early Christians. Even so, at first the Christian community was comparatively small, and the power and authority of the Roman government was often set against it. If Christianity was to survive and prosper, it would have to find new homes in places far from its origins, adapting to new cultural forms and traditions that it encountered.

During the *Pax Romana*, Roman authority reached across Eurasia, and many Romans thought its power was invincible. During the first century C. E., most of the leaders in government, trade, and the arts did not even consider whether this strange and otherworldly religion would pose any threat to such a powerful and prosperous empire. However, the new faith was gaining converts among all classes, and missionaries were spreading the Good News throughout the hemisphere to Africa, inner Asia and India. We now turn to examine how cross-cultural exchanges, such as the spread of Christianity and Buddhism, are promoting a hemisphere-wide zone of communication and interaction, as people exchange not only commercial goods but cultural values as well.

SCENE FIVE

ROADS AND ROUTES ACROSS AFRO-EURASIA

Setting the Stage

Although cross-cultural trade had existed for millennia, after 200 B.C.E. the volume of trade increased dramatically and continued to grow until about 400 C.E. Between about 200 B.C.E. and the beginning of the common era, merchants and traders carried on regular exchanges across central Asia from China to the eastern Mediterranean. A brisk seaborne trade also developed as traders sailed back and forth across the Mediterranean, through the Red Sea and Persian Gulf, across the Indian Ocean to South and southeast Asia, and from there northeast to China. By the start of the common era, the relative absence of war and the expansion of communication networks provided by the Han, Parthian, Kushan, and Roman empires made travel and trade much safer and more profitable and facilitated the spread of ideas across the hemisphere.

This hemispheric trade and cultural exchange spawned a number of cosmopolitan cites and aided the growth of political centers. Cities such as Changan, Patna, Taxila, Persepolis, Alexandria, Constantinople, and Rome provided arenas where traders, merchants, artists, scientists, and philosophers could freely mingle in streets, markets, rest houses, and universities and share ideas. Zoroastrians, Jews, and later Christians, could exchange views with one another and with Buddhists, Hindus, and devotees of Isis. Greek geometry met Indian mathematics and metallurgy, while Indian concepts of yoga and renunciation mingled with Christian notions of prayer and martyrdom. Scholars could discuss Roman law with followers of Confucian ideas of social harmony. Moreover, important contributions from various centers of civilization were available to people throuhout Eurasia and areas of Africa.

Trade within the Roman Empire

Trade contributed to Rome's strength and stability in several ways. Trade made merchants rich, provided markets for goods that farmers grew, and gave the empire a strong tax base. Rome instituted a uniform currency, and Latin became the common language of trade, enabling businessmen from a variety of cultures within the empire to understand one another.

Like the Persians before them, Romans were great road builders. They constructed 60,000 miles of roads to connect the 100 million people in the empire. Using the arch that made it possible to span vast spaces, they constructed impressive aqueducts and bridges, many of which are still in use today. Traders transported their goods on the excellent roads and bridges, and soldiers made travel fairly safe.

Trade made the entire Roman empire interdependent. Bread sold in Rome was made with flour imported from Egypt. Taxes collected in Syria helped finance Rome's monumental building projects. Merchants financed pottery commissioned in Greece. Contact and exchanges also extended well beyond the borders of the Roman Empire to the far reaches of the hemisphere.

The Han Tributary System

Many Chinese communities were self-sufficient, so trade was not as critical within the Han Empire as in Rome. Han officials put traders and other businessmen next to the bottom of their social hierarchy, viewing them essentially as parasites that lived off the honest labor of farmers and artisans without adding any value to the goods they sold. Despite this official Confucian view of merchants, the Chinese created a complex trading system in which the roles of merchants and court officials were often interchangeable.

Officially the Han claimed they had no desire to trade with their inferior neighbors and demanded tribute instead. However, the Han used several methods to exchange goods. In order to keep the nomads from invading, Han leaders would often send them gifts. They also arranged marriages with nomadic leaders, sending large dowries, which could include money, cloth, animals, and other goods, with the Chinese brides. When a nomadic group was strong, it might require the court to provide a fixed amount of goods each year.

The most significant means of exchange was the tributary system. The Han required neighboring groups to pay regular visits to the Han court, bringing gifts and kowtowing (bowing) before the Son of Heaven to acknowledge his superiority. But while they were at the court, the Han entertained these visitors lavishly and then gave the "ambassadors" even more valuable gifts in return. A great deal of informal bartering and exchange went on with their guards and retainers as well.

This tributary system seemed to please the Han leaders because it symbolized that they were superior while still allowing an exchange of goods. Some nomadic groups resented the demand for tribute, but if they got what they needed from China, they often played along with what they considered the myth of Han superiority. In addition, respect from the Han leader, which came from having visited the court, could enhance a nomadic leader's status.

Parthian Cavalry Ensures Safe Travel

The relative peace the people of Han and the Romans established enhanced hemispheric contacts. In between these two empires lay the Parthian and Kushan empires (or should we call them kingdoms?), which also contributed to cross-cultural contacts. The Parthians were a central Asian nomadic group that had originally lived near the Caspian Sea. In the middle of the third century B.C.E. they defeated the Seleucids and established control over the Iranian plateau, in part because they appealed to the local people's pride in the former Persian Empire. Claiming to be related to the Persians, the Parthians promised to reclaim Persian, not Hellenic, glory.

The Parthian Empire flourished from 248 B.C.E. to 224 C.E., almost exactly the same period as the Han. Initially little more than a loose confederation of small areas, at its height Parthia controlled land from the Tigris and Euphrates rivers across the Iranian plateau. Like the Persians before them, Parthian leaders allowed people to keep their own beliefs, and areas such as Armenia remained more or less autonomous as long as they paid tribute to the Parthians.

The Parthians perfected heavily armored cavalry as a new military defense. Their horses were much larger than other horses and could also move quickly, even clothed in heavy armor and carrying a heav-

Romans fighting heavily-armed cavalry

ily-armed rider, in part because they were fed on hay and alfalfa in the winter months, rather than being left to search for scarce edible grasses. Maintaining these horses was expensive, so the government sent the cavalry out to the countryside, where soldiers supported themselves and their animals by collecting rent on land they supervised.

Because much of the land under Parthian control was not suitable for agriculture, the Parthians financed their government by taxing merchants traveling along the Silk Roads. The government did its best to keep the Chinese, Romans, and other groups from trading directly, which would have threatened their control over this lucrative commerce. Exaggerating the dangers of crossing Parthian territory, they carried the goods themselves and collected tolls on all goods. In exchange, the Parthians provided rest houses and protection for the traders. When the Sasanids took over the Parthian Empire in the third century, they continued to control this portion of the trade routes.

The Kushan Empire Completes
the Hemispheric Trading System

After the demise of the Mauryan Empire, a series of nomadic groups
from central Asia invaded northern India. The most significant of
these groups was the Kushans who originated in western China. By
the first century of the common era, Kushan nomads had united the
largest five tribes, invaded areas now in Afghanistan and north India,
and established a foothold in the subcontinent. The Kushans became
another link in the crossroads of trade between East and West, exchanging and borrowing freely from various traditions. Their empire
lasted from the first century to about 240 C.E.

Not only did the Kushans control areas of central Asia, including
part of the Silk Roads, their dominion extended down the Gangetic
plain to Varanasi. They ruled over Greeks, Parthians, Iranians, and
Chinese as well as Indians. Modeling their system of government
after the Persian Empire, the Kushan rulers divided their territory into
satrapies and relied on a huge army to keep the peace. Perhaps their
most impressive ruler was Kanishka who ruled around 100 C.E. He
called himself the Son of Heaven, in imitation of Han rulers.

Religion played an important role during this period. The invading
Kushan nomads tried to use both Brahmanism and Buddhism in an

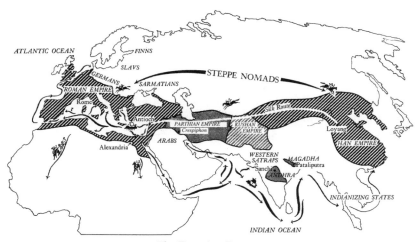

The Eurasian Ecunene

effort to establish their legitimacy. Some Kushan leaders were devout Buddhists and supported the arts. King Kanishka became a patron of Buddhism and helped spread that faith to central Asia. Elements of Christian thought, such as worshiping a savior, may have mixed with Buddhism at this time as well. Until they were defeated by the Sasanids, who sacked and destroyed the wealth of major Kushan cities at the end in the third century C.E., the Kushanas made major contributions to the flourishing trade.

Movers and Stayers

Long-distance trade was usually carried out in relays; one merchant seldom made the entire trip himself. Philip Curtin, identifies traders as either "movers" or "stayers." Stayers lived together in communities, receiving, sorting, and passing goods on; movers traveled back and forth along the trade routes, picking up goods from one stayer and carrying them to the next. After journeying far from home, movers relied on other movers to take their goods the rest of the way. Besides buying and selling, stayers often had to explain local customs to incoming traders and negotiate with the local people on behalf of foreign traders.

Merchants involved in long-distant trade tended to create diaspora communities along the trade routes. In these homogeneous communities, traders could find individuals who spoke their language, performed familiar rituals, ate the same food, and made them feel less homesick, even though their real home might be thousands of miles away. Diaspora communities, where stayers lived and where movers found temporary shelter and companionship before starting on the next lap of their journey, developed along well-traveled trade routes. Sometimes the trade settlements became autonomous, self-governing communities, trying to stay aloof from local rivalries in the larger urban area, or even became independently powerful and took control of areas around them.

Watch Out for Those Merchants

Despite the importance of trade, people throughout Afro-Eurasia during this period often looked down on merchants, viewing them with suspicion. Local authorities wanted to isolate foreign traders and

Nubians bringing tribute to the Egyptian court

diminish their influence. Foreign merchants had little loyalty to the people with whom they traded, especially when the merchants were skeptical or even disrespectful of local customs.

Greeks respected landowning farmers more than either traders or non-farming laborers. Hermes was the Hellenic god of both thieves and merchants. Greeks preferred to leave long-distance trade to the Phoenicians who, starting from Tyre and Sidon, had established a significant trading network in the western Mediterranean by 800 B.C.E. Carthage was the major Phoenician trading port in the western Mediterranean until 149 B.C.E., the end of the Third Punic (Phoenician) War with Rome.

Merchants were ranked below priests and warrior/administrators in the Indian *varna* system. Indians saw little wrong with getting rich, but they realized that merchants used tricks of *artha*, such as sweet talk or bribes, so trade might make a person prosperous but often brought him little respect.

Trade was important in the development of Nubia and Ethiopia and in trading communities along the eastern coast of Africa, but few records exist that tell how Nubians and East Africans felt about traders. Several trading centers connected Nubia and the interior of Africa with both the Mediterranean Sea and the Indian Ocean. In approximately 300 C.E. Aksum, in present-day Ethiopia, destroyed Meroë, took over its trade routes and dominated the east African cross-cultural trade. The Aksumites transported gold, ivory, animal hides, and spices from the interior through Adulis, their main port. Traders as well as missionaries and refugees also brought Christianity to Axum in the third century C.E.

The Era of the Ancient Silk Roads

When Roman legions fled from Parthian troops in Syria in 53 B.C.E., the Parthians unfurled elegant banners made of Chinese silk. This was probably the first silk cloth the Romans had ever seen, and very soon upper-class Romans were demanding silk clothing, exchanging one pound of gold for one pound of unwoven silk. During the *Pax Romana*, Romans could buy imported luxuries, such as silk and wigs, from as far away as India and China and spices from southeast Asia, although silk probably accounted for as much as 90 percent of what Rome imported from China. China's favorable balance of trade helped to weaken Rome economically.

Although traders and other travelers had been exchanging goods and ideas throughout inner Asia for a very long time, during Han Wu Di's reign (140–87 B.C.E.) contact and exchanges all the way from

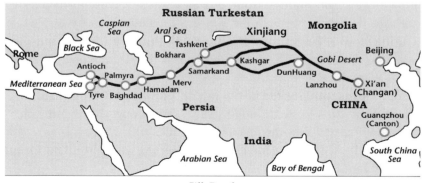

Silk Roads

China to the Mediterranean were established. At the very start of the Han dynasty, the Chinese had made peace with the Xiongnu, the federation of pastoral nomads living along the frontier between China and Mongolia. But as the Han got more powerful, so did the Xiongnu, and they were a constant threat. To appease the Xiongnu and try and keep them from attacking, the Chinese court agreed to send a fixed number of gifts each year, but periodically the Xiongnu raided anyway. Hoping a marriage alliance would improve relations, Wu Di arranged for a Chinese princess with a large dowry to become the bride of the Xiongnu leader, but they still continued to raid. So Wu Di decided to employ other diplomatic and military tactics.

First he tried to "use barbarians to control barbarians" by stirring up rivalries among the various nomadic groups. Because the Xiongnu had recently killed the ruler of a group living near Ferghana and used his skull as a drinking cup, Wu Di believed they would want revenge. Hoping to convince them to attack the Xiongnu from the west while the Chinese attacked from the south, he sent Zhang Qian to work out an alliance. Carrying silks as gifts for people along the way, Zhang Qian left Chang'an in 138 B.C.E.. After being captured and held by the Xiongnu for about ten years, he finally reached Ferghana and proposed the alliance.

The people in Ferghana were not too keen on the idea of attacking the very powerful Xiongnu, so they sent Zhang Qian back. When he returned to Chang'an in 126 B.C.E., his trip appeared to have been a failure because he had not gotten an agreement, and most of his men had been killed. But he told Emperor Wu Di about the sturdier, faster, so-called blood-sweating horses he had seen in Ferghana, stressing that that they were superior to any Chinese horses, and he had given silk presents to leaders in Central Asia, stimulated their interest in obtaining silk. The Chinese wanted horses, and the central Asians wanted silk, so his trip helped establish the network of Eurasian trade routes that became known as the Silk Roads (although that term was not used until the late nineteenth century).

Starting in Chang'an on the eastern end, travelers and traders went west through Mongolia and Turkestan (modern Xinjiang). They had to go along either the northern or southern borders of the Taklamakan Desert, and then through Central Asia. From there one branch led southeast through the Khyber Pass to the Kushana kingdom in north-west India, where Indians traded spices and precious jewels for Chinese silk. The main route continued west through Parthian, and later Sasanid, territory, all the way to Syria and the Roman Empire.

Silk and other rare and precious goods were not the only things that people carried along these ancient routes. Monks, traveling to religious sites, shared religious insights. Women, going to be married, carried their dowries. Armies used the routes in their military campaigns. And people all along the way shared and exchanged many different ideas and customs.

Ideas Flow Between South Asia
and the Mediterranean World

Considerable contact had existed for a long between the Mediterranean world and the Indian subcontinent. Historians have the reports Ambassador Megasthenes sent back to General Seleuces (late fourth century B.C.E.), including requests that Athens send the Mauryan court figs, wine and two Sophists. About fifty years later, Emperor Ashoka directed one of his edicts to rulers of various west Asian kingdoms. There is evidence that Western concepts of medicine and astronomy mixed with Indian ideas of the cosmos and the body. Especially during the Hellenistic Age Indian ideas may have influenced Greek thinkers such as Pythagoras, Plato, and the Stoics and Skeptics.

Images of the Buddha offer a dramatic example of the way Greek and Roman art may have influenced some Indian artists. Although

Riderless horse and wheel symbolize the Buddha and his message

Indian sculptors had been making beautiful representations of nature deities early in the first millennium B.C.E., especially tree spirits represented as sensual women, they did not make any images of the Buddha. Because the Buddha had told his followers to focus on his message, not on himself, early sculptors in India used an empty seat under a bodhi tree or a riderless horse to represent the Buddha's enlightenment, or a wheel to represent his teachings.

Some traders coming through the Khyber and Bolan passes into the Kushan Empire brought along anthropomorphic images (human-like) that Greek and Roman sculptors were making of their gods. These examples influenced sculptors from the Gandharan school of Indian sculpture in north India who began to make images of the Bud-

Gandharan Bodhisattva

dha that looked very much like Greek images of Apollo or Roman likenesses of senators.

Cross-cultural Influences on Early Christianity

Historians can only speculate on possible cross-cultural influences around Jesus and his early disciples. Palestine at the beginning of the common era exemplified the mixing of cultures that characterized the cities and towns along the major trading routes of the hemisphere, and it seems clear that one reason Christianity was able to survive and spread was its ability to adapt existing beliefs and rituals, including those practiced by people known as pagans (from *payus,* meaning rural or countryside).

Because Christianity had its origin in Jewish reform movements, it

Jesus separating the sheep from the goats

was permeated with important Jewish concepts including the Messiah and monotheism. Christians and Jews worshiped the same God, and they both believed that God acts in history. Early Christians also followed the Jewish custom of meeting in small groups and reading sacred scriptures together.

Jesus' message resonated with several important Zoroastrian beliefs. Zoroaster, in the sixth century B.C.E., had preached about the end of the world and a final judgment. The Christian Good News was the promise of life after death. Dualism, which had already spread through the Roman Empire, found a significant place in Christianity as well. Christians made a distinction between body and soul, the material and spiritual world, and this life and life after death.

Christianity also resembled aspects of Hellenistic philosophy, especially Stoicism. In the face of a seemingly capricious universe, Stoics had taught, people could not expect to control events. If, instead, they controlled their own reactions to what happened, they could find peace. Christians were advised to concentrate not on the hardships of this world but rather on the Good News of the life to come. St. Paul also stressed the community of all believers that was similar to the Stoic idea of a universal brotherhood.

Christian holy days often merged with existing celebrations. For example, people began to celebrate Jesus' birth during the winter solstice. Religious rituals involving trees and light gradually drifted into Christian practices as well. So did incense and having priests wear vestments and use holy water, common practices of the so-called mystery religions of western Asia; and churches often sprang up on sites of earlier goddess temples. Images of Mary and the Christ child are almost identical to those of Isis nursing Horus, which had been familiar throughout west Asia for centuries. And Christian saints frequently replaced local pagan deities, fulfilling some of the same functions, such as preventing illness and protecting towns and travelers. All these similarities must have made it easier for some people to move from their own faith to Christianity.

It is intriguing to wonder about the contact between Indian thinkers and early Christians, especially in regard to such things as similarities between stories of the early life of the Indian god Krishna and Jesus and those between Buddha's story of the prodigal son and the biblical version. St. Thomas, known as "Doubting Thomas" because he insisted on feeling Christ's wounds, is said to have spent his last years in Southern India and his remains were buried in the cathedral in Madras. When early Christians despaired of

*Goddess Isis nursing
her son Horus*

living a Christian life in the midst of what they saw as a corrupt and degenerate world, some began to drop out of society and live alone in the desert, earning the name "desert fathers." This practice of extreme asceticism may have been influenced by Indian religious ideas that featured the practice of dropping out and "going to the forest."

Indian Concepts Travel to Southeast Asia

Traders, and the brahmins and monks who accompanied them, were also carrying ideas from India as they traveled to ports along the coasts in southeast Asia. Local leaders who dominated these ports were eager for the wealth and increased status that trade with these men from the subcontinent brought, and for the luxury items they were selling, so they willingly provided shelter and provisions for them.

Local chiefs also hired some of the educated brahmins and monks to keep records at the court and to adapt local languages to the Sanskrit alphabet. Some leaders even took Sanskrit names as a sign of status. They learned how King Ashoka had ruled by moral authority rather than military might and how rulers in southern India attracted support by distributing gifts and holding lavish rituals. These ceremonies symbolized the ruler's control not only over his own kingdom but over the whole cosmos and made him seem godlike. They probably also learned how these performances impressed people in villages clustered around these royal centers, how allies were drawn to the rulers, and how south Indian leaders, through intense religious devotion to one of the Indian gods, became divine kings.

Before the arrival of these outsiders, many of the southeast Asian leaders had claimed their legitimacy rested on their ability to ensure a sufficient supply of sun and water for agriculture as well as their identity with renowned ancestors. The kind of ritual authority practiced in the subcontinent, a civilization they regarded as culturally rich and powerful, could enhance their authority, so they tried to adapt some of these Indian ideas.

In doing so, they were able to link some important Indian concepts with similar local ideas. For example, mountains were sacred according to both southeast Asian cultures and the Hindu and Buddhist worldviews. People in southeast Asia worshiped divine spirits and revered ancestors whose spirits were associated with sacred mountains. The stupa, which was becoming the most sacred Buddhist symbol, resembled a mountain. Local leaders realized they could commission the building of stupas to enhance their legitimacy, as Ashoka had done, and that reverence for a stupa would seem like worshiping spirits on a sacred mountain. In addition, people in both areas worshiped the sacred power of the *naga,* or snake, and images of the Buddha being sheltered by a *naga* became popular.

Most important, the idea of a ruler whose power rested on ritual or even divine authority echoed in both cultures. "Controlling" rain and sun rests on spiritual power, not on commanding armies or directing large bureaucracies. The Indian idea of ritual authority rested on spiritual power, so by adapting Indian ideas and performing similar ceremonies, leaders were often able to claim that they, too, were or divine kings, allowing them to build up their authority over large areas.

Theater States

In other areas we have considered, leaders often used religious power to establish their legitimacy, but this was usually backed up with strong armies. However, the kingdoms that began to develop in southeast Asia were based on people, not land. They had no definite borders where leaders stationed troops nor strong standing armies. Instead, they relied on trade and rituals to attract people and maintain their authority.

Historians have called this type of centralized control a "Theater State." Legitimacy comes from "divine kings" who, because of their spiritual power and lavish rituals, draw people to their courts. In this form of rule, the monarch relies on his court's ability to dazzle and enchant less powerful princes and subjects with extravagant rituals, ceremonies, and feasts.

Perhaps the rains would come anyway and the harvest would be rich regardless of who was king. However, many believed that if the leader performed the proper rituals and his court were a model for the larger society and the cosmos, he could ensure the peace and prosperity necessary for his people. Ideas and rituals from the Indian subcontinent fit well with the needs of southeast Asian leaders and provided the cultural symbols that shaped the early states in this area.

During the era from 200 B.C.E. to about 400 C.E., the empires that governed much of the land mass from the Mediterranean to the Pacific supported a vast network of exchange and trade. Within that framework many people moved across the land, bringing with them goods to sell and ideas to share. The cross-cultural contract resulted in political innovations such as the theater state, new religious expressions such as Christianity, and the exchange of many goods. People in the west began to use silk from China and cotton fabrics from India, porcelain from China, and glass products from Rome. Spinach and eggplants from India, lemons and apricots from China, nutmeg and ginger from southeast Asia, and pistachios, walnuts, and pomegranates from Parthia — all became additions to the increasingly cosmopolitan Eurasian diet.

But this expanding hemispheric system of interaction and exchange depended in large part on the stability provided by the major empires, which was always fragile. We now turn to consider the inner contradictions and external threats that challenged the continuity of these political systems and the cross-cultural contacts they had made possible.

WHY DON'T EMPIRES LAST?

Setting the Stage

Many factors contributed to the strength and endurance of both the Roman and Han empires. But after several centuries of glory, both began a period of decline and political decentralization. Why did these great empires disintegrate? What caused the central governments to lose control, trade to diminish, and creativity in the arts and literature to fade? Historians often write about the fall of Rome. Starting in the third century, the authority and legitimacy of the Roman government began to weaken, and it could no longer control the provinces. By that time the Han Empire had lost much of its hold over its territory as well.

We can only speculate to what extent people living through these periods of decline realized what was happening. Most subjects within an empire, we have noted, are unaware of what is going on in the capital. Local bureaucrats demand taxes and corvée and carry out the will of the central government as best as they can. Although the central government's vast network of control and communication is impressive, the daily lives of most people, especially those in distant provinces, are hardly affected. However, when people no longer feel secure and are not "left in peace," they begin to care a great deal about "who rules the land."

Why Did the Roman and Han Empires Disintegrate?

Chinese historians constructed the concept of a dynastic cycle to explain why the Shang, Zhou, and Qin dynasties — as well as the Han — had lost the Mandate. They focused on the quality of leadership and suggested that T'ian (Heaven) blesses a moral leader and gives him and his family the Mandate to rule. The people follow his example, obey the rules, and share their labor and produce with the central authorities. But when the emperor does not set a good example, officials become corrupt and try to get rich rather than serve the people. Corrupt officials award bureaucrats who have not passed the examinations honestly positions in the government. These officials, no longer carefully schooled in the Confucian classics, care little about decorum and moral example and use their positions to build their own power base.

Although Chinese historians stressed the personal and moral aspects of the dynastic cycle, more recent world historians tend to emphasize economic and political reasons for the collapse of the Han and later dynasties. These historians cite peasant uprisings and the idea that troops were used to put down these internal threats instead of defending the country. To pay the army, the government levied increased taxes, which led to more unrest and revolts. Additional soldiers were needed, so the government forced poor farmers and others to fight, or hired nomads as soldiers, further angering the people and creating reluctant warriors. Using more soldiers against the people left the borders unguarded, inviting nomad invasions. Sometimes a series of natural disasters, such as floods, earthquakes, and droughts, also helped bring down a dynasty.

Studies of the disintegration of the Roman Empire do not emphasize moral leadership or countrywide examinations, but many of the other reasons for the fragmentation of the Han are similar to reasons for the breakup of the Western Roman Empire. With increasing expenses and a shrinking tax base, both governments had to choose between raising taxes or reducing their armed forces and social services. Population declines added to the growing fiscal crisis. Because of social unrest, trade was decreasing, lowering profits. Both governments experienced a major breakdown in their efficient administrative systems and tried to control corrupt officials and court intrigues. Finally, both faced treats from nomadic groups on their borders.

TAXES

The financial base in both empires eroded as peasants had difficulty paying taxes. Rates were high in part because many large estates in both areas were no longer taxed. Rich Roman landowners resisted paying taxes to a government that was no longer providing services, and often a landlord's armed guards drove tax collectors away. In addition, much church land was not taxed. In China many of the large estates scholar-officials owned were tax free. When local officials in both areas tried to force peasants to pay their taxes, some fled to local landlords for protection from tax collectors and marauding bandits, asking to live on their estates in exchange for working the land. Landowners welcomed these additional laborers, who worked for almost nothing. In Rome large estates attracted craftsmen who were having trouble finding markets for their goods. These artisans made tools and other implements, and the estates became increasingly self-sufficient.

POPULATION

Changes in population added to the problem of collecting enough revenue. Beginning in 165 C.E., a series of plagues (perhaps smallpox or measles) killed hundreds of thousands of people in the Roman Empire, drastically reduced the farming population. When farmers died, their lands often lay fallow, producing no crops that could be taxed. In China population increases in certain areas led to smaller family plots. Some peasants who were unable to pay the tax fled south to the Yangzi (Yangtze) valley, far from the reach of efficient tax collectors.

TRADE

Decline in trade was more of a problem in Rome than in Han China. Many Chinese communities were self-sufficient, and most trade was carried out as part of the tributary system. Many within Roman territories, on the other hand, relied on trade, so when the legions spent less time repairing roads and bridges and guarding travelers, bandits and pirates attacked travelers and ships, leading to a sharp decline in trade. Less trade further reduced tax revenue. In addition, the Roman government minted money not backed by silver, causing prices to soar, and this inflation also hurt trade.

THE BUREAUCRACY

Administrative problems plagued both empires. The Roman government had trouble recruiting bureaucrats who could enforce laws and collect taxes. Instead of being able to keep some of the tax revenue

for themselves, as officials had done earlier, they now had to make up
the difference between what they collected and what Rome required.
No wonder it became almost impossible to find talented people who
were willing to serve as provincial governors. The Later Han was
unable to check the power of the large private estate owners, who
were gradually becoming very wealthy and powerful. Many were able
to bypass the exam system by buying positions in the bureaucracy,
which elevated their status.

SUCCESSION

Establishing an orderly system for selecting the new ruler had always
been problematic for Roman citizens who wanted to hold onto the fic-
tion that the Senate chose the new emperor. In reality would-be rulers
usually fought for the throne, and soldiers, hoping for shared rewards,
supported their generals. Once in power, the new emperor concentrated on winning the loyalty and protection of the Praetorian guards
and then the entire army. Even with this loyalty, however, being emperor became a dangerous job: between 235 and 284 C.E., 25 out of 26
emperors died violent deaths.

Emperor Diocletian, who ruled as an absolute monarch from 284 to
305 C.E., tried to stem the political and economic decline by introducing reforms that improved tax collection, froze prices, and required
sons to perform the same job as their fathers. To govern more effectively, he divided the empire in half, making two separate administrative units. He ruled the western half from Rome, and a trusted
colleague ruled the eastern half. After Constantinople became the capital of the eastern half of the empire, the stronger emperors ruled from
that city, and trade, manufacturing, and cultural creativity were concentrated in the east, further weakening the western half.

COURT INTRIGUES

Unlike Rome, where conflict among military leaders hurt the government, in Han China the constant intrigues of corrupt palace officials,
especially those close to the emperor, created instability. Because a
hereditary monarchy ruled, the battles over succession took place
mainly in halls and bedrooms inside the palace, not on streets or bat-
tlefields. Isolated from the outside world, the ruler relied on compet-

ing court officials to find out what was going on, and he had little way to check the accuracy of what they told him. He also had to balance the desires of his consorts, who often sought power for their own sons and families. In addition, eunuchs (castrated men) who guarded the women's quarters and had free access to the emperor, were often involved in palace intrigues.

A good example of an emperor who had difficulty balancing the various factions around the court and getting accurate information to guide his actions is Emperor Han Huan Di (r. 146–167 C.E.) To offset the influence of the consorts, he increased the power of the court eunuchs, even allowing them to kill members of his consorts' families. But soon the eunuchs were telling the emperor whom to reward with titles or honors, whom to send to be tortured or killed, and who should become scholar-officials. The eunuchs made sure that their relatives and friends got positions of power. Others who wanted to be officials had to bribe the eunuchs. To counter the eunuchs' power, the scholars formed their own association. Unfortunately, the next emperor did not trust the scholars and ordered them arrested and executed.

Neither the eunuchs nor the emperor realized that massive unrest was building in the countryside. Feeling desperate, many people rallied around a leader of a Daoist faith-healing sect who seemed to have magical powers. In 184 C.E. his group and another secret society rebelled against the Han. The emperor died, the palace was destroyed, and chaos followed as nomads took advantage of what was happening and sacked the city. By 220 the Han had lost the Mandate. Three smaller states were established in place of the Han, but none was strong enough to bring the empire together again and claim the Mandate.

What Role Did Christianity and Buddhism Play?

In the declining years of the empires, an increasing number of people sought solace for their miseries. Some, thinking it was useless to look for answers, simply tried to enjoy the physical pleasures of life. Many others, hoping for some vision of a better future, began to investigate new sources of meanings for their insecure lives. Many within the Roman Empire concentrated on enjoying luxury goods, dressing well, and showing off their wealth at lavish parties. Moreover, women had fewer children, and parents spent less time and effort teaching them the older values of citizenship and public service. Roman religion, largely inherited from the Greeks, was increasingly unable to satisfy the yearning for meaning that confronted average men and women within the empire and had little to say about civic society and social relations. During the insecurity of the later Roman Empire, many turned to Christianity.

Even so, it is not clear just how much the spread of Christianity contributed to the breakup of the Western Roman Empire. As Christianity spread, Roman rulers tried unsuccessfully to eliminate it. In an attempt to rouse the old sense of citizenship, Emperor Diocletian declared himself the supreme god, the symbol of the state, but his major campaign to wipe out Christianity, despite many deaths and cruel punishments, failed.

A struggle for the throne followed Diocletian's death. Constantine, one of the contenders and a convert to Christianity, believed that the Christian God had helped him win. In 313, after he became emperor, he issued the Edict of Milan, which made Christianity legal throughout the empire, and declared that Christians should be tolerated. During his reign, which lasted from 324 to 337 C.E., Constantine made Sunday a holiday, gave tax-free land to Christians on which they began to build churches and cathedrals, and exempted the clergy and many average Christians from paying taxes, increasing the tax burden on others. By the time Constantine died, Christianity not only had become the major religious faith of Rome but was spreading far beyond the Roman borders to Nubia, India, and northwest Eurasia.

In 380 Emperor Theodosius made Christianity the official religion of the empire. He ordered the statues of other gods destroyed and made it an act of treason to practice any other religion. Those who did not follow orthodox Christian doctrine on issues such as the nature of Jesus were persecuted. More and more people became Christians, and many began to put their faith in the "City of God," not in Rome or other cities within the empire.

By contrast Buddhism was not a factor in the decline of the Han. The first mention of a Buddhist community in China dates only from the first century C.E., and initially the new religion was confined mainly to traders and other outsiders. Because Daoism offered a degree of mysticism, and Confucianism, which had become the official ideology of China, provided the foundation for both private and public life, other worldviews had little appeal. Buddhism was far more popular among the nomadic groups who invaded and came to control some of the territory formerly under Han control, and many Chinese turned to Buddhism to answer the insecurities of life in the years following the disintegration of the Han.

The Second Great Movement of Nomadic Groups

About two-thousand years after the first significant migration of Indo-European and Semitic nomads in 1700 B.C.E., nomadic groups from the Inner Asian steppes launched a second prolonged wave of migration. These nomadic invasions, which added to an existing crisislike atmosphere and threatened the very survival of both empires, were not isolated events but affected all Eurasia.

While the chariot may have been a major stimulus to the dramatic nomadic invasions in the second millennium B.C.E., the stirrup played an important role during this second influx of nomadic peoples and indirectly helped bring about the end of the Western Roman Empire. This important new technology, which gave a rider support for his feet, allowed him to stand in the saddle, and made the cavalry devastatingly effective, may have first developed in the steppes or in India. By 300 C.E. the Chinese were casting iron stirrups.

By connecting various defensive walls and building additional signal towers, the Qin had discouraged nomads from trying to invade China. When the Han Empire was strong, it could use its trade/tribute arrangement to keep the Xiongnu and other nomadic groups from invading. When the

Nomad using stirrups

Nomadic prisoner

Later Han could no longer maintain the tribute system, the Xiongnu had to find other ways to get the goods they needed. As the Han defenses on the walls weakened, in part because Xiongnu served as defensive troops, they increased their raids inside the walls and also moved farther west in large numbers. Starting around 304 C.E., about a century after the end of the Han, nomadic groups invaded and plundered China and established several kingdoms in the north, the most impressive of which was the Northern Wei.

Internal divisions within the Xiongnu confederation, as well as pressure from another powerful nomadic confederation living in Mongolia, caused some of them to move west. As they went, they put pressure on other pastoral groups, causing some, including the Kushans, to move into northern India. These domino-like pressures also helped trigger the movement of nomadic and semi-nomadic Germanic peoples into territories under Roman hegemony.

Sometime before the start of the first millennium B.C.E., Germanic groups, who probably came originally from the Russia steppes where they had been living for perhaps 2,000 years, began to move out of the steppe lands of central Asia and into sparsely settled lands to the west. These Germanic tribes began entering northern Eurasia about 500 years before the start of the Roman Republic. The "Germani," as the Romans called these nomadic bands, split into two main branches: the Teutons and the Goths. Teutons in the west comprised peoples such as Franks, Alamanni, and Saxons; Goths, who settled in the east near the lower Danube and around the Black Sea, included the Ostrogoths, Visigoths, and Vandals. They gradually moved westward, in part because other groups farther east were putting pressure on them.

Although these groups were not very skilled farmers, they had superior military technology and an impressive fighting spirit; by the second century B.C.E. they were threatening Roman forces. During Julius Caesar's rule some tried to conquer eastern Gaul, but Roman legions stopped them. Many settled down near the Roman border, especially along the Rhine and Danube rivers. In general the Romans did not allow them to settle within the empire, although some occupied vacant land. For decades there were many relatively peaceful interchanges. Some even joined the legions, and many who were captured in battle worked as slaves in the empire.

What About the Huns?

But the Xiongnu helped upset this balance. As increasing numbers of Xiongnu moved further west in the fourth century C.E., both Germanic groups and Romans tried to stop the advance of these people they called the Huns. Both considered the Huns violent, savage men who covered vast distances with amazing speed, riding on their wiry ponies.

The Huns were one of the first groups to make extensive use of stirrups attached to their saddles. With a stirrup, Hun warriors could stand erect astride their galloping horses, which made it possible for them to shoot arrows with deadly accuracy. Hun (Xiongnu) attacks

Roman soldiers battle German nomads

made Germanic groups step up their pressure along the borders of the Roman Empire. When the Huns crossed the Volga River in 372, the Ostrogoths (East Goths) begged permission from Rome to cross into its territory for protection. Rome allowed them to cross the Danube River, which many Ostogoths did. But when the Ostrogoths did not get the land and food they believed the Romans had promised, they started to pillage. In 378 the Ostogoths defeated several Roman legions. Some Roman peasants welcomed the Germanic peoples as deliverers from Roman taxation and oppression and a buffer against the Huns.

By the fifth century the center of the Hun confederacy was in present-day Hungary and included much of what is today central Europe. Under its leader, Attila, who led the Huns from 434 until his death in 453, they made repeated assaults against Roman territory, even attacking Gaul. After Attila's death, the Huns continued their aggression, but by the sixth century they disappear from historical record. Many had died in their confrontations with the Germanic tribes, but some returned east and intermarried with other nomadic groups, losing their identity.

In 410 a Visigoth general sacked Rome, and Roman officials bought peace by granting him control of southern Gaul and Spain. By 425 German chieftains had set up many small kingdoms within the territory that had been part of the empire. In 476 Odoacer, a German chief, captured Rome and made himself king of Italy, the date many historians use as the official end of the Western Roman Empire. By that time the city of Rome was a poor shadow of its former greatness. The population had shrunk from around a million in 100 C.E. to 356,000 in 361 C.E., to 40,000 in 476, and grass was growing in the streets and around the once splendid buildings.

Legacies in Roman and Han Territories

The decline of the Han and Roman empires resulted in different legacies. One of the most striking differences likely resulted from the contrasting attitudes toward centralized authority and the legitimacy of the leader. Given the central role of the Chinese family, which served as a model for the state, and the importance of the concept of emperorship, later Chinese leaders would be able to draw upon a strong tra-

order. However, in the aftermath of Rome, whose subjects looked to law and citizenship more than to the family, and where the ruler's legitimacy had often been tenuous, political leaders would have to struggle to establish any kind of lasting centralized control.

The breakup of these empires also had a profound effect on cross-cultural contacts. The vibrant trade across the hemisphere significantly declined, generally lowering the standard of living, and many of the large cities that had been the centers of culture, artistic creation, and commerce faded. In part because of its reliance on trade, major cities in the declining Roman Empire fared far worse than those in areas that had been under the Han. As networks of trade eroded, learning and the arts, as well as the high level of technology that Rome had achieved, declined.

While the Eastern Roman Empire continued to flourish, large, relatively self-sufficient landed estates sprang up no only on the Italian peninsula but also in areas where Germanic groups settled. These autonomous estates could not support high quality artistic, literary, or scientific endeavors or an active trading network. It would be a long time before these areas were able to develop a complex urban civilization and new forms of political legitimacy.

In China, on the other hand, although the central government collapsed and, in 311, nomads captured and destroyed the Han capital at Loyang, many people, including those who fled south, were able to retain their cultural traditions. Nomadic leaders established several impressive kingdoms in the north, while five Chinese kingdoms formed in the south, and these were able to maintain large urban centers and support intellectuals and artists who strove to keep alive the rich scientific, philosophic, technological, and literary traditions of the civilization.

With the increased instability and turmoil, men and women looked for new ways to deal with the insecurities they faced; many sought new religious insights. While many people of Han turned to Buddhism for security in these trying times, they did not fundamentally question the underlying philosophy of the Han synthesis, especially their faith in Confucianism. In western Europe, North Africa, and west Asia, new religious expressions and very diverse political and cultural system would emerge.

Long-term Legacies and Coming Attractions

Before we bring down the curtain on this part of the human drama, we might pause to consider how the collective experiences of men and women may influence some of the themes and choices that lie ahead. The players established the fundamental outlines of our life today. Further, they grappled with certain challenges that still vex us in a new millennium. Although what has happened in the past does not determine what people will do next, it does provide the historical context for the options people have.

Our ancestors, who spent the majority of their time gathering and hunting, taught us to live cooperatively in groups, build families, and institute rules for social interaction. Those who launched the Agricultural Revolution demonstrated how to make more efficient use of the land and produce a surplus, freeing others to pursue the arts, sciences, government, and warfare. Nomadic pastoralists established a lasting ideal of masculinity: courageous and fearless warriors, conquering and controlling people and events. Our concept of the hero in war, business, and sports still owes much to the pastoral nomads of the steppes. Humans who ventured to build the first cities made possible the high degree of specialization that still characterizes urban life. Out of these complex societies emerged impressive art, innovative technology, and new ways of organizing political and social life. The creation of cities was so important that we often think of civilization itself as synonymous with urban life.

As we studied the Axial Age, we heard echoes of moral questions that still perplex us: Is life fair? How can we provide for the welfare of all people? Is it possible to live without wars and violence? How can we live a moral life? What is the ultimate meaning of existence? This period brought insights into such things as right action, dealing with insecurity, finding meaning in the face of death, doing as little harm as possible, balancing harmony and justice, pursuing meaningful work, and establishing meaningful relationships with others. In our own time, as we face these issues, we can draw on insights developed in the Axial Age.

When we looked at the age of empires, we analyzed the basis for their rise and fall. We saw both the challenges and rewards of living in a multicultural society, where all groups are allowed to follow their own cultural values but at the same time strive for common goals. Our study may help us understand why few empires exist now, and to appreciate why various empires, down to our own time, have destroyed millions of people as they have competed for world dominance.

In this initial phase of the human drama, we have witnessed duplicity and violence alongside the highest ethical and moral teachings. We have seen the continuous interplay of nomads and settled peoples and how each group was influenced by the other. We have examined artistic expressions of fundamental human longings, fears, and hopes. We have seen how people of genius have discovered mysteries of the natural world and invented technologies that harness energy and increase wealth and human comfort as well as kill people more efficiently. Finally, we have studied how quickly ideas, cultural forms, and scientific and technological breakthroughs travel to distant places and are adopted and adapted by others.

As we close this first volume and prepare to confront the period from 500 to 1350 C.E., we can anticipate questions and challenges that lie ahead. Will settled and nomadic people continue to interact or will one or the other way of life prevail? Will religions such as Christianity, Hinduism and Buddhism survive and prosper? What new religious ideas and faiths will emerge? What is happening in the Western Hemisphere? Are people there experiencing some of the same historic patterns we have identified in Afro-Eurasia? What new empires will emerge, what will make them strong, and how will they manage the diverse people within their borders? What new nomadic groups will be on the move, and how will they interact with those in settled areas? What new forms of political organization will emerge? What possibilities will new technologies offer and how will men and women use them? Will we learn to live more harmoniously with others?

As you prepare to examine the next acts in the human drama, think about the questions you want to ask and keep your questions in mind. It is also essential that we remember the history and ethos of what has gone before. Change is a common thread of history, and the past helps us understand what is happening in the present. Perhaps the past and present are like the interplay of *yin* and *yang*, moving in a constant dialectic. If we become too fascinated with the past, we grow stale and repetitive. Yet if we think only of the new and discard the past, we are like an anchorless ship pushed here and there by every cultural wind. Understanding the past offers us rich insights into how we live in the present. Furthermore, we are all heirs to the contributions of countless societies that have gone before. The interdependent global world that we sometimes think is so new, has, in fact, had a very long history.

ACT FIVE – ESTABLISHING A SYNTHESIS IN THE AGE OF EMPIRES (500 B.C.E. TO 500 C.E.)

Setting the Stage

1. Define the characteristics of an empire. How does an empire differ from a city-state or kingdom?
2. What is the best way to deal with diversity in an empire? Is cultural pluralism a strength or weakness? Explain.
3. For what reasons does cross cultural interaction increase or decrease when empires exist?
4. List the things that rulers expect their subjects to do. List the things that subjects would like their rulers to do. How do these expectations either jibe or clash?

SCENE ONE
Synthesis in the Mediterranean World

1. How important was geography in the development of empires in the Eastern Mediterranean World?
2. How did the leaders of the Persian Empire handle its diverse subjects?
3. Using the Greek and Persian views of the Persian Wars as your evidence, write an accurate account of that war. What did the Athenian general mean by saying "The Persians came to rob us of our poverty"?
4. What were the characteristics of Athens during the Periclean Age? Which groups prospered? Which groups had a more difficult time?
5. Give a few examples of how art and literature reflect a humanist outlook.
6. What was the purpose of the Delian League? Why did some city-states led by Sparta resent it?
7. Why did Thucydides write about the Peloponnesian War? What did the Melian Dialogue reveal?
8. Summarize in your own words the major ideas of Socrates, Plato, and Aristotle. Would you like to have been one of Socrates' students? Why or Why not? How did Aristotle modify Plato's picture of ultimate reality?
9. What were the accomplishments of Alexander of Macedonia? Argue whether he followed the familiar pattern of conquerors in west Asia or

created something new.

10. What are the major characteristics of the Hellenistic Age? What aspects were Hellenic? What came from Persia? What probably came from Egypt? What might have come from India?

SCENE TWO
India: A Synthesis of Ideas

1. Who was Chandragupta? What was life like in the Mauryan court when he ruled ?

2. Explain how someone could use the Seven Ways to greet a Neighboring State to achieve a goal.

3. Why did Ashoka renounce war as a means to extend his influence and control? What did he mean by *dhamma*? How did he deal with the cultural pluralism in his empire?

4. What evidence is there that Ashoka became a Buddhist or used Buddhist ideas to increase his legitimacy and effectiveness? What were the greatest achievements of his reign?

5. What is the basis for ranking castes? Why are some people called untouchables?

6. Evaluate the statement: "The Hindu four goals of life offer something for everyone."

7. Explain the four stages of life. When may a person move from the first to the second half of life?

8. List the reasons why Arjuna should fight. What finally convinced him to go back to the battlefield? If someone in the United States did not want to go to war, would you try to convince him he should fight? If so, what reasons would you offer? If not, why not?

9. Identify several ideas from Jainism and Buddhism that were absorbed into Hinduism. Which ideas might have come from the Indus Valley civilization? From Brahmanism?

SCENE THREE
The Middle Kingdom Defines Itself as the People of Han

1. Support the idea that Emperor Shih Huang Di was a Legalist.

2. What reforms did Shih Huang Di put in place? How did they either strengthen or weaken the Qin government?

3. Why did Shih Huang Di want an army of clay soldiers? What does that clay army tell you about the Qin?

4. Explain how the Han balanced Legalism, Confucianism, and Daoism.

What did the Han keep from the Legalists? What aspects of their rule followed Confucian philosophy? What did they use from the Daoists?

5. What were the Han Empire's greatest achievements?

6. Why did the Han establish an examination system? On what were scholars examined?

7. What was the role of women in Han China? How does it compare to the lives of women in Periclean Athens or the Mauryan Empire?

8. Did Emperor Wu Di really follow Confucianism as his official philosophy of rule? What is your evidence?

SCENE FOUR

The Triumph of Law and the Military in the Roman Empire

1. Identify some of the important features of the geography of the Italian peninsula. How did the Romans take advantage of these features? What challenges did the geography present?

2. Rome created a republic. What does that mean?

3. Why did the patricians have so much political power initially? How and why did the plebeians get more political power?

4. What impact did military success have on the Roman Republic?

5. Was Julius Caesar trying to preserve or destroy the republic? Explain your answer.

6. In creating an empire, what elements did Augustus and his followers take from Greece and from west Asia? Why did the Romans try to claim they were still a republic?

7. What contributed to the strength of the Roman Empire?

8. Which aspects of the Roman Empire did the Romans adapt from other areas and which ones were unique to Rome? What were the Roman Empire's greatest achievements?

SCENE FIVE

Roads and Routes across Afro-Eurasia

1. Why was there such a great deal of trade during the period from 200 B.C.E. to about 400 C.E.?

2. Why did diaspora communities develop? How did they facilitate trade?

3. Why do you think so many groups during this period of history looked down on merchants?

4. Draw the Silks Roads on a map of Afro-Eurasia. Identify the areas of the world that were linked by the Silk Roads.

5. What made the Silk Roads possible and profitable? How did the Silk Roads affect the Roman balance of trade?

6. How did the Parthians take advantage of the geography of the Iranian plateau? What role did they play in the Silk Road trade?

7. What did the Jews hope Jesus would do? What was his message?

8. Why did Christianity survive and spread? Who is attracted to it? Who opposes it? What made it appealing?

9. Why did local leaders in southeast Asia welcome traders, brahmins, and monks from the Indian subcontinent?

10. How did local southeast Asian leaders adapt Indian ideas to enhance their own legitimacy and power?

SCENE SIX
Why Don't Empires Last?

1. In what ways and to what extent do you think the Chinese dynastic cycle might fit the rise and fall of all empires? Which aspects were unique to China? What should historians be looking for in explaining what happens to empires?

2. Compare the role of trade in the Roman and Han empires.

3. What was the basis of Parthian strength? What role did the Parthian Empire play in the Silk Road trade?

4. List the factors that weakened the Han Empire. Put the ones you think were most important on the top and the ones you think were less important on the bottom. Compare your list with lists made by the other members of your class. Discuss any differences.

5. List the factors that weakened the Roman Empire. Put the ones you think were most important on the top and the ones you think were less important on the bottom. Compare your list with lists made by the other members of your class. Discuss any differences.

6. What reasons appear on both lists? What reason are unique to each area?

7. What impact did nomads have on the Roman and Han empires? Discuss whether they were the cause of the decline or whether their invasions were a result of the decline, or both?

8. If you could go back in time, in which of these areas would you have most liked to have lived? What job would you want to have had? Would you rather have been a woman or a man? Explain the reasons for your answers.

ILLUSTRATION SOURCES

Page: credit

4: Cheryl Fink
10: Lotus–Carol Radcliffe Bolon with permission Archaeological Survey of India; Path–A. J. Gayet, 1894; Athena–Olympic Museum
12: Neg. No. 388315 (Photo by J. Beckett) Courtesy Dept. of Library Services. American Museum of Natural History
18: Neg. No. 336184 Courtesy Dept. of Library Services. American Museum of Natural History
20: Neg No. 326475 Photo Boltin. Courtesy Dept. of Library Services. American Museum of Natural History
23: © Longman Group Limited, 1984 Reprinted by permission of Pearson Education Limited
24: James Mellaart. *Catal Huyuk A Neolithic Town in Anatolia.* (Thames & London, 1967)
34: The Metropolitan Museum of Art (30.4.48)
37: Asa Davis and Matt Atkatz, Friends Seminary
40: Helen Chapin Metz, ed. *Iraq, A Country Study.* (Federal Reserve Division, Library of Congress, 1990)
47: Wills Davis-Held
48: *Djoser, KLM*
51: The Metropolitan Museum of Art. (detail)
52: ISL Culture Tours
54-5: The Metropolitan Museum of Art (30.4.2) (detail)
55: Rosellini, 1834
57: Harappa Archaeological Research Project
58: Archaeological Survey of India, New Delhi
59: Archaeological Survey of India
60: Donald Johnson
61: J.M. Kenoyer (www.harappa.com)
62: Priest–Pakistan Mission to the United Nations; yogi–Archaeological Survey of India, (1421/56)
63: Pakistan Mission to the United Nations
68: Richard Wilhelm, 1929
73: Aegean Trade From European History on File by Diagram Visual Information Ltd. Copyright 1997 by Diagram Visual Information Ltd. Reprinted by permission of Facts on File, Ind. (detail)
75: Greek National Tourist Organization
76: Greek National Tourist Organization
77: Scala/Art Resource, NY

84: Denis Sinor. *The Cambridge History of Early Inner Asia.* Reprinted with permission of Cambridge University Press.

88: Courtesy of the Metropolitan Museum of Art. (372.5578.205)

92: Willa Davis-Held

99: Giraudon/Art Resource, NY

103: Hatshepsut The Metropolitan Museum of Art, Rogers Fund and Edward S. Harkness Gift, 1929. (29.3.1)

104: Photograph, Courtesy of The Metropolitan Museum of Art.

109: temple–Derek A. Welseby; Queen Amanishakheto–C.R. Lepsius, 1849

112: Helen Chapin Metz, ed. *Israel A Country Study* (Federal Research Division Library of Congress, 1990)

115: Drawing by Bela Petheo in William McNeill. *The Rise of the West.* (Chicago: The University of Chicago Press, 1963)

120: Professor P. Lal

122: Archaeological Survey of India

124: Patricia Buckley Ebrey. *The Cambridge History of China.* Reprinted with permission of Cambridge University Press

125: British-China Friendship

131: Glenn E. Curtis, ed. *Greece A Country Study.* (Federal Research Division. Library of Congress, 1990)

133: Greek National Tourist Organization

136: Angel Antonio Mingote. *History for Beginners.* (New York: Thomas Nelson and Son, LTD, 1960)

149: A.H. Layard 1849; Giraudon/Art Resource, NY

163: Indonesian Embassy, Washington, DC

171: Derk Bodde. *Chinese Ideas in the West.* (Washington, D.C.: American Council on Education, 1948)

183: The Metropolitan Museum of Art, Rogers Fund, 1914. (14.130.12) (detail)

188: Greek National Tourist Office

189: The Metropolitan Museum of Art, Fletcher Fund, 1931 (31.11.10)

192: *The Cambridge Illustrated History of Ancient Greece.* Reprinted with permission of Cambridge University Press

205: Willa Davis-Held

206: Giraudon/Art Resource, NY

209: Greek National Tourist Organization

212: Apollo–Greek National Tourist Organization; Discuss thrower–Alinari/Art Resource, NY

213: Greek National Tourist Organization

220: Alinari/Art Resource, NY

221: Willa Davis-Held

230: Marian McKenna Olivas

232: Archaeological Survey of India

233: C. Collin Davies *An Historical Atlas of the Indian Peninsula.* (Madras, India: Oxford University Press, 1949)

234: Donald Johnson

242: Archaeological Survey of India

243: Archaeological Survey of India

248: Harrison Elliott

250: Donald Johnson

251: National Tourism Administration of the People's Republic of China

254: The Metropolitan Museum of Art, Gift of Douglas Dillon, 1991. (1991.117.2) (detail)

258: Drawing by Bela Petheo in William McNeill. *Op, cit.*

261: Harrison Elliott

263 & 266: maps designed by Tsering Wangyal Shawa, Graphic Information Systems Librarian, Princeton University

267: Foto Marburg/Art Resource, NY (detail)

274: map designed by Tsering Wangyal Shawa, Graphic Information Systems Librarian, Princeton University

277: Alitalia

286: Alinari/Art Resource, NY

287: Drawing by Bela Petheo in William McNeill. *Op. cit.*

289: The Metropolitan Museum of Art. (30.4.21) (detail)

290: Willa Davis-Held

292: Archaeological Survey of India

293: The Metropolitan Museum of Art, Purchase, Lita Annenberg Hazen Charitable Trust Gift, 1991 (1991.75)

294: The Metropolitan Museum of Art, Rogers Fund, 1924. (24.240)

295: Alinari/ Art Resource, NY

305: Drawing from map of silk road by Michael Grimsdale, in *Aramco World*, July/August 1988

306: Alinari/Art Resource, NY

307: Alinari/Art Resource, NY

QUOTATION SOURCES

40: Samuel Kramer. History Begins at Sumer: thirty-nine firsts in man's recorded history. (Philadelphia: University of Pennsylvania Press, 1981)

42: *Smithsonian* Vol. 19, Number 9, December 1988. (Washington, DC: Smithsonian Associates) p. 134

45: Wolkstein, Diane and Samuel Noah Kranmer. *Inanna Queen of Heaven and Earth Her Stories and Hymns from Sumer.* (New York: Harper & Row, Publishers, 1983) p. 37

50: Linole Casson. *Early Egypt.* (New York: Time-Life Books, 1967) p. 95

50: Linole Casson. *Early Egypt.* (New York: Time-Life Books, 1967) p. 95

51: Quoted in Durant, William and Airel. *Our Oriental Heritage.* (New York: Simon & Schuster, 1935) p. 165

52: Quoted in Gay Robins. *Women in Ancient Egypt.* (Cambridge: Harvard Univ. Press, 1993) p. 69

85: Quoted in Jagchid, Sechin & Paul Hyer. *Mongolia's Culture and Society.* (Boulder: Westview Press, 1979) pp. 2–3

86–7: *Ibid.*

87: *Ibid.*, p.305

96: Kramer and Wolkstein, *Op.cit.*, p. 32, 33

96: Herbert Mason. *Gilgamesh A Verse Narrative.* (New York: A Mentor Book, 1972) p. 43

99–100: Pritchard, James B., ed. *The Ancient Near East Vol .I An Anthology of Texts and Pictures.* (Princeton: Princeton University Press, 1973)

105: Quoted in Durant. Op cit.

116: O'Flaherty, Wendy Doniger. *The Rig Veda.* (New York: Penguin Books, 1981) p. 236, 240–41

119: Ibid., p. 31

119: Quoted in Bhagwat Saran Upadhyaya, *Women in Rigveda.* (New Delhi: S. Chand & Co., 1974) p. 213

128–9: Waley, Arthur. *The Book of Songs.* (New York: Grove Press, 1996) pp. 120–22

129: Waley, Arthur. *Three Ways of Asian Wisdom.* (Garden City: Doubleday Anchor Book, nd) p. 36

134: Homer. *Iliad.* Michael Reck, trans. (New York: IconEditions, an imprint of New York: HarperCollins Publishers, Inc., 1994)

135: Barnstone, Willis. *Sappho Lyrics in the Original Greek with Translations by Willis Barnstone.* (New York: New York Univeristy Press, 1965) p. 111

136: Slavitt, David R. and Oalmer Bovive. *Euripides, 3.* (Philadelphia: University of Penn Press, 1998)

138: Hesiod. *Works & Days and Theogony.* Translated by Hackett.

(Indianapolis, IN: Hackett Publishing Company, Inc., 1993) p. 29

151,152,153: The Holy Bible. New Revised Standard Edition. (New York: Oxford University Press, 1989)

159–60: Olivelle, Patrick, trans. *Upanishads.* (Oxford: New York, 1996) p. 154

165: Henrich Zimmer. *Philosophies of India.* (Princeton: Princeton University Press, 1951

169–70: Sun Tzu. *The Art of War.* Translated by Samuel B. Griffin. (New York: Oxford University Press, 1971)

170–71, 173–75: *Confucius. The Analects.* D.C. Lau, translator. (New York: Dorset Press, 1979)

177: McNaughton, William. *The Taoist Vision.* (Ann Arbor: The University of Michigan Press, 1971) p. 10, 15, 17, 23

177: Lau, D.C., trans. *Lao Tzu Tao Te Ching.* (London: Penguin Books, 1963) p. 85

178: Bynner, *The Way of Life According to Laotzu.* (New York: The John Day Company, 1944) p. 35

186: Quoted in Marjorie Wall Bingham and Susan Hill Gross. *Women in Ancient Greece and Rome.* (St Louis Park, MN: Glenhurst Publications, Inc., 1983)

187: Barnstone, Willis. *Sappho Lyrics in the Original Greek with Translations by Willis Barnstone.* (New York: New York Univeristy Press, 1965) p. 101

201: See McNaughton, William. *The Confucian Vision.* (Ann Arbor: The University of Michigan Press, 1974) p. 129

212: Brendan Kennelly. *Sophocles' Antigone. A New Version.* (Bloodale Books, 1996)

215: Jennings, Whitney and Charles Theophilus Murphy. *Greek Literature in Translation.* (New York: Longmans, Green and Co., 1944) pp. 763–64

228: Susan Murcott. *Translations and Commentaries on the Therigatha.* (Berkeley: Parallex Press, 1991) p. 51

229–30: See Henrich Zimmer Philosophies of India. (Princeton: Princeton University Press, 1951) pp. 120–123

231–35: Rock Edicts adapted from Balkrishna Govind Gokhale. *Ashoka Maurya.* (New York: Twayne Publishers, 1966)

240–41: Barbara Stoler Miller. *Bhartrihari: Poems.* (New York: Columbia University Press, 1967) pp. 95, 99, 137

245: Miller, Barbara Stoler. *The Bhagavad-Gita Krishna's Counsel in Time of War.* (New York: Bantam Books, 1986) pp. 108–9

259: Lau. *Lao Tzu Tao Te Ching. Op. cit.* pp. 52, 36

260: Chinghua Tang. *A Treasury of China's Wisdom–A Story for Everyone.* (Beijing: Foreign Languag Press, 1996) pp. 79–80

261–62: Quoted in Alfred Andrea and James Overfield. *The Human Record Sources of Global History*, Vol. I. (Boston: Houghtom Mifflin Company, 1994) p. 151

288: Philip D. Curtin. *Cross-Cultural Trade in World History*. (New York: Cambridge University Press, 1984).

INDEX

ABOUT THE AUTHORS

DONALD JOHNSON, New York University, directed a Master's Degree program in Teaching Asian Studies for twenty-two years. He is the author of several books and numerous articles on Asia and teaching history and is currently concluding a study of historical representations of the world in American schools.

JEAN JOHNSON, New York University, taught world history at Friends Seminary, where she piloted this text. She directed TeachAsia, a staff development program for middle school teachers sponsored by the Asia Society.

Together the Johnsons have created many teaching units and co-authored *Through Indian Eyes*, now in its fourth printing, and *God and Gods in Hinduism*.